D-DAY

About the Author

John Sadler has had a lifelong interest in Scottish military history. He now combines writing with lecturing in History at Newcastle University and working as a battlefield tour guide, living history interpreter, and heritage consultant. He is a keen re-enactor and a long-time member of the Sealed Knot Society. He lives in mid-Northumberland.

D-DAY

THE BRITISH BEACH LANDINGS

JOHN SADLER

AMBERLEY

Dedicated to the memory of Jack Whitmore Rasmussen (1922–1989), a Danish soldier and patriot who first enlisted with the Buffs then transferred to No. 4 Commando; he served both at Dieppe and on D-Day. I knew him.

All of Amsterdam, all of Holland, in fact the entire western coast of Europe all the way down to Spain, are talking about the invasion day and night, debating, making bets and – hoping.

Anne Frank, diary entry, 22 May 1944

Soldiers, Sailors and Airmen of the Allied Expeditionary Force; you are about to embark upon the Great Crusade, toward which we have striven these many months. The eyes of the world are upon you. The hopes and prayers of liberty-loving people everywhere march with you. In company with our brave Allies and brothers-in-arms on other Fronts, you will bring about the destruction of the German war machine, the elimination of Nazi tyranny over the oppressed peoples of Europe, and security for ourselves in a free world.

Eisenhower's Order of the Day

This edition published 2022

Amberley Publishing
The Hill, Stroud
Gloucestershire, GL5 4EP

www.amberley-books.com

Copyright © John Sadler, 2019, 2022

The right of John Sadler to be identified as the Author of this work has been asserted in accordance with the Copyrights, Designs and Patents Act 1988.

ISBN 978 1 3981 1243 8 (paperback)
ISBN 978 1 4456 4463 9 (ebook)

British Library Cataloguing in Publication Data. A catalogue record for this book is available from the British Library.

Typesetting and Origination by Amberley Publishing.
Printed in India.

CONTENTS

PREFACE

The human heart is the starting point of all matters pertaining to war.

Maurice de Saxe, Count of Saxony

TO ALL IN FORCE 'S'

The great day for which we have all been training is at hand. The task allotted to us is a formidable one, and calls for all that is best in every one of us.

The 3rd British Infantry Division has been entrusted to our care. They are old friends of ours; we have grown up together; we have come to look on them as our own. Let every officer and man in the Force feel a personal responsibility for the comfort, safety and maintenance of his 'opposite number' in the 3rd Division.

And, above all FIGHT
    FIGHT to help the Army;
    FIGHT to help yourselves;
    FIGHT to save your ship;
    FIGHT to the very end.

A. G. Talbot
Message from Rear Admiral Arthur George Talbot
to all the sailors and crew of Force S

On a visit to Normandy as a guide on a brilliant summer day in June 2018, I'd taken the group to the wide expanse of Utah

Beach, a long sweep of perfect sand. Aside from the squat, huddled remains of German blockhouses, abandoned in the dunes, there was nothing to suggest this tranquil, gilded shore had ever been a battlefield. As we scaled the concrete roofs, a pair of charioteers propelling racing carts along the beach dashed by, like some scene from an altogether earlier age. And that's the trick with Normandy – trying to conjure up the awfulness of battle, which wasted so many towns, villages and farms and which brought the full, crushing, smashing power of industrial war to this beautiful landscape.

This book is the product of a lifetime's obsession with the Second World War and the role of the British and German infantryman. As Montgomery pointed out, the Britisher was not, in the main, the member of a professional *corps d'élite* as their adversaries in the *Wehrmacht* might claim to be but essentially a citizen under arms. In the main, these young soldiers were a conscript army, dragged from occupations and professions that had nothing to do with fighting a war.

For most on both sides, this experience would be challenging, infinitely tedious, often disagreeable and occasionally terrifying. The task facing Tommy in spring 1944 was to break into Hitler's Fortress Europe, *Festung Europa,* perhaps one of the most daunting challenges any British and Allied army could possibly face. Fritz had the job of stopping him. And the Tommies included not just Brits but also Free French, Poles, Czechs, Belgians, Danes, Dutch and Norwegians. Our fathers and grandfathers did it; they won. The world post-1945 may not quite have been Churchill's 'broad, sunlit uplands' but democracy and humanity survived. The careless freedoms and liberties we take for granted today are their legacy. I have focused on the experiences of ordinary men and women who were caught up in these momentous events rather than on the grand strategy; there are many excellent books that do the latter, particularly my own favourites, the great John Keegan's *Six Armies in Normandy* and David Howarth's *Dawn of D-Day.*

During the last 40 years I've spent many hundreds of hours with tour groups of all ages in Normandy, on the British, Canadian and American beaches, at Pegasus Bridge, Merville Battery *et al.* So I've walked, crept and crawled through Atlantic Wall defences throughout Normandy and Brittany, handled and fired most of the small arms and made a career out of talking to veterans.

D-Day was the single greatest military undertaking of all time, carried out on a scale that today would be unimaginable: a superbly convoluted deception plan, *Fortitude,* a vast and complex naval armada, *Neptune,* and the amphibious assault, *Overlord.* The job was to breach the mighty walls of Hitler's Fortress Europe and begin the liberation of all of Germany's victims, beginning with France, Belgium and Holland – and then push on through the Siegfried line and into the heart of the Reich, which would be inexorably squeezed from two sides. Stalin would get his Second Front, and the Russian offensive in the east, *Bagration,* would be astonishingly successful. If, as Churchill so memorably described, El Alamein was the end of the beginning, then D-Day was the beginning of the end.

Failure would have been disastrous – it would have taken the Allies years to rebuild their strength sufficiently for another attempt. Hitler could have swung his Normandy garrison eastwards to hold the line there. He could have continued building up his Atlantic Wall defences to the point that they would have been truly impregnable. The war might have ended in an armistice, with incalculable consequences for mankind. So the opening airborne assaults on the night of 5 June 1944 and the invasion of the beaches the next morning could be said to be the decisive hours of the Second World War and perhaps of the 20th century.

At the time of writing, it will be nearly 75 years since D-Day, and fewer and fewer veterans survive. I did speak to the son of one; his father had been a beach-master on Gold and had never spoken about his experiences. Only when the old man was clearly nearing the end of his long life could he be persuaded to speak of his experiences on 6 June 1944. But all he would say was: 'Well son, it was all very noisy and I got the very distinct impression we weren't at all welcome.'

As single-sentence histories go, that's pretty hard to beat.

ACKNOWLEDGEMENTS

Thanks are due to a great many people without whose willing and generous contribution this work could not have been completed. These include: Steve Shannon, curator of the former Durham Light Infantry Museum; Peter Hart and Emma O'Brien of the Imperial War Museum; Richard Groocock of the National Archives; Amy Cameron of National Army Museum; Ian Martin of the King's Own Scottish Borderers Museum, Berwick-upon-Tweed; Steve Erskine and the Trustees of the Green Howards Museum, Richmond; Roberta Goldwater of *Charge!* at the Museum of Northern Cavalry; the staff of Durham County Record Office; the staff of Northumberland County Archives at Woodhorn; staff and trustees of the Fusiliers Museum of Northumberland, Alnwick; colleagues at the North East Centre for Lifelong Learning at the University of Sunderland; staff at the Literary and Philosophical Library, Newcastle; staff at Central Libraries, Newcastle and Gateshead, Clayport Library Durham, Northumberland Libraries at Morpeth, Alnwick, Blyth, Hexham and Cramlington; Lindsey and Colin Durward of Blyth Battery, Blyth, Northumberland; the curator and staff of the Royal Engineers Museum and Archives, Chatham; Andrew Whitmarsh of the D-Day Museum in Portsmouth; David Fletcher of the Tank Museum Bovington; Rod Mackenzie of the Argyll and Sutherland Highlanders' Museum; Thomas B. Smyth of the Black Watch Museum; Paul Evans of the Royal Artillery Museum; Natalie Worthington of Juno Beach Centre; Mark Worthington of the Memorial Pegasus; David Kelly; the

Acknowledgements

late Sir Laurence Pumphrey; Timothy Norton; John Stelling; Mark Pinkney; Sir Paul Nicholson; Major Chris Lawton, MBE; Colonel Arthur Charlton; Major Samuel Meadows, 2nd Battalion The Royal Gurkha Rifles; Trevor Sheehan of Defence Photography; Graham Trueman; Neville Jackson; Colonel Anthony George; John Fisher; John Shepherd; Brian Ward; Sarah Reay; Jennifer Harrison; Johanna Sheehan; Chloe Rodham, for the maps; and to Samantha Kelly, for original verse.

Naturally, the author remains responsible for all errors and omissions.

John Sadler

Credits

Stand To is reproduced by kind courtesy of the Fusiliers Museum of Northumberland.

Poor Bloody Infantry is quoted in Mallinson, A., *The Making of the British Army* (London, 2010), p. 480.

I Will Come Back to You is reproduced by kind permission of the Fusiliers Museum of Northumberland.

Keith Douglas' *Desert Flowers* is from https://www.theguardian.com/books/2014/jun/09/poem-of-the-week-keith-douglas-war, retrieved 20 March 2018.

Beach Casualty by kind permission of Durham County Record Office.

Vale appears by kind permission of Joan Venables.

Hitler Has Only Got One Ball is reproduced by kind permission of Tyne and Wear Archives and Museums.

The poems of the late Maurice Pinkney appear by kind courtesy of Mary Pinkney.

Bill Millin appears by kind courtesy of Tony Church (www.warpoetry.com).

Waiting is reproduced by kind permission of Samantha Kelly.

As the author I have, at all times, attempted to provide true acknowledgement of all the material quoted. If, however, I've have failed to do so, or have incorrectly credited any extract or account, then I'd be very pleased to hear from anyone affected thereby and will undertake to correct any errors or omissions.

LIST OF ILLUSTRATIONS AND PICTURE CREDITS

LIST OF MAPS/PLANS

Map 1. Map of 6th Airborne Division area of operations 5/6 June 1944.

Map 2. Sketch of Pegasus Bridge operations 5/6 June 1944.

Map 3. Sketch of the attack on Merville Battery 5/6 June 1944.

Map 4. Map of Sword, Juno and Gold Beaches, 6 June 1944.

TIMELINE

I was three years old and my father stood me on the windowsill looking out. The sky was black with aircraft and I must have been woken by the noise. His exact words escape me, but he said that this marked the coming of the end of the war. I can see that sky now.*

June 5th

18.00 hrs: A seaborne invasion force of five Allied assault groups, consisting of 130,000 men, leaves the English coast, sailing through prepared channels cleared by minesweepers.

June 6th

00.05 hrs: German coastal batteries between Le Havre and Cherbourg are bombed by Allied aircraft as part of the deception plan.

00.20 hrs: British airborne troops secure Pegasus Bridge, over the Caen canal, and other bridges over the River Orne.

04.30 hrs: US airborne troops capture St Mère Eglise and secure roads leading up to Utah beach.

05.00 hrs: 9th Parachute Regiment destroys guns at the Merville Battery, thus protecting troops who will be landing at Sword Beach.

05.30 hrs: Allied warships begin the bombardment of the Normandy coastline and landing craft leave mother ships, bound for the shore.

06.00 hrs: Allied bombers pound German shore defences. More than 5,300 tons of bombs are dropped.

06.30 hrs: US troops begin landing on Omaha beach and face devastating German fire, which pins them down until 1100 hrs. Americans begin landing at Utah beach.

07.30 hrs: British troops land on Gold and Sword beaches.

07.35 hrs: Canadian troops land at Juno Beach.

09.00 hrs: General Eisenhower, as Supreme Commander of *Operation Overlord*, issues a communiqué announcing that the invasion of France has begun.

11.00 hrs: The British and Canadian troops secure beachheads on Gold, Juno and Sword beaches.

12.00 hrs: Winston Churchill, the Prime Minister, speaks to the House of Commons about the landings.

13.30 hrs: US troops on Utah and Omaha beaches begin to secure the beachhead.

14.30 hrs: The German *21st Panzer* Division unleashes a counter-attack towards the coast.

16.00 hrs: The British secure the coastal town of Arromanches so that the Mulberry Harbour can be laid to facilitate rapid disembarkation.

18.00 hrs: Leading elements of 69 Brigade (7th Green Howards) approach the Caen–Bayeaux Road to the south, their objective for the day.

20.00 hrs: Allied patrols at the outskirts of Bayeux.

23.00 hrs: All the beaches are secure. By the end of the day, the Allies have disembarked 135,000 men and have established bridgeheads of varying depths along the Normandy coastline. By sunset, a total of 10,000 men have been killed, wounded or reported missing.

*https://witness.theguardian.com/assignment/53884eeae4b0bd8f3 5189225?page=2 retrieved 29 March 2018

I

INTRODUCTION

I would say that I was fighting the war to rid the world of fear – or the fear of fear is perhaps what I mean. If the Germans win this war, nobody except little Hitlers will dare do anything. England will be run as if it were a concentration camp, or at best a factory. All courage will die out of the world – the courage to love, to create, to take risks, whether physical or intellectual or moral. Men will hesitate to carry out the promptings of the heart or the brain because, having acted, they will live in fear that their action may be discovered and themselves cruelly punished. Thus all love, all spontaneity, will die out of the world.

Richard Hilary, *The Last Enemy*[1]

A New B.E.F., which includes you, is going to France. You are to assist personally in pushing the Germans out of France and back to where they belong...

Instructions for British Servicemen in France 1944[2]

It was at 11.00am on 3 September 1939 that Britain entered a new era. The transition from peace to war was swift and dramatic. The country had put on uniform. The sky over the cities was dotted with balloons. Everywhere people were digging trenches, filling sandbags. Gas masks were given out. There was a rush for black paper and cloth to cover windows and skylights. Grim, grey vehicles thundered along the roads on mysterious errands. There was in the air a feeling of change – complete, inevitable and tremendous.

Off to war

A generation before, war had come in cloudless August, greeted by vast, thronging crowds intoxicated with an almost transcendent spirit of patriotic fervour. Young men queued to volunteer in their tens of thousands. Their children, who listened to Neville Chamberlain's radio broadcast, greeted the business of war in an altogether different mood. The Prime Minister's voice, scratchy and somehow rather feeble over the airwaves, conveyed a sombre note of resignation. This time there would be no great rush of enthusiasts off to biff the 'Beastly Hun'.

That the Hun was still beastly was beyond question: their conduct in Poland, swiftly overrun and then murderously oppressed, hammered into a Dark-Age vision of servility, left no room for doubt. Appeasement was definitely out of fashion:

> I remember the bother with Czechoslovakia, and we thought there was going to be a war. My father certainly did – and we were quite prepared for it. Then of course it all blew over temporarily, and I remember Dad bought us a dolly each to celebrate, because it seemed as if it was going to be alright – and of course, it wasn't.[3]
>
> I remember vividly 'Peace in our Time' – Neville Chamberlain coming back from Munich. We thought, 'Thank God, it's going to be peace, it's not going to be war.' But of course events proved [*sic*] wrong. I began thinking, 'Is it going to be like the First World War, when thousands of men were killed? In a way they were human fodder.' I thought, 'Is it going to be a repeat? What's going to happen to my brothers?'[4]

Britain was two very different countries in the 1930s. Both north and south had been badly affected by the Great Depression, with unemployment in the industrial north reaching 13.5 per cent. But the decade had seen a revival of economic prosperity throughout the Home Counties, with new manufacturing such as electrical goods and a burgeoning motor industry. Leafy, pleasant suburbs spread outwards and standards of living soared; electric cookers, washing machines and radios filled kitchens in garden townships. In the north, a very different picture emerged. Here, traditional industries such as coal mining, shipbuilding, textiles and engineering were in marked decline; unemployment spread like contagion. Millions existed in cramped, unsanitary housing on means-tested handouts, eating in communal soup kitchens. With poverty and squalor, disease spread: scurvy, rickets and tuberculosis.

The Great War of 1914–1918 had been billed as 'the war to end all wars' and David Lloyd George had promised a 'land fit for heroes'; this was wrong on both counts. The 'heroes' of the Western Front were seen begging on street corners and pawning their medals to survive, and now another war was brewing. Guernica had shown what indiscriminate horrors modern strategic bombing could unleash. The only thing certain about this war is that it would be very much worse than the last: 'Looking around, I could see that we were quite unprepared to enter a war of any magnitude – we just weren't ready. We never had the kit and we never had the men. We never had anything – we had so far lagged behind.'[5]

Britain had 'won' the First World War but what was the face of victory? A whole generation of young men blighted in what seemed, in retrospect, the bickering between members of a dysfunctional pan-European royal family. There was a feeling that the titanic effort expended during the war was somehow a one-off. The scale, suffering and sheer pointlessness of the whole ghastly mess had led to a view, not surprisingly, that such a thing could simply never again occur, must never be allowed to recur:

It is not therefore surprising that, as the horrific experience of war receded, to be replaced by the onerous problems of peacetime soldiering, the feeling should grow that the unprecedented war effort of 1914–1918 had been unique, even an aberration.

No less an authority than the Chief of the Imperial General Staff, Sir George Milne, endorsed this view in 1926 when he described the recent war as 'abnormal'. At present, he added, the army couldn't even mobilise a single corps; it was most unlikely ever again to be required to fight a European War. The phrase 'Never Again' was frequently used about such a nightmarish prospect; politicians implied scornfully that they would not send troops to 'the trenches' and even the use of the term 'Expeditionary Force' was deplored in government discussions and official reports.[6]

Facing the jackboot

Life was hard in the north-east during the Depression, and after. In such difficult times, Sir Oswald Mosley's British Union of Fascists was able to make significant gains in terms of a popular following. Modelled on and extolling the perceived virtues of Mussolini's Italy, membership rose as high as 50,000 and produced an equally aggressive response from Jewish leftist groups. There were violent clashes between both factions in Newcastle upon Tyne and other cities. On 10 September 1933, Stockton-on-Tees became an unlikely battlefield in the ideological clash between forces of the far right and moderate left in the UK.

Sir Oswald Mosley was a baronet, Great War veteran and MP but, notoriously, he had become leader of the British Union of Fascists (BUF) in the hungry '30s. He had founded the BUF in 1932, heavily influenced by Mussolini's bully boys in Italy – nationalistic, anti-left and anti-Zionist, militaristic and pro-authoritarian.

In 1933 Hitler came to power in Germany, and Europe began to look down the long tunnel into war. It was a bad time for north-east England: Depression, the death of traditional industries, mass unemployment, hunger and despair.

On Sunday 10 September, in the early afternoon, the BUF contingent motored up to Stockton in a convoy of hired coaches, about 100, led by their spin doctor Captain Vincent Collier. Their column halted by Victoria Bridge, on the south side of the Tees. Some of the BUF were from Manchester, others Tyneside. Paramilitary in their distinctive black shirts, the fascists dressed ranks and marched along the High Street to just north of the Town Hall. It was here they intended to hold a rally.

If they'd hoped to succeed through stealth, they were going to be sadly disappointed. Local activists had got wind of the planned demo and trades unions had taken up the gauntlet, organising a counter-rally with perhaps 2,000 participants drowning out Collier's vitriol as he tried to stir the crowd. Even his loud-hailer couldn't help. The only people who did not seem to be aware of an impending crisis were the police. Those few officers on duty attempted to calm a crowd rapidly running out of patience, and increasingly hostile to the Blackshirts.

Collier was ordered to stand down and disperse his *abteilung* (battalion) who, realising the odds were pretty much stacked against them, decided en masse upon a rapid tactical withdrawal to the lee of Silver Street to regroup. With the river at their backs, they attempted to make a stand. Both sides were now very much 'tooled up' with batons and pick-axe handles. Battle was joined, the confined space became a local Thermopylae. Arrows didn't darken the Sunday afternoon sun, but rocks, half-bricks and spuds neatly ornamented with razor blades certainly flew. At least one of the fascists, Edmund Warburton, lost an eye.

By now more police were being drafted in and deployed to create a barrier between the combatants. The BUF were delivered from annihilation and hustled back down High Street to the refuge of their transport. Stragglers got a good send off from their tormentors. Collectively they didn't get off scot-free; it's thought at least a score of them required hospital treatment and many more would carry the bruises for a while. The BUF didn't hurry back to Stockton.

The Jarrow March has passed into legend as the totem of despair. Only three years later, in October 1936, the Jarrow hunger marchers, 'crusaders', a hundred and more of them, would set out on their historic if hopeless march.

The Battle of Stockton is less celebrated than the later clash at Cable Street in East London, on 4 October 1936. Numbers were greater; perhaps as many as 20,000 Jews, Socialists and trades unionists clashed with about 2,000–3,000 Blackshirts.[7]

One further consequence of hard times, particularly for northern regiments such as the Durham Light Infantry, was an abundance of recruits. Economic necessity was, as ever, a powerful driver to enlistment:

Durham being one of the counties hardest hit by the economic depression as well as being one in which unemployment gave a welcome, however regrettable, stimulus to enlisting; the Regiment could have recruited itself six times over. Recruiting had even to be suspended for several months in the year. As it was, recruits were so numerous that the old militia barracks at Barnard Castle were opened up as additional accommodation.[8]

I make no apology for a rather northern-centric view. Besides, from 1939 to 1945 the experience of the men serving in the Durham Light Infantry ('DLI') and other regional battalions mirrors that of the British Army as a whole. They fought in France in 1940, throughout the Desert War, battled across Sicily, slogged through Italian mud, struggled through the bocage when they returned to France in 1944 and then fought in the jungles of Burma. When it all seemed to be over, in 1945, one of their battalions uncovered the horrors of Belsen in northern Germany.

Not all of Britain's youth were un-blooded – those who had already fought in the Spanish Civil War (17 July 1936–1 April 1939) knew what to expect:

We had no illusions on that score. However, I answered the call the same as many thousands of others and reported myself at Winchester, and we were there a total of two days. Everything was in chaos ... You can imagine the chaos as literally hundreds and hundreds were pouring through the gates those first three days – all reserves answering the call.[9]

Arthur Bryant, the distinguished popular historian, writing in 1948, described the context:

John Moore's[10] tradition, though often neglected and obscured, survived in two great branches of the army – the Rifles and the Light Infantry. Widely applied in 1914 and still more in the years after 1940, it enabled men untrained in war to become superb soldiers and to defeat the finest veterans of the

Continent. Their victories are now as much a part of history as Waterloo and Agincourt. Though wars pass, the British soldier remains. His weapon and uniform may be changed, his tactics superseded, his body threatened with death and mutilation by new, though not more fearful weapons, but the factor of his spirit is constant.[11]

It's a bit gung-ho, but essentially true.

It was Haldane's reforms of the early 20th century that created the basis for territorial forces but these have an ancient, militia lineage, in the case of the Durhams, certainly as far back as 1685. Alarums during the Napoleonic Wars when it seemed, as later in 1940, that Britain might be invaded by a strong Continental enemy, spurred recruitment of Volunteer Companies, though this faded away rather after the demise of the threat in 1815.

A general revival occurred in the late 1850s and after 1908 four Territorial Battalions (the 6th, 7th, 8th and 9th) were formed into 151 Brigade, which was to serve with considerable distinction in both World Wars.[12] The Second World War would arguably be the most testing time of all for the Durhams and the whole of Britain's citizen army, pitted against one of the most monstrous tyrannies in history. The years 1939–1945 would witness both the nadir and zenith of military achievement, from the scarred and bitter sands of Dunkirk, the crucible of the Western Desert, the long slog up the spine of Italy, to the Normandy beaches and beyond.

Unlike those resounding fanfares of 1914, the nation came to arms in 1939 with an air of weary resignation. Many had accepted for some time that war was inevitable and that Munich was just a stopgap. Despite 'Peace in our Time', the number of Territorial Battalions had been doubled from 13 to 26 in March 1938. Partial mobilisation had been anticipated by the passing of the Military Training Act 1939[13].

In training
No sooner had Chamberlain issued his mournful declaration of war than the National Service (Armed Forces) Act – conscription[9] – came into immediate effect. If there was to be no spectacular rush to the colours this time around, there was at least a steady trickle. Men came forward voluntarily

to enlist, more in a spirit of stoical acceptance than in any marked swell of patriotic fervour: 'It was a silent audience which heard the Prime Minister announce quietly that a state of war existed between Great Britain and Germany, and just that evening the various companies heard HM the King speak to his people throughout the British Empire. The challenge from Nazi Germany had been accepted.'[11]

In September 1939 there was a total of eight DLI Battalions; the 1st was in distant Tientsin, whilst the 2nd was rather nearer to hand in less exotic Woking. Of the five territorial formations, two (the 5th and 7th) had been diverted to Air Defence Great Britain; the remaining three (the 6th, 8th and 9th) would form 151 Brigade with a further three reserve Battalions, the 10th, 11th and 12th (Tyneside Scottish).[13] All who served in these units were by definition volunteers: professionals and Territorials. There would be no Second World War equivalent of the Kitchener formations. The DLI would be on the beaches at Dunkirk and back again in Normandy. The 'Dunkirk' Battalions, raised by conscription, might be the nearest in concept, and of these DLI formed the 14th, 16th and 17th Battalions which were to serve as the 206th Independent Infantry Brigade:[14]

> As one of the three DLI battalions of 151 Infantry Brigade of 50 Division, the 8th, like so many other territorial units, had its teething troubles during those first hectic weeks after the declaration of war. To Captain A. B. S. Clarke the adjutant and others on the administrative side must go much of the credit for the smooth running of the unit.
>
> They brought order out of chaos during that critical period of the Battalion's history. September was indeed a month when there was so much to do and so little time in which to do it. Trenches were dug and sandbags filled as part of the air defence scheme, dozens of indents were sent in by the harassed Q.M. [Quartermaster] for the many and varied stores needed to bring the unit up to its war establishment and the medical officer was busy all day, inspecting, inoculating and vaccinating hundreds of tough-skinned miners.[15]

Despite the exigencies of a life-and-death struggle, the army's capacity for bureaucratic officiousness never dimmed:

> When, for instance, in a practice, all the fire hoses were found to be defective, the barrack-master at Shorncliffe, an old soldier of some 40 years' service, issued a new one but 'on condition,' as he said, 'you never use it for water but let it stand on the wall.' Views, too, on the advantages and disadvantages of the various defences were apt to change with each new commander. One liked such and such pillboxes; another did not; and one day spent painting them with the letters A (approved), B (requiring strengthening), C (not wanted) or X (loop-holes not wanted) might be followed by another spent in painting C on those already marked A or B or in painting out the Xs. But one of the most rewarding moments in a commanding officer's service came on 10 May 1941 when the Battalion was visited by the General Officer Commanding the XII Corps, General Bernard Law Montgomery, whose decided opinions on all matters had already made a refreshing impact on his command. After watching the Battalion for some time he rose to go, saying as he did so, 'Well, that's very good. You could do anything with that lot.'[16]

It had not been anticipated that a shrunken and emasculated army of those grim inter-war years would need to answer a fresh and all-consuming summons. The UK was divided into a total of eight military districts, each of which could field its quota of regular and Territorial divisions. The whole of the north-east region was within Northern Command. At the outset, virtually all available regular and TA formations would be required to fill the ranks of the BEF being sent to France.[17]

At the same time, Britain still maintained vast overseas commitments within the creaking Empire. The Second World War is now sometimes viewed in the rosy glow of hindsight as a crusade, the Western democracies tilting against a totalitarian regime, the most brutal and repugnant in history. This was not necessarily immediately apparent at the time:

When war was declared, I was in bed having a lie in, which one did after a late Saturday night. My mother called upstairs to tell me, and said there was someone using a rattle, which was the signal for gas being used.

This was the state of tension which existed at the beginning. But no gas was ever used so here was I, in a reserved occupation, wanting to go into the armed forces, but unable to do so ... The recruiting officer asked us our occupations, and told us we were in reserved jobs, and he couldn't take us. So that was the first rejection. One might ask why did I want to go into the forces, when I could continue in a fairly safe job? Well, the forge work was very hard and dirty, and the thought of getting away from it, without considering the dangers, was all I could think of. It must be remembered having a job before the war was something to hold onto...[18]

Peter Williams was a youthful volunteer with an ambition to serve in the Royal Armoured Corps. He found his introduction to the soldier's life something less than Homeric:

Thus began our eight weeks of basic training, which was to make a young offender's institution seem like a holiday camp by comparison. Each hut had 20 two-tier bunks to hold 40 troopers but no other furniture except for the scrubbed trestle table which was in the central pathway. At reveille we had to fold our blankets and lay out our kit on the bunk ready for inspection. Then we had to sweep the hut, 'bumper' the floor, scrub the table and we even had to scrub the back of the scrubbing brush (this latter took some ingenuity and we resolved it by co-operating with the next-door hut).

We were drilled from 6.00am to 8.00pm and, apart from marching drill on the parade ground, we had to go everywhere at the double. We were marched to all meals in the cookhouse; to the camp barber's shop that first week; to the camp tailor (a German Prisoner of War) to have our best battledress altered to fit; to the medical officer for fitness tests, inoculations, tetanus toxoid, TAB, typhus; and we were even marched to the ablutions block for a daily cold shower. The haircutting parades were probably a racket as we were deducted 6*d* (2½p) from our pay for each haircut and I'm sure that the infantry sergeants in charge of us had some sort of rake-off. Because of lack of earlier dental hygiene, (we had only visited the dental clinic if we had toothache), I spent many sessions in the dental chair during those first weeks and I have every reason to be grateful to the Army for correcting many years of neglect.[19]

Part of the limitations in British and French tactical thinking throughout 1939–1940 was that this war would be a re-run of the last and that it would become a static affair of trenches. That the break-in battles of 1918 had shown potential for the use of mass-armoured forces seemed to have been overlooked. Tanks were to be used in penny packets for infantry support, rather than in large independent formations, capable of exercising strategic impact: 'I think we rather thought that it would be very like the First War – there'd be the rush forward by the Germans – we'd hold them. Then trench warfare would come about as it was. We did realise that there'd be much more bombing from the air – in fact, we thought it would be much greater than it was to start off with. Gas – so everybody had gas masks.'[20]

No amount of training, as the draft manual readily concedes, could offer a substitute for action: 'Everything else is make-believe. It follows therefore that the more practically and realistically troops are taught when they are not fighting the better they will perform when they are, and the impact of battle will be less strange to them.'

The British Army of 1939 would go to France as the most mechanised in history though, tragically, virtually all the vehicles and equipment would be lost there. So much British kit was abandoned in Norway, France and later Greece that, when attacking Crete in 1941 from the air, the *Luftwaffe* parachuted in crates of spare parts for Allied vehicles! Despite this, and despite the fact the vast majority of Axis forces still relied upon transport of the equine variety, British arms were defective in certain key respects. Infantry tanks, the Matilda particularly, were slow-moving and under-gunned, though their thick armour would give Germans a fright at Arras.

Anti-tank weapons relying upon the same two-pounder gun were ineffective and the anti-tank rifle obsolete. The Bren light machine gun was a fine weapon but the *Wehrmacht* possessed the fast-firing MG34 and lots of them. British Lee-Enfield rifles were, as ever, rugged and reliable, but our infantry lacked handy and versatile submachine-guns.[21] 'One of the things we were told – the sort of rumour that was going around – was that the Germans couldn't possibly have built up an army since 1933, in six years. People even said that, when the Germans paraded their tanks through the cities of northern Germany, some of them were made of cardboard. That is the sort of rumour one heard.'[22]

There was also the problem of space: where were all these hordes of khaki-coloured heroes going to sleep? Britain, unlike the Continent, had no tradition of mass armies; unlike the USA, there was no abundance of ground where vast, tented cities could spring up unimpeded. Barracks were relatively few and more could not be constructed overnight; most of those standing dated from the 18th or 19th centuries. These rapidly swelling legions had to be accommodated on a rather ad hoc basis, billeted in private homes, large country houses, hotels, village halls and schools, an administrative nightmare and grossly inefficient. As a nation, we tend to pride ourselves, not without justification, on our capacity simply to 'muddle through'. At this point, Britain was on the cusp of experiencing her most severe test of nationhood since Bonaparte.

In 1939, the introduction of Infantry Schools lay three years distant. For that first desperate half of the war, Britain remained on the defensive. One disaster followed another: Norway, France and Belgium, Greece, Crete, the fall of Malaya, Burma and Singapore. Cities were pounded during the Blitz, wolf packs stalked Atlantic convoys; defeat, starvation and ruin filled our horizons. It was not until October 1942 that the 'End of the Beginning' heralded the 'Beginning of the End'. Montgomery's great victory at El Alamein, though costly, ended Rommel's long run of successes, and disaster in the east at Stalingrad gave

Germany a taste of what lay in store. Fortress Europe no longer seemed impregnable.

> Will young soldiers pause, while I tell them two laws
> Of the rear, which should cause no surprise.
> The first of the two is called 'cover from view',
>
> And the second is 'cover from flies'.
> When you've done all you can in a bucket or pan,
> Don't think it a terrible bore
> To sprinkle some sand on the top with your hand,
>
> From a box you'll find on the floor.
> Now flies may with ease spread a lot of disease,
> So from this it's perfectly clear,
> Conceal your excreta, it looks so much neater,
> And keep flies away from the rear.
>
> *Laws of the Rear*[23]

For those answering the call-up at the outset, training took place at Infantry Training Centres, essentially just a reclassification of regimental depots. Training was 1914–1918 vintage. 'Battle Drill' did not appear until after 1942 when the School of Infantry was established:

> On receiving my call-up papers, I started to prepare for the life ahead. I had not much idea of army life, but I did my best to visualise it. The fateful day came ... I left home about 7am, which had meant getting up at what, at that time, seemed an unearthly hour but I was soon to learn that reveille at 06.00 hours was quite the usual thing in the army.
>
> We changed trains at Durham and boarded a train to Brancepeth Castle. Spirits were high and there were some real characters. On arrival at Brancepeth we left the train and began our tramp down the straight road to the castle. At the castle we were hanging about for quite a time before being issued with a meat pie. I remember that more than half the lads left theirs, while some finished off a second. We also received a mug of cocoa which I think was made of red limestone![24]

These training centres (a total of 64 in 1939),[25] by their very nature, tended to be situated in large urban areas so unsuited to coping with a substantial influx of untrained recruits: Peter Anderson continues:

> At this point we were issued with kitbags, which were soon to be filled up with kit. We followed each other through the corridors having equipment and clothing thrown at us from all directions. When we had got all the kit we were marched away to the camp, which was about half-a-mile away.
>
> It was a Durham Light Infantry camp and the Duke of Wellington's Infantry, (No. 4 Infantry Training Camp, 54 Primary Training Wing). After we had managed to carry all our kit to the camp, we were sorted into companies. Each of the four companies had two squads each. I was in 'C' Company 19 Squad. We were then given palliasses, which we had to fill with straw, quite a job that was! We then received a mug, plate, knife, fork and spoon and other equipment, including a bed!
>
> During the next few days we were marched all over camp for various things. We went to the tailor who marked one of our battledress suits for altering where necessary. We also went to the shoe repairer who put 13 studs in each of our boots. We went to the barber's and all had haircuts. It was really funny to watch some of the chap's expressions when they felt their hair being separated from their heads: some of them looked as if they hadn't had their hair cut for months! We were then taken to the M.I. room for inoculations: TAB and TT, and were confined to barracks for 48 hours. We found out why the next day: our arms were very stiff and everyone felt ill, with one or two chaps passing out during the day.[26]

Such rapid expansion inevitably resulted in an acute shortage of officers. An initial response was to establish cadet formations nationwide 'where the emphasis was placed more on technical efficiency and physical endurance rather than on character and leadership.'[27] As the war progressed a more considered approach was adopted, with those selected being sent to Officer Cadet Training Units; for infantry, the course duration was normally 17 weeks.[28]

Quite often infantry recruits would find the training and fitness regime extremely tough. For many, this was their first taste of regular exercise and equally regular rations:

> I was drafted to an infantry training regiment in Scotland. Every recruit had to have basic infantry training. I weighed only nine stone when I went into the army, that being due to the working conditions and food shortages. I did really thrive on the fresh air, exercise, food and training. I can honestly say that I have never felt fitter than at that time, or since in my life. It was hard work but interesting, and it suited me down to the ground.[29]

Peter Anderson recalls how little leeway was afforded to new recruits:

> We had fairly decent meals at the camp, all cooked by ATS cooks. We had kit inspections every week. The army authorities watched our every move during this part of army training. One night some of us went into nearby Crook for the evening and walked home eating fish and chips. We were stopped by army redcaps (military police) and told in no uncertain terms that this was not acceptable behaviour.[30]

The period of the 'Phoney War' that followed the fall of Poland, the 'First Ally' as the exiled government would come to be known, did not long endure. Germany's triumph there had been the product of superior infantry tactics employing stormtroopers based on what was erroneously labelled the Hutier model from the last war.[31] Though the world had yet to witness *blitzkrieg*, the Allies, now Britain and France, would not be kept waiting unduly.

2

OVERTURE

... Having seized the initiative by our initial landing, we must insure that we keep it. The best way to interfere with the enemy concentrations and countermeasures will be to push forward fairly powerful armoured force thrusts on the afternoon of D-Day. ... I am prepared to accept almost any risk in order to carry out these tactics. I would risk even the total loss of the armoured brigade groups – which in any event is not really possible.[1]

Remember that Continental France has been directly occupied. In consequence it has been stripped of everything by the Germans. Almost all French civilians (including French children) are under-nourished, and many have died from exhaustion and hunger, because the Germans have eaten the food. The Germans have also drunk the wine ...

Instructions for British Servicemen (bold emphasis as in the original)[2]

It's said the Calvados coast of Normandy gets its name from a Spanish galleon, the *Salvador*, fleeing from the defeat of the Armada that came to grief on rocks just off Arromanches. This was in 1588. Much later, as a foretaste of 1940, the *Department* was occupied by the Prussians after Napoleon's defeat in 1815. It is a lovely region where small, mellowed stone settlements rise from a wide, flat coastal plain, long stretches of pale and perfect sands with, certainly in 1944, a dark, enclosed interior of myriad tiny, deeply hedged fields bisected by sunken lanes, the bocage country. Tommy in 1944 would come to know it well. Many would not emerge.

The beaches

Remy Douin was 13 as he cycled along the emptied lanes that spring with his artist father Robert. Theirs was an artistic lineage and just because it was wartime that didn't stop Douin *pere* from sporting his artist's beard and pointed moustache, nor, indeed, did it deter him from wearing a loud, very un-wartime velvet suit, colourful cravat and elegant, wide-brimmed fedora. Robert's flamboyance went with his art, of course. Although he had a badly damaged arm from the last war, he still followed his vocation of teacher, church artist and restorer. This meant he could travel along the coast inspecting ancient churches pretty much without comment, and church towers commanded an excellent view. What he sketched, cleverly disguised, was the dangerous and forbidden mass of the Atlantic Wall. Each sketch, like a giant mosaic, was a piece in the jigsaw he was building.

He'd joined the fledgeling Resistance at the very outset in November 1940, in his native Caen. Two years later, he was a fully committed activist and leader of a local *réseau*. He used his cover and *Mousquetaire* bravado as a disguise in plain sight. It was very dangerous work. A year before D-Day, he knew he was a marked man; the *Geheime Staatspolizei* (Secret State Police, the Gestapo) and their collaborators were on his tail. Still, although he could have been, with his family, spirited away to England, he chose to stay, teaching fine art classes in *l'ecole des Beaux-Arts* in Caen. The work, his greatest creation, was paramount. Robert Duin was a very brave man.

Remy knew what his father was about; as the pair rode their bicycles through the lovely Norman spring, using the turns of their pedals to calculate distances between bunkers, the net inexorably tightened. At last Robert sent Remy south to stay with relatives. On 16 March 1943, Robert walked to the station to meet a contact. Nobody turned up – not until next day when the *Milice* kicked in his door. Robert, with many others, was dragged to the prison in Caen where he was interrogated and systematically tortured.

His left arm, the one he'd damaged last time around, was broken and he was mercilessly beaten before being chucked into the cooler.

When he was at last dumped in an ordinary cell, most were crammed with captured resisters. He managed to confer with another prisoner, Bernard Duval, a teenage carpenter who'd suffered similar torture – ironically he'd been the one who fitted the heavy timber door to Cell 27, the one he was now incarcerated in! Robert managed to salvage some scraps of parcel paper and laboriously crafted letters to his wife and son using a series of innocuous-looking dots. These were got out weekly via the laundry basket. On 6 June, in the morning, Robert was among 75–80 other resisters who were taken out of their cells and shot in batches against the walls of a blood-slicked courtyard. His body was never found.[3] Remy returned, becoming a civil servant and businessman; Bernard Duval also survived. Both continued to keep alive the memory of those who'd sacrificed their lives.

A hard-won lesson

Earlier, on 19 August 1942, St Oswin's Eve, the Allies launched a major amphibious raid on the coast of occupied France aimed at seizing and then, for a limited period, holding Dieppe. Operation *Jubilee* was the curtain-raiser for Operation *Overlord*. Even at this early date the Americans, anxious to be done with war in the West so they could concentrate upon the defeat of Japan, were pressing for a full-scale invasion of Hitler's 'Fortress Europe'. It was one of those raids, such as the ill-fated Operation *Agreement* launched against Tobruk that September, which comes under the fateful heading of 'it seemed like a good idea at the time' – it wasn't.

Some 6,086 Allied troops, mainly Canadians, went ashore at Dieppe and, of these, 3,623 became casualties, a loss of nearly 60 per cent; the RAF lost 96 planes and the Navy lost 34 vessels of all types. The images one retains of Operation *Jubilee* are those of wrecked British tanks, hopelessly bogged down on the shingle, with the bodies of dead Canadians strewn around. The raid was an unqualified disaster yet many lessons, vital to the subsequent success of *Overlord* on D-Day, were learnt. It could be argued, though many would disagree, that the Canadians' terrible sacrifice wasn't wholly in vain.

When the Japanese bombed Pearl Harbor on 7 December 1941 they answered Churchill's prayer, for now surely the New World must come to the assistance of the Old, even if the US preferred and prioritised the fight in the Pacific. We needed them. Hitler's fatal blunder in opening a second front by attacking the Soviet Union that June had taken the pressure off Britain and her empire but there was, at that stage, no prospect that Churchill's slice of the Old World could, on its own, liberate Hitler's massive portion.

Success had so far eluded British forces, harried out of Norway, hustled out of France and Belgium, fleeing from Greece and beaten on Crete. Operations against the Italians in the Western desert had brought victory but only very temporarily; Rommel's *Deutsche Afrika Korps* had seen to that. General Auchinleck had fought the Desert Fox to a standstill and clawed back the empty miles of desert with his *Crusader* offensive of November 1941 but lost it again just as quickly, British forces reeling backwards with alarming alacrity in the 'Gazala Gallop' and 'Msus Stakes'. Tobruk fell with a huge bag of Allied captives. Pretty soon the 8th Army was dug in along its last line of defence 60 miles west of Alexandria at El Alamein.

Meanwhile, the Japanese overran Malaya and Burma, contemptuously scooped up Singapore and sank the pride of the Royal Navy. They were soon knocking at the doors of India but that was as far as they'd get. Island by bloody harsh and barren coral outcrop, the Americans clawed back the Pacific. MacArthur memorably vowed he'd be back (before abandoning his men in the Philippines) and the Japanese now began to feel the heat. The Battle of Midway paid them back for Pearl Harbor and dusk very slowly came to settle over the Empire of the Rising Sun.

Finally, in October 1942, General Bernard Montgomery opened the Second Battle of El Alamein, a grinding, costly attritional struggle that would, nonetheless, herald the end of those constant swings of the desert 'pendulum'. In November, British and American forces invaded French North Africa and the Axis powers were pushed back and back until a final capitulation at Tunis on 13 May 1943. The tide had begun to ebb on Hitler's Thousand Year Reich. Disaster at Stalingrad was followed by defeat at Kursk and a very long retreat that would end with the storming of the Reichstag.

Atlantic Wall

Meanwhile there was Fortress Europe. From 1942, even though Dieppe was a disaster, *Oberkommando der Wehrmacht* (*OKW*) was well aware the blow must sooner or later fall against the Atlantic Wall, that string of fortifications rising like fresh scars along the coasts of north-west Europe. Churchill didn't like the idea. He preferred peripheral, potentially less costly strategies, hopping from North Africa to Sicily and then onto the toe of the Italian Peninsula. It brought Il Duce's new Rome crashing down but the fight up the inhospitable spine of Italy was long and hard, bloody, exhausting, contested yard by yard in a defender's paradise.

Our former colonies were getting restless. The Americans wanted done with Hitler and fully on to Hirohito. Dieppe and wise counsel convinced them it couldn't be done in 1942 or even 1943. Britain was still, if only just, the senior partner in the western reaches of the Grand Alliance. In the east, too, the natives were agitating. Stalin wanted, demanded, the Allies open a second front to take pressure off the Red Army. Much as we might dislike him, the Russian dictator had a point. It was his armies that were bearing the brunt of the fight, the most terrible in history, which would claim the lives of perhaps as many as 27 million Russians; that's nearly 100 times greater than the UK or US sacrifice.

Breaching Hitler's Fortress wouldn't be easy. All amphibious operations carry huge risks and the Germans would be waiting – but waiting where? Germany had 2,800 miles of occupied coastline to defend and to cover this great length was beyond Hitler's shrinking resources, but beginning in March 1942 a series of stout, well-constructed bunkers, artillery and anti-aircraft emplacements were built in concrete and steel – covering ports, landing groups and dominating sea-cliffs.

By 1944, Hitler's slaves, nearly 300,000 of them, were labouring in France and on the Channel Islands under the whips of the Todt Organisation.[4] Approximately 17 million cubic yards (13 million cubic metres) of concrete and 1.2 million tonnes of steel went into the build. Coastal batteries deployed 700 guns. Inevitably, the Pas de Calais was the most defended sector. It was closest and the German command assumed the Allies would aim, as a primary objective, to seize a major Channel port, a deep-water harbour. The Dieppe debacle did have the effect of reinforcing this assumption.

What *OKW* didn't know was that the Allies had a very significant ace, or pair of aces, up their sleeve – the Mulberry Harbours. These were an astonishing innovation. The idea dated from 1942; the Allies would take their own harbours with them, vast pre-fabricated structures, each as big as Dover, comprising 73 floating concrete caissons that would each be towed over the water, then assembled off the Normandy coast. IKEA on an epic scale. One was intended to serve the British and Canadians just off Arromanches, with the other reserved for the Americans. Despite their enormous size and complexity, the Germans never found out about the Mulberries, one of the great Allied successes of D-Day.[5]

In mid-April 1944, 9th Battalion, Durham Light Infantry moved to their pre-embarkation base about 5 miles from Southampton, as Eric Broadhead describes:

Life on the whole was pleasant. It was summertime at its best. Our evenings found us in Southampton, where the servicemen outnumbered the civilians by seven to one. The walk from Southampton back to camp was a pleasant one, and often I and my mates would stroll back talking of home, parents, wives and sweethearts and of the day that must surely dawn soon, the day when we sailed for a destination that only a few men knew.

We discussed our ideas of where it would be, but the question was when? Sometimes the question got on our nerves. We all had our own theories as to when it would be. Around May 10th a drastic move took place. The camps were sealed, our training was over. The days that followed were strange to be sure. Barbed wire skirted the camp area, armed guards too. We received no mail, but were still allowed to write home, subject to strict censorship.

Our briefing took place in a Nissen hut, which was heavily guarded. Inside was similar to a schoolroom and had a huge map on an equally huge blackboard. On the map we could see a small strip of coastline, the names of towns and villages were false, New York, Istanbul etc. So we learned little as to the exact whereabouts of the assault. All we knew was that our objective was to capture the beachhead and press on to high ground and above all, hold our ground until armoured divisions were ashore.[6]

By the time Tommies were clambering aboard ships on 5 June, more than 12,000 Atlantic Wall fortifications had been completed and 500,000 beach obstacles, sown like the Hydra's teeth, were laid; there were also 6.5 million landmines, inland areas were flooded and the drenched polders bristled with stakes designed to impale gliders or paratroopers – 'Rommel's asparagus'.

To defend the Calvados coast 7,800 *Wehrmacht* of the 716th Infantry Division, with their HQ in Caen, were deployed. This formation wasn't too impressive; the ranks were, in some places, made up of renegade Russians or Poles, even Indian Army survivors from the Desert War who'd swapped sides as a less bad alternative to POW status. It's hard to blame them; the Germans treated their *Ostfront* captives very badly.

Someone who knew an Allied invasion was inevitable was Field Marshal Erwin Rommel; Hitler had appointed him late in 1943 as Inspector of the Atlantic Wall defences. The Desert Fox quickly realised the cheerful and bombastic propaganda newsreels showed a very different picture from the reality. His preferred strategy was at odds with that of Field Marshal Gerd von Rundstedt, overall commander in the west, who favoured a massive counter-punch rather than trying to sweep the Allies off the beaches as they came ashore. This was bad enough but Hitler insisted on making the final decision, and the Fuhrer liked to sleep late. His habits would be of enormous help to the British and Americans on 6 June. Some German officers were considering a rather more radical solution for a leader they now considered a liability.

On 15 January 1944, Rommel was promoted to command Army Group B, in charge of the defence from Calais to Rennes. Normandy sat squarely within his watch. By March he'd set up his HQ in the old fortress of La Roche-Guyon. As ever, his restless energy and all-seeing eye galvanised the defences and the defenders. He harried his men relentlessly: more wire, more mines, more obstacles. What he really, really wanted was to keep the six reserve *panzer* divisions as close as possible to the landing grounds. Von Rundstedt fretted that his tanks would be too exposed to naval bombardment and demanded they be held further back. Berlin temporised, allowing Rommel only half of what he wanted, and even those divisions were not fully under his hand. Like most compromises, this pleased nobody and hampered an effective response.

Monty

General Bernard Law Montgomery had replaced General Morgan, whose COSSAC[7] Group had been planning the invasion, codenamed *Overlord*. Amphibious landings would be supported by a vast naval armada, *Neptune*, and the enemy kept guessing by a brilliant deception plan, *Fortitude*. American General Dwight Eisenhower would lead SHAEF.[8] Monty, in charge of land forces and as abrasive as ever, wanted to expand the initial 30-mile landing zone to 50 miles and to commit five divisions rather than three as previously.

The author has been within the precincts of Kirkham Priory in North Yorkshire, a 12th-century Augustinian foundation, now sympathetically managed by English Heritage. A site of such calm pastoral beauty and ancient provenance, it appears as far from the realities of industrial war as you could get. Yet in the build-up to D-Day, Churchill himself came north to the ruined priory where some innovative ideas on armoured warfare were being put to the test in giant ponds excavated by the river.

The then prime minister was joined by King George VI in a visit that was first brought to English Heritage's attention by a local elderly resident. 'The visit to Kirkham by Churchill and the King shows that this was a key training area.' A rare photograph came to light after *Country Life* published an article referring to the priory's war-time service. A reader came forward with the image, showing Churchill talking to his grandfather, who had served in the army. 'The British 11th armoured division was amongst the units moved to Kirkham to give drivers experience of manoeuvring and to test various waterproofing compounds. Vehicles ranged from tanks to jeeps. During the build-up to D-Day the A64 was a massive car park for all kinds of military hardware.' Troops also gained some useful experience by tackling Kirkham's ancient walls using clambering nets, this was fitting practice for the rubble-strewn towns they were to encounter in northern France.[9]

Major General Percy Hobart ('Hobo'),[10] a mercurial if gifted officer, had been appointed to command 79th Armoured Division, a creative rather than fighting formation. He had been born in 1885. Commissioned into the Royal Engineers, he was an early enthusiast of armoured warfare. In the 1940s, he had fallen foul of Field Marshal Wavell and been pensioned off into obscurity. However, Hobo was Monty's brother-in-law. Monty was a man who loved his wife very much and never fully recovered from her early death. For a while Hobart's eclipse meant he was relegated to the ranks of the Home Guard and the defence of Chipping Camden. It was Viscount Alanbrooke[11] who, in March 1943, rescued Hobart. He'd got back into regular service and commanded 79th Armoured, which had been on the point of disbandment but was again facing the axe. His enemies, who were legion, hadn't forgotten him either, but the lesson of Dieppe was that specialised armour was needed for a successful beach assault. Hobo's hour had come and he didn't fail the test.

His tank designs, if unconventional, were brilliant and thousands of Allied servicemen on the British beaches would owe their lives to him. He created the fearsome 'Crocodile' flame-throwing variant, the mine-bursting 'Flail', bunker-busting 'Petard', and the remarkable 'DD' (for 'duplex drive') swimming tank, using Shermans, Valentines or Cromwells fitted with canvas skirts that enabled the vehicle to be launched at sea and literally swim to the shore. A tanker veteran Tom Walling recalled training with DD tanks in the Lake District: 'We got pretty good with 'em too, the training gave us confidence. Not like the Yanks mind, they hadn't a clue!'[12]

The Plan

Paratroops were a Second World War innovation. German General Kurt Student had shown what his *Fallschirmjager* could do in 1940 when they brilliantly took the great Belgian fortress of Eben-Emael.[13] Allied planners were hoping for a masterful *coup de main* in 1944. At 02.00 on 6 June, the 6th Airborne Division, coming in by glider, would attempt to seize the vital bridges over the Orne River and Canal, a task allotted to D Company of the Oxford and Buckinghamshire Light Infantry (*see* Map 1). Other elements of 5th Para Brigade would take and hold ground around Ranville, (Map 1). To 3rd Para Brigade fell the tasks of knocking out the Merville Battery and destroying the Dives River crossings at Varaville, Robehomme, Bures and Troarn. Sorting out the battery was paramount as it was feared the big guns there could command the length of Sword Beach and wreak havoc among the landing craft. With the Dives' crossings gone, the Germans would struggle to get reinforcements in from the east; the paras, if successful, would effectively seal off that flank (for a full Order of Battle *see* Appendix i).

The most easterly beach, Sword (*see* Map 4) would be attacked at 07.25, the same time as men would go ashore at Gold Beach further west, and with the Canadians going for Juno between the two British beaches. The 3rd British Division had last seen action on rather different beaches, at Dunkirk; much of their time in the intervening four years had been spent in getting ready so as to ensure this time would be different. Lead elements going ashore first would be the 8th Infantry Brigade Group with armour and DD tanks. Lack of naval gunfire wouldn't be a limiting factor as it had so tragically been at Dieppe; 2 battleships, a monitor,[14] 5 cruisers and 13 destroyers would be there to lend their enormous combined barrages.

On the division's eastern flank, the Orne River and Canal created a formidable wet gap, and it was intended that the paras, backed by the Special Service Brigade, would have secured those two vital crossings at Bénouville. 'Queen' Beach was divided into White and Red Sectors and would be clobbered by the attacking brigade. Time was very much of the essence; if the Germans got their tanks in the 21st *Panzer* and 12th *SS Panzer* moving, then the British could be in for a very rough ride indeed. Getting inland and doing it quickly was the key to consolidation.

The infantry had to relieve the paras at Pegasus Bridge while No. 4 Commando moved east on Ouistreham. No. 41 Royal Marine Commando would head west to link with the Canadians coming ashore on Juno Beach (*see* below). Once Pegasus was secured, 1st Special Service Brigade would advance eastwards from the crossing, with 185th Infantry Brigade following – their objective was Caen itself. The troops landing on Sword Beach would only achieve their objectives if they took the city of Caen on 6 June. This was asking a very great deal.

Juno Beach was assigned to the Canadian 3rd Division (*see* Map 2) and they'd go in at 07.45. The beach was split into two sectors. 'Mike', on the right looking from a seaward approach, would be hit by 7th Brigade Group aiming for Courseulles-sur-Mer; 'Nan', on the left, was where the 8th Brigade Group would attack Bernières. Both assault brigades had DD tanks in support and hefty naval firepower. The Canadians' objectives were to take the coastal settlements Courseulles, St Aubin and Bernières. Beyond the beach they had three operational bounds to make, taking them inland. The first wave would be followed by part of 4th Special Service Brigade, whose main job on D-Day was to hook around and link up with 3rd British Division Commandos who'd assaulted Sword Beach.

West of Juno, on Gold Beach (*see* Map 4), 50th Northumbrian Division would more than have their work cut out. Their multiple objectives included reaching Bayeux, interdicting the main N13 highway to Caen, taking out the powerful battery at Longues and throwing out flankers to link up with Canadians to their east and as far west as Port-en-Bessin to hook up with the Americans advancing (hopefully) from Omaha.

Gold Beach itself was divided into an easterly sector, 'King', to be assaulted by 69th Brigade, and a westerly 'Jig', targeted by 231st Brigade. Their job was to land east of Le Hamel (Asnelles), take and secure the settlement, then push west towards Port-en-Bessin, which Commandos would already have grabbed. In the east, 69th Brigade would come ashore west of La Riviere (Ver-sur-Mer), clear the place, and then forge inland to reach the N13. So what would happen was that the two assault brigades would effectively veer apart as they gained their initial objectives allowing, at 10.00, two fresh brigades, 56th and 151st, to get ashore and push straight on to Bayeux.

If Eisenhower lacked Monty's battlefield experience, he was an inspirational leader and was able to cope with the precious ego and fractious temperament of his subordinate. Sergeant-Major

William Brown, serving with 8th Battalion Durham Light Infantry, was one of the thousands who found the Commander-in-Chief a powerful and heartening presence:

> Eisenhower came to have a chat with everyone, he was great. The finest general there's ever been. We formed a whole square right round this great big field. And he walked into the middle of it and said, 'Right, gentlemen; when I give the signal, all come in and sit down. Never mind the officers; they'll walk in with the men. I want everyone to hear what I have to say.' That pleased everyone. There was no bullshit about him. He was immaculate; he could have been made from chocolate. He said he'd heard all about us down in Southampton, how we'd been living it up and now the time had come to get aboard ships and fight alongside each other. He did more to lift morale – certainly mine, than anything else.[15]

Not all of the Durhams enjoyed such cordial and uplifting relationships with our US allies. Sergeant George Self, also 8th Battalion, formed a rather different impression:

> We moved to a camp near Romsey. We had battles with the Yanks nearly every night in Southampton. The main cause of this friction was money and their arrogant behaviour. Eisenhower came to see us and gave us a lecture about the American soldier. He agreed they were overpaid, oversexed and over here – but when we got over the other side, they would show us the road home – how to fight. That was the worst thing he could have said; that night blood flowed in Southampton.[16]

This would be the greatest invasion ever planned or carried out. Everyone involved from Eisenhower down to the least bright Tommy or GI knew this coming battle would be decisive. The Allies faced a fearsome challenge. To marshal the great armada, 6,000 vessels of all types needed to transport so many men, tanks, vehicles and supplies, was an unprecedented task. Yes, we had form with North Africa, Sicily and Italy, but this operation would be on a scale never before attempted, subject to fickle weather and the Channel's notorious swells. Keeping the umbilical cord of supply going was as essential as taking the beaches; maintaining the momentum, breaking out inland and sweeping through France would determine victory. The fate of the world hung in the balance.

Embarkation

Sergeant Mackenzie, serving in the Royal Signals, prepared to embark at Tilbury:

> We were issued with a new AV battledress (stinks, awful) and two 48-hour ration packs, 20 cigarettes, a life belt (such as you learn to swim with!) and two 'spew bags'. We are also paid 200 francs, so it is France after all. My own feelings are very mixed. Sometimes I feel that I am going to certain death, then at other times I think I shall make it. I shall soon know, for we are on our way to the Docks. It seems the local population don't realise that they are witnessing the beginning of what may well be the greatest moment in the history of war.
>
> Eventually we got onto the ship, a Belgian trader called 'Leopold'. When I saw the hold that had been allotted to us, my spirits sank to zero and I think this was my most miserable moment. We had the bottom hold, right in the bows, with only one exit which joined all other exits after the first stairway had been mounted. We were crammed like sardines. Twenty-eight feet below water, what chance if we were hit, either by shell, bomb or torpedo![17]

Another of the Durhams preparing for the invasion was Lieutenant William Jalland, again of 8th Battalion:

> I'd been on a sniping course at Llanberis, with instructors from the Lovat Scouts, Lord Lovat's private army![18] They were all ghillies and absolutely first class ... Then we were moved down to Southampton prior to the invasion. I knew

what we'd be doing, I'd taken part in exercises SMASH 1 and 2.[19] Well, we were open-mouthed at all the equipment; we saw part of PLUTO,[20] it was enormous, and sections of Mulberry, there were crab, scorpion and flail tanks. We knew we must be going, we weren't confined to base just at that point but soon we were. We finally embarked on an LCI, which had ramps on either side of the prow; it could accommodate the entire battalion.

My company would be one of the first off and we carried loads of equipment; [Major] Ian English and his company were kitted out with bicycles, I had to carry a folding bike and extra magazines for the Bren guns. I had a plentiful supply of condoms, not for what you might think but for waterproofing grenades and other kit. Our loads were very heavy and we were given these enormous chest waders so we'd come ashore dry, in theory at least. I wore my pyjamas under battle dress, helped to prevent the wool from chafing – just as well – I didn't take mine off for 28 days as I recall![21]

Major (then Lieutenant) K. P. Baxter (who we'll meet again on Sword Beach), serving in 5 Beach Group, described his experiences on the way to the beaches:

From the sealed camp at Rowlands Castle, we were driven under security escort to the docks at Portsmouth. Our waves to passers-by were cheerfully returned with a 'see you tomorrow' air, as none thought that this was anything but a routine exercise.

Once in the docks we were rapidly embarked on the *Empire Battleaxe*, an LSI equipped with assault landing craft suspended in davits on both port and starboard sides. This vessel was one of a small group carrying the assaulting companies of infantry together with specialised units making up breaching teams and beach signal communications.

The ship was well into the Channel when we were issued with further maps, photographs and the last briefing instructions, this time with full place names instead of code references, and any doubts amongst the many guesses as to the true landing areas were finally dispelled.[22]

British troops would be landing to the east on Sword beach, west of the Orne estuary, then Canadians on Juno and 50th Division at Gold. West of the British beaches, the Americans would land firstly on Omaha, then Utah on the flank of the Cotentin Peninsula. Paratroops would precede both British/Canadian and American seaborne landings. In the British sector Red Devils would secure the vital Orne River and Canal crossings to be immortalised as Pegasus Bridge, the high ground by Ranville and eliminate the ostensibly formidable Merville Battery overlooking Sword Beach.

Robert Millan was a signalman in the Royal Navy:

I was sent with my best mate, a freckle-faced Yorkshire lad called Foley, to the busy signal station in Gosport called Fort Gilkicker, to augment the regular signal staff prior to the invasion of Europe. The build-up was tremendous, a spectacle never to be forgotten. The Solent waters gradually filled up with every type of naval craft, from battleships down to corvettes and motor torpedo boats.

Meanwhile with all the constant reading and sending of signals by 10-inch signal lamps, my mate and I were suffering terribly from conjunctivitis. When we complained about the long 24-hours stretch of duty to the chief yeoman in charge of our watch, we were consoled by how lucky we were; that all that lot out there in the Solent (pointing out to the massive gathering of ships) were going to die, while we would survive. So we had to crawl back into our shells and just get on with life as it was.

Then it all happened. I was off duty the night of 5th June, and about 9pm noticed a steady stream of naval craft underway, making for the open sea. As daylight dawned, the whole sea area seemed still. Everything had gone, apart from one ship, HMS *Alresford*, anchored nearby, and an array of small craft, mostly used for ferrying duties. The invasion had begun. It was indeed D-Day, 6th of June 1944.[23]

Kay Martin was a Wren based at Fort Southwick, just north of Portsmouth:

> The [Fort] was the Combined Headquarters, Commander-in-Chief Portsmouth, and stood on a high road overlooking Portsmouth Harbour. Down below, a long way down, was a network of tunnels and various departments, plotting room, Cypher office, tele-printers, wireless office, telephone exchange and so on.
>
> On the morning of D-Day, I, as a Wren, had been on duty as a telephonist. A buzz went round as news of the invasion filtered through the tunnel, as it was affectionately called. But it was the run-up to D-Day which is printed deep in my memory after all these years. All around the area, inland, the troops were camped in woods and anywhere where there was space for them. Each in turn was moved on towards the embarkation area, and another took its place, like a game of draughts. Then the telephone number which was for 'X' Regiment one day, would be for 'Y' Regiment the next day. It was all a bit confusing, and difficult to keep up with![24]

Diana Granger was a Wren Petty Officer Quarters Assistant stationed in Southsea:

> I was a Wren housed in one of the seaside hotels in Southsea, overlooking the Solent, very near South Parade Pier. June 6th dawned. We Wrens woke up to the sound of military boots marching along the pavement across the road from the hotel. We soon looked out of the windows to see some of the first of the men preparing to land on enemy territory. Their progress followed a regular pattern – men carrying arms, men carrying pickaxes, more arms. At regular intervals a stretcher was carried (this sight giving us deeper thought than that accompanying our wild cheers). By now, the sash windows at the front of the hotel had been thrown up to help us shout our encouragement, and we knew the big day had started.[25]

For most, the embarkation and waiting, and waiting, in cramped conditions onboard was far from the uplifting version portrayed in movies. Eric Broadhead again:

> By mid-day on the 2nd [June] we were aboard a small flat-bottomed craft holding around 150 troops – LCI 501, US Navy – which was to take us across to a still-unknown destination. Comfort aboard was almost nil. Bunks were six deep and each hold held around 50 men. The water we used for washing was seawater, and getting soap to lather from seawater is almost impossible. Killing time was our worst problem. We only went ashore once a day, for a meal.
>
> At 9pm Monday evening we were issued with seasickness pills. That was enough, we knew by morning we should be in less peaceful waters than we were then. That evening, 501 weighed anchor. As darkness fell, we went below decks and lay on our bunks fully clothed. Outside the wind was howling even more as we turned out to sea. I dozed off before we really turned on full steam, only to be awakened by a horribly sickly feeling inside. 501 was rolling in every imaginable direction. The seasickness pills had failed if ever anything did fail. There was only one thing to do, that was to lie still, even that was dreadful and only served to make one feel worse.[26]
>
> .... People who heard the noise on the 5th June remember it as different from anything that had ever been heard before. Life in the war had made them adept at guessing what was happening from what they could hear, and as they listened that night, with increasing excitement and pride, they knew that by far the greatest fleet of aircraft they had ever heard – and therefore the greatest fleet that anyone had ever heard – was passing overhead from north to south.[27]

The weather gods, fickle in the Channel even for spring, had provided an opening, that crucial window, and Eisenhower had taken the greatest, most momentous decisions of his life – of anyone's life ever. It was on.

All at sea

Lieutenant Jalland remembers the embarkation process:

When we went down to the harbour and embarked, it was too rough to sail that night; next day was 5 June and we had a visit from a group of dignitaries, VIPs, several cabinet ministers, Churchill himself, Attlee, Eden, Bevan and Herbert Morrison, Jan Smuts and Prince Bernard of the Netherlands, all there to see us off. Once on board we were told where we were going and we sailed past the Needles as it was getting dark. The sea was very rough and people were being sick everywhere. I started feeling queasy so I left my bunk and went up on deck; this wasn't really allowed but I found a corner and huddled down up top. We were a flotilla of three LCIs and a tiny minesweeper. An awful lot of aircraft were going over and there was clearly a great deal of bombing. Naval vessels were hooting to each other and the occasional MTB motored between us.[28]

Sergeant William Brown was also on the LCI:

They gave us these enormous gas trousers, they went on last over all of your kit, and we carried everything you could imagine – three days' rations, toilet paper, cigarettes, sweets and our damned folding bicycles. I went up on deck as we crossed the Channel. We seemed to be the only ones then, all of a sudden, as we rounded the Isle of Wight, there were thousands of ships, thousands of them. Downstairs, below decks, the smell was pretty horrible, vile in fact, and the chewing gum they gave you just made it worse; the spew bags were handy though and you just threw them over the side.[29]

Brown, a highly experienced NCO, was serving with Major Ian English:

The 'O' – Orders Group involved all the officers and NCOs above the rank of corporal; Major English, Ian he was called, though he always got 'Pat', not sure why, asked me to sort out some tea so I went to find our cooks and orderlies in the bowels of the ship but they were too busy spewing up. I was looking for tea; the tins had no labels but the one I opened contained fat bacon! Well I retched and retched, I'd had nowt to eat really for a couple of days so I just retched! Now 'Pat' English was a hell of a soldier, the men had total confidence in him. He wasn't the smartest soldier in terms of turnout but he always needed to be in charge, I was sure he was after a VC![30]

Once we were all on deck, even with these gas trousers on, it was easier, the air was warm but the ship was still rolling dreadfully. Next to us a rocket ship was blasting away, salvo after salvo, the recoil was juddering the ship, great bloody noise. The LCIs were coming in on Gold beach but we stuck quite a bit out, about 500 yards off, in fact – quite a swim.

Major English said to me 'Right, Sergeant-Major, lead the way.' 'Not bloody likely,' I replied, 'I'm not taking men into that depth of water.' The LCI captain said 'Right, we'll give it another go.' So he backed up and charged in again. This time we got to within 200 yards before we stuck, the prow of the ship digging in. 'Come on Sergeant-Major,' said Major English, 'Now's the time.' 'I'm still not taking men into that,' I replied. Just then a young US sailor offered to get a rope ashore, he stripped off down to his singlet and in he went, great lad he was. The rope was secured and we started going ashore, got everybody off OK, though the damned gas trousers immediately filled up with water. We couldn't hang around, had to get up that beach as quick as possible![31]

Mr R. Haig-Brown, 93rd Light Anti-Aircraft Regiment, Royal Artillery, crossed the Channel in an LST and describes the joys of the crossing on the night of 5/6th June:

Much the most memorable impression I had that night was, seasickness apart, the terrific morale of the troops. Such was their training and briefing, and so muddle-free the assembly;

that none of us thought it possible that anything could go wrong or that we were on anything but a rather super exercise where live bullets would not actually be aimed at us, but so as to miss, and death never really happened. At 2am on 6th June, I was sent for and given an envelope by the ship's captain.

In it was the key to the code on the maps I had seen at briefing; for the first time did I know that Nan Beach in Juno Sector was at the village of Bernières-sur-Mer, just west of Ouistreham, and that the river was in fact the Orne. We had already been told we were to land at H-Hour plus a half; now we knew that H-Hour was 7.30am, just a few hours hence. I spent the rest of the night poring over my maps, translating the codes on them, telling the men all about it and issuing them with a couple of hundred francs each in new notes.[32]

And there were the big guns of the RN. One of the lessons learnt from Dieppe was that a serious weight of naval gunfire was needed to help suppress shore defences. John Abbott was serving on HMS *Largs*:

I was a young Sick Berth Petty Officer in HMS *Largs*, the senior sick berth rating aboard. She was an HQ ship, flagship of S Force, Rear Admiral Talbot flew his flag in her, and the beach that we were to take the 3rd British Infantry Division into was to become Sword Beach. Most of us had done it before, but this was the biggest yet and we felt our luck might run out after all the Mediterranean invasions.

That Tuesday morning we were chugging along steadily keeping station and the sea was full of ships. It was very early and I was up top with the Jaunty, somebody or something was making smoke, I think it was to starboard of us. We both looked, and looked again, and there were two tin fish [torpedoes] heading straight for us. What a panic, the lookouts were going mad, somehow the old *Largs* went astern, and those two fish whizzed across our bows slap into the Norwegian destroyer *Svenner,* stationed on our port side. She broke in two halves and went under, making a 'V'. It was awful, and under orders no-one stopped for survivors.[33]

G. L. Haskins:

[I] was a Midshipman RNR in HMS *Emerald* – communications number with the spotter aircraft during the initial bombardment. I had been busy passing on target references, shot times and spotter reports when, about 0730, there was a brief lull in proceedings. I emerged from my cramped position in the bridge chart table well and looked ashore at the coastline through binoculars. We had no idea where we were – only Captain F. J. Wylie and Graham-Brown the navigator seemed to be in the know. What I saw through the binoculars looked rather familiar and I said 'It's Arromanches'. It was Arromanches of course, and the only place in France I had ever, until then, visited. It was when we had our family summer holiday before the war. What an unforgettable day 6.6.44 was – my first ship, I was aged 17, and a front seat view of the lot.[34]

Mr P. H. Humphries was a Signal Officer:

HMS *Glenroy* was a 10,000 ton Landing Ship Infantry. She carried 20 LCAs and was the HQ ship for Force G1. We sailed just before dusk on the 5th [June], going round the Needles and heading up Channel towards the Straits of Dover, this being to deceive the enemy into believing that the invasion would take place in the Pas de Calais area. When darkness fell, we turned south towards the Normandy beaches and just before dawn we could see the battleships close inshore, bombarding the defences. About five minutes after anchoring we saw banks of fire behind us and a sound like a dozen express trains going overhead.

This scared the living daylights out of us as this was something that we hadn't experienced before. It turned out to be the rockets from the LCT(R)s coming up behind us and firing over our heads. When all the LCAs had returned [from delivering troops to the beaches], we proceeded back to Southampton, where we took on more troops. We carried this on, day and night, for four days and during this time the bridge party did not leave the bridge except for emergencies.[35]

A. C. Lamey was one of many merchant seamen who were involved in D-Day:

All through the last war I was serving as first mate on the steamship *Greta Force*. I volunteered for the liberation of Europe and my ship was allotted to the Americans. We were running ammunition and stores to their beaches, Omaha and Utah. We were running from Southampton mostly. We had our sealed orders at 3 p.m. on 6th June and sailed 1 a.m. on the 7th. When we were nearing the French coast the ship that was just ahead of us blew up. She was loaded with ammunition and needless to say there were no survivors.[36]

Walter Palmer served as one of three crew members on a Thames barge that carried petrol cans on D-Day. After this crossing, he was transferred to crew an LCF and was mainly involved with protecting merchant ships against enemy attack:

During the day we patrolled the coast along with LCGs. A new menace appeared in the shape of a one-man sub with a tinfish [torpedo] slung under it. The man on the sub could only see through a Perspex dome which could be seen coming through the water. Our first encounter with one of these was when our skipper opened fire on one with a Lewis Gun, at which the German threw back the hatch and raised his arms in surrender.

We went alongside, took the German aboard and the sub in tow. It was handed over to the naval experts as it was the first to be captured. The next nightmare was the acoustic mine, which exploded under a ship when it picked up the sound of the ship's engine. We really feared this one as all our craft were driven by large diesel engines, so their echo through the water was noisy. We lost a lot of craft this way and a lot of lives. Being a stoker, my job was to look after the diesel engines on my craft, and when I went below in the engine room for four hours I was scared stiff in case we caught a packet from these mines.

In fact I was so scared that I used to take my meals on the upper deck and sleep near the bows, so if we did sink I was ready to jump in the water. One night we were going to join the rest of the craft and I was sat near the bows when there was a hellish explosion and I found myself in the air and then in the water, swimming for dear life; our luck had run out, in the form of an acoustic mine; those of us that survived were picked up.[37]

3

H-HOUR, THE AIRBORNE DROP

The sea at dawn is grey, sombre as metal,
With dull un-burnished strength
The light expands till the horizon,
Once more defined, encircles our day.
In the tufted grass and the sea-pinks
Our rifles lie, clean, with bolts oiled,
Our pouches hard with rounds,
A metal world of rifle, sea and sky
                    Neil McCallum, *Stand To* (1942)

Food, drink, clothes, tobacco – everything has been rationed, but to have a coupon has not meant to get even the meagre ration. Women have queued up daily for vegetables from four in the morning till the market closed at 08.30 – and gone away without any because the Germans had robbed the lorries on the way ...[1]

At 07.00 hours on 6 June, British I and 30 Corps would come ashore on Sword and Gold Beaches. General Crocker, commanding I Corps, was tasked to take Caen, and any failure to seize this vital gateway on the first day would have serious consequences. Bucknall's 30 Corps, which included 50th Division, was to drive 7 miles inland and liberate Bayeux. Within the initial and critical couple of hours, some 30,000 soldiers, 300 guns and 700 armoured vehicles were to be landed, a magnificent achievement if it could be pulled off and, though the sands would be choked with the mother of all logjams, exacerbated by a swelling tide, the British would be firmly lodged; a bridgehead secured. Fortress Europe would look set to crumble. In order to make any of this possible, 6th Airborne Division had to seize their own vital set of pre-dawn objectives, the hinge on which the whole plan must turn.

Tonga

General Richard ('Windy') Gale, CO of British 6th Airborne Division, was tasked to seize the crossings of the Orne River and Canal at Bénouville, eliminate the dangerous Merville Battery, blow up the Dives River crossings to the east to prevent German reinforcements getting up, and hold the key high ground around Ranville. This was a very big ask, yet without these paratrooper successes, the whole flank of the British landing grounds was wide open. Failure, as our US allies would say, was not an option.

Grabbing the Orne River crossings was vital as these would be the open road to Caen and 3rd Division was (improbably) tasked to take the city as a first-day objective. It's been said, quite often, that while Monty had meticulously planned the assault on the beaches, he'd thought less about getting into Caen. This would have consequences.

Operation *Tonga* – midnight plus 20; Major John Howard would lead the spearhead that was to seize the crossings by an audacious and highly risky *coup de main*. A company of 2nd Ox and Bucks Light Infantry, now part of 6th Airborne, would blitz the defences from three Horsa gliders,[2] towed in by Halifaxes[3] and Stirlings.[4] Each fragile aircraft carried 30 men and the glider pilots had to land each of them on the narrow strip of ground between the two bridges. This was a very, very difficult assignment but getting it wrong could, probably would, be fatal, to the men inside and to the mission itself.

C. J. Woodward flew with the RAF and witnessed the vast armada of gliders that would carry the airborne troops over to Normandy:

I was the pilot of a Stirling aircraft of 161 Squadron on a mission dropping spies behind enemy lines on the night preceding D-Day. We had had a special briefing in which it was emphasised as being critically essential that there should be absolute radio silence, no matter what we saw. We were on our way out from Tempsford in Bedfordshire. At about 3,000 feet we were suddenly confronted by the most awesome sight. The whole night sky, high above and filling the whole area in front, was filled with myriads of red, blue and white lights rotating very slowly like one vast coloured whirlpool.

It seemed impossible not to be engulfed, and we were without lights. Although we knew that something was going on, we were not aware that the French landings were imminent, so there was no explanation of the phenomenon. It was, of course, the gliders and their tug aircraft marshalling in the area, I believe, of Benson. All the members of my crew except the rear gunner crowded into the cockpit in amazed disbelief. Because of the dead quiet of the radio silence, the sight was unbelievably uncanny. Suddenly the spell was split wide open. 'What the f...g hell are all those bleedin' lights?' It was a Canadian voice, and he must have accidentally pressed his transmitting button in his excitement. I have always wondered what any German listening watch who picked up that transmission must have thought.[5]

Major Howard had instructed his glider pilot Staff Sergeant Wallwork to drop the Horsa with its nose literally inside the wire defences of the bridge. If ever there was a clear definition of mission impossible, this had to be pretty close. He wanted the other two bunched up behind and to the right. Obviously gliders don't have engines; it was also pitch dark and there would be no visible landmarks. 'Don't worry,' Wallwork reassured him, 'the [defensive] posts will take the wings off slowing us down, so we won't hit the bridge quite as hard.' (They'd be coming in at 100 mph.)

Behind Howard the men were keyed up, their singing a balm for loose bowels and dry mouths. This was what they had trained and trained and trained for. The risks were so many, so varied and generally so lethal as to be hardly worth thinking about. At 12.26 hours the tow was cast off, they were committed, and that last umbilical severed.

The glider was too high as we came in and Jim Wallwork deployed the arrester parachute and adjusted the flaps as he tried to control the unwieldy aircraft and to steer it precisely where he wanted it to come in to land. He had cheekily asked me where I wanted the glider to finish up and, never imagining that he would take me seriously, I had told him 'Ideally Jim, right through the wire defences of the bridge!'[6]

There was no more reassuring sound of engines, just the steady hiss of the wind as they dived down through cloud cover. Lieutenant Den Brotheridge pushed the forward door open, a rush of cold air coming in: 'Hold tight.' Below the golden gash of the canal shone in the fitful moonlight. This wasn't a model, it wasn't training; this was it. The glider hit still doing 90 mph (140 km/h), tore along the ground, ripped itself to shreds like a badly made kid's toy aeroplane and then stopped.

Robert Ashby, Glider Pilot Regiment, describes his part in the operation:

There below us, like a badly-shaped question mark, was the mouth of the River Orne and neighbouring canal, exactly as I expected to find them. Further down into France, quite a way off ... was the blinking red light of the lead-in beacon positioned by the paratroops to mark our LZ [landing zone] ... Our gliding approach required us to half-circle the beacon, and before we got there I began putting on flap as we were very much too high. I dived, with Jim, whose duty it was to keep an eye on the instruments, shouting that we were going too fast, at 100 mph, enough to tear the flaps off.

I seemed to sense rather than see the ground coming up, and at the right moment levelled off and put her down. Once touched, she stayed on her wheels and came to a stop undamaged. We had expected that all hell would break loose when we landed, but it did not. In fact, when, after a very brief pause to catch our breath, we tumbled out, we were in mortal dread not of the enemy but of other gliders. They were landing all over the place, some with spot-lights on, which was a dead give-away, others approaching from the wrong direction, and many crashing into posts or other gliders.

All of this happened within the space of about a minute. When it was all over there was a sudden silence. All that could be heard was the gentle sighing of the wind through the grasses. Typically English, I suppose, but the first thing we did in Normandy was to get out the large Thermos flasks and have a mug of tea ... But there were problems getting the 3-ton bulldozer out of the Horsa glider. It had been brought to clear any obstructions left by the Germans.

By now the pre-dawn light was coming up:

Shouldering our rifles, bandoliers of ammunition and other kit, we gravitated towards the southern end of the sweep of meadowland which formed our LZ. There we found the church of Ranville at the top of a slight slope and the village beyond; this, though we did not know it at the time, was the first village in France to be liberated.[7]

Perhaps the real value of training is you don't have to think, it's all instinctive. Howard and his boys were piling out of the wreckage almost before it shuddered to a broken halt. Howard struggled free, tripping as he got out but, as he looked up, there it was, the lattice tower of the bridge not twenty steps away. They were spot on target.

The door opposite me seemed to collapse in on itself as we came to a halt and the tremendous impact caused me to pass out.

As I came round I fund to my horror that I couldn't see anything. For a frightful second I really believed that I might have been blinded, and then just as quickly realised that my helmet, the battle bowler, had rammed itself down over my eyes as I hit the roof or the side of the glider. Pushing it up I took in my surroundings – the smashed doorway, the air full of dust, the holes torn in the sides of the glider and the sound of the pilots groaning in the smashed cockpit. And then the glorious realisation came to me that otherwise there was silence, complete silence, no gunfire at all – we had achieved our first objective of complete surprise.[8]

The adrenalin rush carried them forward, through the ripped wire. Up ahead, a pillbox erupted in MG fire but grenades took care of that. Up the embankment they went, onto the echoing planks of the bridge, and across. On the far side, another MG opened up. Now the other two gliders came bursting in behind the shell of Howard's, just as they were supposed to do. The paras hit the German trenches guarding the span like a tsunami; those who could, bolted. It was over almost in seconds but that other MG had killed Den Brotheridge, who won the unenviable distinction of being the first British casualty.[9]

The canal bridge was secured in less than 3 minutes, though the attack on the river crossing had run into problems and the drop wasn't as precise. Lieutenant Fox had got to the bridge in time to see its former custodians pelting off into the darkness. A British NCO capitalised on an abandoned MG42 and pointed the fleeing Germans on their way with a series of long swinging bursts.

> Thus within a few minutes, a message was received on Tappenden's [radio operator] wireless from Dennis Fox and Tod Swinney at the river bridge to say that they had captured it without any opposition but that there was no sign of the third glider containing Brian Friday and Hooper's platoon. They reported that the enemy had run off, leaving their guns in weapons pits, still warm from the sentries' occupancy. That the river bridge was secure was good news for me and I instructed Tappenden to send out the success signal for both bridges being captured intact. Jock Neilson and his sappers had searched the bridges, cut all wires and found the chambers ready to receive their charges of explosive but, in fact, no charges had been laid; they were later found in a magazine near the canal bridge.[10]

'Ham' was the code word for success from the canal's bridge and 'jam' for the river. Not very inspirational perhaps, but those two code words meant the first of the paras D-Day objectives had been accomplished. An apocryphal tale tells of the absent German guard company CO who raced back late from a night out in the fleshpots of Ouistreham only to run into a para road-block and capture. When the doors of his staff Mercedes were wrenched open and he and his driver were dragged out, two very scantily clad French girls scattered out of the back like startled hares and took off down the road!

Lieutenant D. J. Wood served with 'D' Company of 2nd Ox and Bucks:

As luck would have it, I was commanding No. 24 Platoon. The company had been given the task of capturing the two bridges over the River Orne and the Caen Canal by a *coup de main*. We went into action in Horsa gliders towed by Halifax bombers. Thanks to the superb timing and skill of the glider pilots, we landed within a very short distance of the objective. Admittedly, in my case, the landing was very rough and the glider broke in half on touching down. Luckily it was made of plywood and we, its twenty-four passengers, more or less came out of the crash unscathed.

What happened next is history; the leading platoon commanded by Lieutenant Den Brotheridge captured the bridge intact. My platoon took on the task of defending the Canal Bridge. Twenty-five minutes after landing, I, my platoon sergeant 'Laces' Leather and my batman Private Chatfield were all wounded by a burst from a *Schmeisser* machine pistol ...[11]

One veteran's family recorded:

Bleaching the date of birth on his identity papers, and getting away with it, my father joined the Royal Ulster Rifles aged 17. He'd also heard they were recruiting for a new section that were going to be part of an airborne brigade, and volunteered for it. Training endlessly, he told me years later that he found it hard, endless, but became incredibly fit. There were runs before breakfast, endless weapon training, assault courses and parachute jumps, often using Stonehenge as a reference point.

He told me of having to jump out of a converted bomber where they had simply cut a circular hole in the flooring. The jumps were precarious as the wind would knock you forward as you went to jump out. You had to gauge it properly to allow for your parachute on your back to have clearance, but not jump too far forward as you would hit your chin on the rim. Many troops in training had broken and cut jaws. He became part of 6th Airborne Division, eventually landing during the night of D-Day right near Pegasus Bridge. He admitted he was petrified, but also excited. This was the first time he'd ever left Northern Ireland. Getting stories out of him was also very hard. He met Madame Gondrée, owner of the now famous café at Pegasus Bridge, but the place was also crowded with soldiers.[12]

Robert Ashby, as a glider pilot vital to airborne operations, was on his way back to Britain the day after landing:

The beach, all things considered, was remarkably tidy. Some disabled landing-craft were washing about in the surf and there was other wreckage. Round the bastions of the seawall were what looked like piled-up stores under canvas sheets. But they were not stores, but the bodies of men who had fallen in the first assault. I noticed a wax-like hand sticking out. It had on it a wedding-ring, token of some poor woman back home who did not know, and would not know for some time, that she was a widow.[13]

Ranville

For the rest of 6th Airborne, things generally weren't going quite as well. Signals gear had gone adrift in the drop so comms were the first casualty; this was really quite bad. No comms was a disaster – airborne ops are fraught with peril by their very nature and for the divisional commander not to be able to even speak to his scattered minions meant he was fighting blind. The landings would achieve surprise, the first vital ingredient of success, but that only lasts for so long; once you've smashed, you've got to grab. It had gone wrong when the initial wave of pathfinders became scattered and then confusion, like Topsy, grew at its own unfortunate momentum. However, by 02.30, 13th Lancs Bn had fought their way into the village of Ranville. This became the first *commune* to be officially liberated by the Allies. Gale himself landed an hour later and set up his divisional HQ there. It wasn't bloodless and several British paras lie in the churchyard and the large adjacent CWGC cemetery.[14]

A medic in the paras, E. Purchese, landed by air on the east side of the main beach landings:

My unit was 225th Para Field Ambulance, 5th Para Brigade, 6th Airborne Division. We were at Keevil Camp for a week before the invasion, being briefed in detail for our drop near the River Orne. Take-off was about 23.00 hours on 5th June. After running into tracer fire, which was returned by our rear gunner, as we crossed the French coast we dropped at about 01.00 hours near Ranville. We made our way to a pre-arranged rendezvous, thence to Ranville where villagers in the dark (approximately 03.50 hours) whispered *Bonjour* from bedroom windows.

We arrived at a chateau (picked previously from aerial photographs). Our second-in-command knocked and asked if there were any Germans inside. There were, and four or five surrendered and were made prisoners. We then entered, and set up our various departments. I was in a surgical team, and we started operating about the time of the main seaborne landing, which was announced to us by a thunderous barrage from the Navy. We operated all day and had two hours' sleep early on 7th June. We used a landing light from a glider for the surgeon to see by. Many lives were saved by plasma, the bottles slung from rigging lines cut from parachutes. We also had some of the first penicillin used for troops.[15]

Another coming in from the skies was R. G. Lloyd:

I was in the 12th Parachute Regiment, 6th Airborne Division, and we took off in converted Stirling bombers from airfields in various parts of southern England at about 21.30 hours on the 5th June 1944. Our flight across the Channel went off without incident, thanks to the supremacy of the Allied air forces. Incidentally our aircraft had a Canadian crew. In the very early hours of D-Day we were dropped a few miles inland, behind the Normandy beaches. As I left the aircraft I could see some light flak coming up, slowly it seemed, like long strings of flaming sausages.

After landing safely in open country, my first impression was not what I expected. It was very quiet. After releasing myself from my parachute and retrieving my kitbag which contained a small radio set, I commenced my stealthy walk towards what I thought should be our rendezvous. I found a crossroads and a few of my comrades. We discovered later that like many of our division, we had been scattered far and wide in the darkness, and so had not time to get to the rendezvous. We then made our way in a small party across open country to our objective, where about 100 of our unit were already in position. From now on, enemy opposition increased, and for a few hours we had a very hectic time. Shells passed overhead – this was HMS *Warspite* firing her big guns at targets well inland. We could hear the noise of the beach invasion. Daylight came. Yes! This was D-Day and I was in Normandy.[16]

'Windy' Gale was 48, old for a paratrooper; he'd won his spurs in the trenches and came back with an MC. He certainly looked the part, 6 feet 3 inches, and sporting a fearsome Blimp moustache. As we have seen, he came in at 03.30 – he'd be the first British general to arrive in occupied France. Cool and level-headed, the inevitable mass confusion didn't faze him, at least the airlifted bulldozers had got through pretty much in the right place and were soon enthusiastically harvesting Rommel's crop of obstacles. Many gliders had rough, if not catastrophic, landings. One barrelled straight through a cottage and burst out the far wall with the hapless occupants still in their double bed, now hung off the bow of the glider! Amazingly there were no serious injuries.[17]

R. G. Lloyd remembers digging in:

Without orders we dug our slit trenches. Little did we know it during our previous training, but these trenches were to play a very important part in our life during the days ahead in Europe. They would afford vital protection, but would for long periods be our homes, where we would eat, sleep, wash, shave, write letters, in fact do practically everything. Unfortunately they were not weatherproof, and when the heavy rain came, you just sat with a wet backside and hoped that the incessant drip-drip would stop soon, and mostly it did; in the morning you dried out the best you could and hoped that you'd find a better hole next night.[18]

The Galloping Major

Now, what about those other bridges? Blowing the Dives crossings was as vital in its way as Pegasus (as the Orne bridges would be known). If these weren't dealt with, the Germans had a perfect conduit for rushing in reinforcements. Engineer parties had been widely scattered but in small ad hoc groups, in one case a solitary sergeant, they got to their objectives and set about destroying them. The most important and, inevitably furthest away, was the one that carried the main road from Caen to Rouen and Le Havre, lying just past the settlement at Troarn. The bridge was in fact 4 miles (6.5km) beyond the perimeter that the division intended to hold. Nonetheless, it had to go.

Major J. C. A. Roseveare would lead the assaulting engineers, backed up by an infantry detachment. They'd move fast and hard, dashing forward in jeeps with loaded trailers. Anyway, that was the plan. They came in at 01.50 and were widely scattered. He could only find about 40 of his own men with 6 officers and not much more than a single squad of the infantry with no officers. Explosives they had but of jeeps, there were none. They did have trolleys but these would have to be manhandled. They toiled up hill and down dale, many nursing injuries from the landing. It was heavy going and when they finally found a road sign, it confirmed what the major had feared, they were 7 miles (11 km) from their objective. Regular if random MG and mortar fire enlivened their journey.[19]

Fortunately, a single RAMC jeep and trailer appeared *deus ex machina* and was quickly commandeered, unloaded and re-packed with an altogether different kind of cargo. It was an hour before the summer dawn. Roseveare sent the bulk of his scratch force off to find another bridge; they'd never make it to Troarn on foot before first light. He drove, the Willys jeep burdened with a lot of explosives and 8 hefty troopers. They were a lone spearhead in what was very much enemy ground, a few atoms at the very sharpest point of a very big spear.

Off they roared over a level crossing where a lone sentry loosed off a single round before decamping. The galloping major galloped straight into a barbed-wire obstacle and it took 20 vital, ticking minutes to free the entangled jeep. But they got close to Troarn without seeing another German and Roseveare sent a couple of blokes off to scout. This pair bumped into a single enemy on a pushbike, and as he wouldn't shut up they disposed of him. Ill-advisedly they killed him with a burst from one of their Stens; a knife might have been preferable as the shooting roused the whole town.

In best Cagney style, the major just floored the accelerator and bowled down the main street. But as the jeep was carrying a ton-and-a-half, flat-out meant barely crawling above 30 mph and it seemed every window bristled with Germans. One of the team simply fell off and there wasn't time to recover him, the rest blazed away with Sten and Bren. It was a long road of more than a mile down to the bridge.

Incoming rounds careened off the cobbles, skittered from walls, smashed glass and pinged off the Willys; tracer seemed to dance like fireflies along the street. The only good news was that it was downhill to the river and gravity came to the aid of the over-worked engine, the vehicle jinking wildly to confuse the enemy gunners who now had at least one MG on their case.

Somehow they made it to the bridge; they'd lost another man, he had been Tail End Charlie on the Bren. Though there was a hornet's nest buzzing angrily behind, nobody was guarding the span. Not much more than 10 minutes later, the bridge was blown. Nobody would be passing armour that way through Troarn any time soon. Roseveare and his team ditched the faithful jeep and made their way back to the Allied perimeter, a pretty good night's work, very much against the odds, behind them.[20]

Merville

Not far from the mouth of the River Orne, where sandbanks and a sloping shore seemed to stretch to infinity (guarded by 18th-century redoubts), and on the pleasant rolling pastures of the coastal plain, stood Merville Battery (*see* Map 3). Just south of the town and about 1½ miles (2.4km) from the beach, it had the potential to slice withering fire along the length of Sword Beach. Four 100mm guns with a 5-mile (8-km) range, in powerful casemates, at least a company of infantry, AA guns, searchlights, trenches, MG posts, wire and mines meant it would take a full battalion with heavy weapons to knock the place down and silence those guns.

Lieutenant-Colonel Terence Otway, 29, commanded 9th Para. It was their job to do for the battery. Otway had 750 men in his battalion and he'd trained them well, well and hard and tirelessly. He knew from aerial reconnaissance what the place looked like so he'd chosen a stretch of UK farmland and built a full-scale replica. His men bounced the facsimile time after time after time – observing the old maxim, 'sweat saves blood'. Otway was more than ordinarily thorough, he shifted and cut down the local woods to match, took over acres of farmland (the owners had to be compensated) and replicated every known point of the defence.

As with Howard's men on the bridges, surprise was key so he decided he'd mount three-score paras in three gliders and aim to skip these over the outer perimeter to park directly against the bunkers. Now, even with the justly famed skills of the glider pilots, this was going to be tricky. This leaping Trojan Horse would be flown by A Company. He called for volunteers but didn't need to. Prior to the op, he'd imposed a 24-hour drinking ban, (though he was careful to take his own bottle of whisky with him).[21]

Planning only gets you so far, what you really need is luck and Otway had none on the night. Persistent and heavy AA fire rattled the pilots, who began to take fairly violent evasive action. That's understandable and Otway soothed his men, who were being chucked around in the fuselage, by passing the bottle around. This helped the nerves but the drop was already in bother. As his plane jinked and turned Otway's men couldn't keep to their tight jump sequence. Otway left what was in the bottle to the dispatcher, and hurled himself out into the night.

It's one thing to practise endlessly but quite another to pitch out over enemy territory, even when there are familiar landmarks, the ones you've spent hours looking at in photos. But yes, it was all there, laid out like a map table, though he could see, as tracer reached up like fingers of fire, that he was headed for a set of buildings he knew to be a German command post. Despite his best efforts to control the descent, he smacked off the wall of the place and ended up, as he thought, in a cultivated area, perhaps the garden. Two other troopers had come down with him and one para chucked a brick at an inquisitive German officer who'd poked his head from a window and then they pelted clear.[22]

Overall, the drop was a shambles, a total mess. Otway's batman Wilson, an ex-boxer, had crashed straight through the roof of the greenhouse but he'd got off without a scratch and the horde of enemy now streaming out of the building had missed him. So had some nearby Canadian paras who'd mistaken him for one of them! Not everyone was so lucky, at least one poor sod drowned in the cloying ooze of the flooded Dives wetlands. By the time Otway and Wilson reached the RV it was 02.00, already behind schedule. Men came in in dribs and drabs, but not enough, nowhere near enough. Half-an-hour later he had 150 men, four times that many were scattered, God knew where, and he had little or no heavy kit. The RAF raid designed to soften up the Battery had missed the target and blasted the village. Of the three assault gliders there was as yet no sign, they weren't due until first light. One thing that was sure was that the Germans would all be wide awake and Merville Battery was fully open for business. Otway was a mile-and-a-half from the perimeter – very little chance of an undetected approach. Yet if he didn't move and the gliders swooped in on time, his men inside would be trapped.

Otway had to decide. It was mission impossible but, after agonising for a precious hour, he gave the order to move out. He was going to throw his company-sized unit into what should have been a battalion attack, with no heavy weapons, no support, no gliders inside the wire and no surprise whatsoever. At 02.50 they marched off. He was crossing his own personal Rubicon.

They had to creep past an AA position, the gunners lit by the flashes of their own flaming muzzles, shooting at the aerial armada passing overhead, a very tempting target but one that had to be resisted. One bit of good luck, long overdue, was that they came across the pathfinder group whose officer had managed to recce the battery.

They'd done well. Despite having no mine detectors, the engineer squad had probed, and poked, and managed to lift a pathway through the mines, all without alerting the sentries. The recce group had come nearer to being killed by the RAF, as their drop had plonked them on top of and then under the falling bombs.[23] The only fresh hazard facing the 150 paras as they crept closer was a stampeding herd of cattle, which charged straight through.

The gliders were on time but Otway couldn't signal to them. Without the reassuring mortar flares the gliders couldn't risk dropping directly onto the battery, they'd sheer off and land nearby. With that, seeing these big birds come to roost so close, the defenders would be fully alerted. So he gave the order to attack.

This was not the battle he'd planned or trained his men for. Once he'd committed to the attack, there wasn't very much he could do to affect the outcome. His attacking force had to go in against a heavily defended position, the enemy fully alerted and almost equal in numbers. It was confused, very violent and very bloody. A rapid staccato chorus of automatic weapons crashed through the night air, grenades banged and flamed. Despite the amount of sophisticated firepower about, much of it was bayonet work, a butcher's trade performed in the red mist, a screaming, shrieking barbarity, with men writhing and pinned by repeated thrusts.

Otway properly had kept his tiny HQ section and another in reserve. Then it was their turn and they went forward through the wire and maelstrom of fire. His adjutant went down, but most of them got through. He'd ordered the lead troops to make straight for the casemates and leave any German infantry to the follow-up. Those he'd kept in hand went for the trenches and outposts. The fury of the attack carried them through and soon shocked defenders were throwing their hands up. Despite staggering odds, the Merville Battery had been captured.

Madam Gondree, who still hosts the family café by Pegasus Bridge, will tell visitors how, when some of Howard's paratroopers knocked politely on their door in the wee small hours of 6th June, Papa Gondree immediately went into his garden to dig out some very good bottles indeed, which had been hidden from the enemy since 1940. It seemed to be a suitable occasion for a shared libation to celebrate liberation. The wine went down very well indeed.

4

SWORD BEACH, MORNING

Hail, soldier, huddled in the rain,
Hail, soldier, squelching through the mud,
Hail, soldier, sick of dirt and pain,
The sight of death, the smell of blood,
New men, new weapons, bear the brunt;
New slogans gild the ancient game:
The infantry are still in front,
And mud and dust are much the same.
Hail, humble footman, poised to fly
Across the West, or any, Wall!
Proud, plodding, peerless P.B.I. –
The foulest, finest, job of all.

A.P. Herbert: The Poor Bloody Infantry

So the French, after the German occupation, are, generally
speaking, in no position to entertain you lavishly, though
families may get up from the cellar in our special honour a
long-hidden bottle.[1]

Can a tank swim? Hobo had proved they could, if all went well
and the seas weren't too rough. The Americans would have a very
bad experience off Omaha but the Brits hitting Sword Beach did
better. DD tanks of 13th/18th Hussars would come ashore ahead
of the infantry (Monty's doctrine formulated in the wake of the

Dieppe debacle), while more of the 'Funnies' crewed by engineer assault troops would disembark from LCTs.

Forward the Hussars

Lance-Corporal P. L. M. Hennessey was serving in 13/18th Hussars with Sherman DD Tanks:[2]

Well before dawn on 6th June we heard aircraft of the airborne spearhead. We were up and about our tanks, stowing kit and making last-minute checks, of air bottle containers and our under-water escape apparatus. The barrage started and there was plenty to see. Most impressive were the rockets fired from the LCRs on our port quarter.

Then came the order to mount and inflate. Everything seemed to work – the canvas screens rose around the DD tanks and we busied ourselves securing struts and securing the periscopes. The LCT hove to some 5,000 yards from the shore. The ramp was lowered and the first tank of 4th Troop wallowed off the ramp into a heavy sea. We were the second tank off and as we righted ourselves in the water and began to make way we could see other DD tanks launching on both sides of us. There was much smoke, much noise and quite a struggle to keep the craft on course. Apart from our driver we were all on deck at that time and looking to my right I remember vividly witnessing the tragedy which overtook Captain Denny's tank as it was run over by its own LCT.

After what must have been well over an hour amidst heaving waves and a growing crescendo of noise we came in close to the beach. As we felt the tracks grind on the shelving bottom, we took post, dropped our screen and opened fire on the line of houses which were our target. We halted with tracks just out of the water and added our contribution to the hail of bullets which were flying in all directions. There was much discussion as to whether we should move on up the beach and chance the mines which had not yet been cleared.

Suddenly that problem was solved for us because having landed on an incoming tide, the longer we sat there the deeper the water became. One large wave swamped our engine compartment and that was that! For a few minutes longer we continued to engage targets inland but the tank was becoming flooded so, taking the .30 cal. Brownings, and as much ammo as we could, we took to the rubber dinghy and began to paddle for the shore. It was barely a minute before some German put a burst of fire through our frail craft.

Our co-driver was hit in the ankle and we were deposited into the sea. We lost the guns and ammo but somehow managed to get Gallagher and ourselves onto the beach. I remember hanging on to a post sticking out of the water to get a breather and, on looking up saw an ugly black Teller mine attached to it!

We finally dragged ourselves ashore, cold and soaking wet and from somewhere there appeared a self-heating tin of soup. As we lay there gasping and gulping down swigs of soup, I remember an irate captain of Engineers saying 'get up corporal – that's no way to win the 2nd Front!' He was absolutely right of course and we began to make our way inland with some infantry. We had only our pistols and a discarded Sten gun which we found.

Much later we met up with some other un-horsed [this archaic expression was a hangover from the cavalry] tank crews and it was then that we saw our first German POWs, some wounded, all looking shocked and frightened, not the supermen we had imagined. Towards midday Major Wormald found us and directed us to make our way to the village of Hermanville where, that evening, we were reunited with the survivors of 'A' Squadron and their five remaining serviceable tanks.[3]

Some family TLC for Trooper Farrell, survivor of an LCT:

Our dad, Trooper Jack Farrell – 14289714, of the East Riding Yeomanry – left from Gosport, Hampshire, on a Tank Landing Craft. He was part of the 'First Wave' of troops to land in Normandy on Luc-Sur-Mer sector of Sword Beach. The first thing he saw was, 'the water coming to meet us through the periscope!' Whilst many vehicles sank immediately, his made it to the beach. 'The beach was littered with various tanks and other vehicles, burning or broken down ... a lot of shelling and aircraft bombing ... sadly, we immediately lost two ... wounded in a short space of time.' We are very proud of him and are remembering him, especially today.[4]

Another Hussars' DD tank was commanded by Sergeant Harry Morris. As with most of their comrades they suffered from sea-sickness during the crossing, nerves already frayed by the prospect of launching in a rough sea. Even once they'd successfully got into the water, it was a race for survival steering their unwieldy half-boats to shore before they were swamped or their bilge pumps gave up the unequal struggle. Their maritime mini-odyssey was accompanied by the wailing, deafening chorus of big naval guns hooting overhead and artillery support closer behind.[5]

It was the screaming banshee horde of rockets which led to that tragic confusion of LCTs actually running down two of their tanks. The commanders, aloft in their turrets, were rescued. Both crews plummeted to their watery deaths before they'd even fired a single shot in anger. Sergeant Morris didn't see any of this, he was fixed on the shoreline looming ahead and wondering if they'd make it before the tank was swamped, his driver was already waist-deep. They chugged in the last 100 yards, a whipping storm of small arms fire and thumping mortars, their hello from Germany's Fortress Europe. Almost directly ahead, he spotted the big Boche gun firing from the fortified cellar of what had been a seaside hotel, though there'd be no ice creams today. Tracks ground onto the shingle bottom and the tank strained forward till the hull was pretty much clear and they dropped their canvas screens, firing a single aiming round just to announce their arrival and entry into the contest.[6] Morris' tank engaged and took out their target though he had to return to the waterline and help drag another bogged vehicle in.

Germans weren't the only enemy, there was the tide racing in, sweeping over half-submerged obstacles, festooned with their deadly crop of mines. DD tanks were soon competing for space with the mine-busting Flails of 22nd Hussars, coming in behind.

The assault engineers had two main jobs: clear the beach exits and get rid of these obstacles.

Colonel R. W Urquhart and his engineers became temporary frogmen as they took to the water to clear the stakes of their lethal harvest. One enterprising sapper hopped onto a DD tank having persuaded the commander to effectively submerge so he could stand on the turret and lift mines. Mindful of a helpful MoD directive to salvage mines for future re-use he stacked his catch on the tank, till an inconsiderate sniper winged him and he had to be dragged clear by the tankers.[7]

Gunners across the water

It was just as dawn was rising at 05.30 that men from 2nd East Yorks and South Lancs clambered into their LCAs, weighed down with their heavy kit. And down indeed they went, into the heavy seas. Most, even good sailors among them, were queasy from the choppy crossing; the bucking and sawing of the ungainly landing craft just added fresh misery. But as the flotilla motored in towards the enemy shore, an East Yorks bugler sounded the General Salute. The Battalion 2I/C Major 'Banger' King rose to the occasion by reading aloud from *Henry V* – the bard's inspiration blasting out over the tannoy speaker.

> The [Battalion] War Diary includes a breakdown of the objectives as well as the 'intention' which was that the '2nd East Yorkshires Battalion Group will land on Queen Red Beach at H plus 5 minutes, destroy the beach defences, capture CROSSLEY 3816 and secure RUGGER 399148 and CRICKET 404146.' 'A' and 'B' Companies would land in the initial assault, with 'C' and 'D' Companies landing twenty minutes behind them.
>
> It was the task of 'A' Company to land about the middle of Red Beach, swing west and destroy the beach defence codenamed 'Cod', together with 'C' Company the South Lancashire Regiment. Cod was a formidable strongpoint, comprising twenty separate positions, including a 75mm gun, two 50mm anti-tank guns, and five different machine gun posts. On D-Day, this strongpoint was not fully subdued until 10am and casualties were heavy.

'B' Company would land on the left of Red Beach and swing east to destroy all beach defences except 'Cod'. It would hold the defensive position codenamed 'Skate' until No. 4 Commando passed through. The role of the follow-up companies, 'C' and 'D', was to assist the forward companies on the beach if needed, or to assemble at point 'Pike' to move inland straightaway. Once inland, the companies would attack the strongpoints 'Sole' and 'Daimler'. The planners considered these objectives sufficient progress for the battalion to achieve on the first day. It was the role of the other, follow-up battalions within the Division to progress.[8]

The infantry were wet, nauseous and crammed shivering in their LCAs, the hostile beach looming, the divisional guns barking behind them. Major Hendrie Bruce commanding 9th (Irish) Field Battery, 7th Field Regiment, watched those flimsy hulls battling the waves and looked at the distant shoreline. It appeared deserted, rows of seaside villas abandoned, B&Bs boarded up, a derelict resort. The gunners could make out the Orne Estuary and the lighthouse at Ouistreham but could not detect 'Cod' as yet. LCTs carrying the Hussars tanks were ahead. Bruce watched as the ungainly leviathans took to the water, it seemed impossible that they should float. Finally, the gunners spotted 'Cod', their objective; they were about 3,000 yards out. The guns themselves, carried in 18 LCTs, were a further 12,000 yards back, shaking out into a spearhead formation. The barrage would be radar-guided and at 06.44 the first salvo erupted. The Royal Navy was already on the job, their big shells passing overhead like the wrath of ancient gods, heralding the *Gotterdammerung* of *Festung Europa*. The divisional artillery, seventy-two guns firing at 10,000 yards, now added their own dawn chorus. These self-propelled guns, 'Priests',[9] had been staked on their LCTs to maximise fire> Decks were stacked with shells and now 200 rounds a minute were blitzing the defences, mostly HE, and by the time they fell silent 6,500 shells had been fired.[10]

As wake-up calls go, this one was pretty loud. The Germans weren't slow to respond, gouts of water spurted like geysers around the landing craft, which started to swerve and several DD tanks appeared to be hit – for their crews a plummeting watery death. It was clear some of our own shells were dropping short, though these were, in fact, rockets shot from an LCT(R). The stonk continued, lifting as the troops neared shore. The guns fell silent and veered away, waiting their turn to land.[11]

Another gunner, Acting-Major Robin Dunn, commanding 16th Battery, 7th Field Regiment, was also an eyewitness to this extraordinary armada, this vast, dazzling canvas of projected power, the whole might and focus of the Allies concentrated on these Normandy beaches. He could see the DDs bobbing along on their ungainly approach, they and AVREs crawling up the beach, tiny stick figures running up behind, the bright firefly of tracer zinging off armoured hulls, shells and bombs pulverising the ground ahead. As General Brian Horrocks commanding XXX Corps said during a later operation, the ill-fated Market Garden: '"Gentlemen, this is a story you shall tell your grandchildren and mightily bored they'll be" ... Oddly we never were.'[12]

Lieutenant Baxter of 2nd Middlesex was one of those approaching. His job would be to secure the beach exits. As they chugged in, he could see the buildings nearly swamped in dust and the lightning flashes as the artillery and naval rounds struck home; there was a crescendo of noise and flame. Rockets added their demonic wail to this devil's chorus. As they went in, an LCT was coming out, its AVRE tank, complete with extended Bangalore Torpedo, still onboard. These were there specifically to blast an exit and the fact one of them had gone astray, missing its proper landfall, was more than a little discouraging.

At 400 yards the divers slipped over the side, their heroic mission was to clear the deadly apparatus of Rommel's nasty surprises, risky enough at any time but with dozens of slicing propellers set to decapitate the unwary, even riskier than usual. Bullets began pinging off their landing craft and Baxter really had very little idea as to where they actually were, except that the beach was now dead ahead. Down went the ramp and off into the knee-deep surf they waded. Lieutenant Baxter would find he'd landed pretty much on top of 'Cod' and this area of beach would soon be very disagreeable indeed.[13]

Poor bloody infantry

Mighty as this huge fleet was, the weather and tides were mightier still. The sea wasn't playing fully on-side and this meant the armour, assault engineers and first wave of infantry were competing for space on the shrinking beach-head. Major A. R. Rouse of the South Lancs was one of those who came ashore first. As the landing craft cruised in towards the shore at a steady 4 knots, those dreaded obstacles reared up like the hideous tentacles of some undersea monster, the stark ribs hung with garlands of black Teller mines, LCAs ducking and shearing past. Mortar bombs were sprouting on the beach and an 88mm gun was shooting in enfilade along the sands. A lone DD ahead on the infantry, despite being partly ablaze, was still firing back.[14]

'Shimi' Lovat (*see* below) was pretty scathing about 3rd Division generally. Not all would agree, of course. The division had been one of the last to leave France the first time round at Dunkirk. They'd been Tail End Charlies then, with the thankless task of forming part of the rearguard:

> Something secret and inexpressible was born within the deepening exhaustion of those calamitous days for men learned far below consciousness, a steely determination never to give in and an implacable resolve to humble the victorious Nazis, at however great a cost of toil and patience and suffering ... that was our finest hour; the hour of naked refusal to submit when we were torn and enfeebled, was a finer hour than we have ever known.[15]

Overall 3rd Division was taxed to hit the beaches at Colleville-sur-Orne, Lion-sur-Mer and St Aubin-du-Mer, to fix links with 6th Airborne (Lovat's job was to get to Pegasus) and the Canadians on Juno. Their final objective for 6 June was to press on and take both Caen and Carpiquet Aerodrome by dusk. Merville wasn't the only heavy battery that had to be knocked out, so were those at Rive-Bella, Ouistreham and Colleville-sur-Mer. The Tommies would be up against both 716th Infantry Division and the all-powerful 21st *SS Panzer*, based just south of the city. *Panzer* Meyer commanded a second armoured formation, *12th SS Panzer*

(Hitler-Jugend), near Evreux. The youth of these troops (average age 17–20), wouldn't impair their fighting prowess.

Lieutenant-Colonel Burbury, OC of the South Lancs, had thought it might be a good idea to carry a personal banner, showing the regimental colours as a rallying point, a bit like the knights of old. However, their opponents didn't have machine guns and the Colonel was dead before he even reached the wire. His 2I/C took over command but left the guidon where it had fallen. Infantry were inextricably mixed up with tanks and both were receiving the enemy's fully dedicated attention. Several officers went down and by the time 'A' Company got through the obstacles lining the dunes, only one was still on his feet.[16]

Meanwhile 'C' Company were aiming for the 'Cod' strongpoint. They should have had a second wave behind them but these had landed well to the east. Major Harrison, 'B' Company commander, was killed straight-off and Lieutenant Bell-Walker picked up the gauntlet. He identified an enemy emplacement which was hosing fire along the beach from a perfect defilade position. The lieutenant got close enough to chuck a grenade through the slit and then squirted the insides with his Sten. This did the trick but a long range burst from 'Cod', did for him too. 'Cod' was mighty strong and the remnant of 'B' Company was stuck right in front of it and had no choice but to rush the place.[17]

Lieutenant Baxter, who as mentioned was charged with securing the exits from the beach, could see just how tough a nut the German complex was to crack. It stood at the hinge of the two beach areas, Queen Red and Queen White. It wasn't just one single bunker but nearer a score, strung out with wire and trenches. It housed one 75mm gun, a brace of 50mms, three 81mm mortars, one 37mm cannon and a hand span of MG posts, all with several automatic weapons. It was a mini-fortress. It would need the attacking infantry, tanks and supporting troops from No. 5 Beach Group, including 4 Commando, to tackle this lot.

Baxter hadn't fully grasped just how powerful this beach-head Verdun actually was. Men he thought were up against the mini-dunes in front lining up for an attack were in fact dead or wounded. Mortar and MG fire was lacerating the beach; whoever moved instantly attracted a whole raft of hostile intent. 'Cod' completely dominated the sands in front but Baxter could see parties of infantry to his right moving up and off the cursed beach. Survivors, in *Saving Private Ryan* style, dashed forward to the cover of a knocked-out Sherman. Baxter counted heads; there weren't many to count.[18]

German 'potato-masher' grenades now began landing among them, soft sand deadening their effect. Tommies threw back whatever grenades they could find. When Lieutenant Tony Milne came up leading the MG Platoon of 2nd Middlesex in carriers[19] equipped with Vickers guns, they charged, spraying the trenches. This was enough; by a quirk of war, the defences of 'Cod' crumbled and survivors were yelling *kamerad*. By now the SPGs were due to be coming ashore and the beach exits had indeed been secured. The cost had not been light.

By 0830 it was pretty much job done, vestiges of 'Cod' wouldn't be cleared for another hour-and-a-half but the South Lancs pressed on south to take Hermanville, 'A' Company made for Lion-sur-Mer to the west. They had to secure Strongpoint 'Trout' at the end of Queen Green. The East Yorks were converging on another redoubt – 'Sole'. As these lead elements pressed inland, the Suffolks were coming ashore. Private Harris remembered the gut-wrenching moments as the landing craft nosed in. Down went the ramp, off went Private Harris sprinting ashore, determined not to expose himself for any longer than was strictly necessary.

What he saw wasn't pretty, eddies of acrid smoke drifted from charred and gutted buildings, twisted wrecks of tanks stood mute as did those dozens of sack-like figures in khaki, puddling red the sand beneath them. They'd breached Hitler's Atlantic Wall but would never know it or live to bore their children with the tale.[20]

The KOSBs came through the heavy seas, great green troughs of waves, craft rearing and plunging. A distant coastline seemed grey and quiet, just odd puffs of smoke as long-range naval shells erupted. Great streams of aircraft, thicker than flocks of gulls, came swooping towards the land. All they could really hear was the wind and clamour of the waves, plus the odd dull thuds of explosions. It seemed unreal. But then features became more distinct, emerging as landmarks learnt from maps.[21]

Our landing came with surprising suddenness and simplicity. As we moved rapidly onto the shore, where we could see that the houses were still burning, the landing craft slackened speed, and drifted smoothly on until the bows, with scarcely a jerk, softly grounded. The gangways were lowering as we moved in and quickly touched down. We elbowed our way forward, grabbing our cycles as they were swung off the pegs and handed down to us, and splashed through the surf barely wetting our ankles.[22]

It wasn't a pretty sight, Sword Beach; surfaces churned by tank tracks, an incoming tide forcing men to bunch up, making perfect targets. Broken glass, rubble and smoking debris from still burning buildings, dead men shrouded in their own gas capes, wrecked and charred vehicles, but above all the din. The pipes played the Borderers ashore, echoing Piper Laidler's epic rally at Loos in 1915 (which won him a VC).

At last we cleared the beach, turned left through the smashed and burning houses and moved off to the right along the road to Lion-sur-Mer. A few French civilians stood at the roadside, pressing cider and wine upon the men and cheering feebly and, as we entered the outskirts of the village an old woman leaned from her window, slowly waving a couple of little knitted flags – the French Tricolour and the Union Jack.[23]

The Normandy civilians were paying a heavy price for their freedom. War had arrived shockingly on their doorstep, shells as big as wheelie-bins shrieking in from far out to sea, heralding the devil's chorus of strafing planes and smashing bombs, their ancient tranquil settlements, already old when the Conqueror departed in the other direction, wiped out in minutes, many dead beneath their own rubble.

This was still very much a 'hot' LZ. Random mortar fire plunged down the battered streets while the crack of snipers competed. Commandos were still at work, winkling out diehards, and a trickle of wounded in their green berets was coming back.

The KOSBs passed through 2nd Lincs. And found the rest of their battalion, their assembly area 'in a rich meadow, full of lush grass, bright with poppies and other flowers'. For a moment, the war seemed far away from this late spring idyll. But it wasn't, even though birds sang and butterflies danced. That afternoon orders came through to move on up to St Aubin d'Arquenay. On the road they met their first bunch of dejected POWs, 'poor looking troops', with listless groups of traumatised civilians, wandering dazed.[24]

My dad landed on Sword beach on D Day with the Lincolnshire regiment, he was 19 years old, he was part of a 2 man Bren gun team, he told me of his feeling of fear of the landing and how he followed an older soldier up the beach, zigging and zagging inches behind him. His group made it to Caen where they were camped in an orchard that came under German shelling, he wouldn't say much about the experience but he remembered running through the trees with the crowns on fire, a shell landed close by him and he woke up in England, he spent 6 months in hospital and rest homes. Another anecdote of the experience was that during his experience in the orchard he saw a comrade's body at the bottom of a shell hole with his arm blown off (one of many), 6 months later he bumped the same chap walking down the street of the town his hospital was in, all dapper in a double breasted suit with an empty sleeve.[25]

Death of a destroyer

Major-General Rennie had his HQ aboard HMS *Largs*. The best planning in the world can very quickly go horribly wrong and while there had been setbacks, the first wave were ashore and holding. From the great ship, however, it was difficult to make any accurate assessment due to the biblical pall of smoke cloaking the beach. The general was raring to get ashore to be with his men but Rear-Admiral Talbot was all for caution; for one thing, the formidable Le Havre Battery, which posed such a threat to the troops, seemed interested in duelling with the Navy. *Warspite* that 'Grand Old Lady', was nearly three decades old, her huge 15-inch guns bellowed back, keeping the Axis gunners fully occupied.

Lieutenant-Commander Tore Holthe was a native of Trondheim and the same age as *Warspite;* he was proud to command his nippy new Norwegian destroyer *Svenner.* She and her sister ship *Stord* had the honour of riding point for the bombardment fleet. Enviable as this distinction might be, it was also dangerous. *Svenner* had a displacement of 1,800 tons, four 4.7-inch guns, eight torpedo tubes and a complement of 200. As well as covering the bombardment, she would come in as close as 3,000 yards to shoot at shore targets.

Early delays had caused frustration but now here they were, striking a blow for their captive Norway. Holthe was proud of his ship and of his crew, he had every right to be. Every shell they fired brought the liberation of their homeland that one step closer. Hitler's *Kriegsmarine* had been a formidable force; their fast, lethal E-Boats had duelled in the Channel with British MTBs since the start of the war but the German navy was depleted, not the burnished instrument of war it had been.

Nonetheless, three of these sleek craft had come out to fight despite the odds. Heinrich Hoffman commanded a vessel some 400 tons lighter than *Svenner* but, as he reckoned, the sheer size of the Allied armada offered opportunities for a spot of hit-and-run. He had no idea just how huge a target or how unfortunate the odds were but he'd led his trio of little ships in a real Balaklava charge through the smoke screen.

They shot off a total of 17 torpedoes and one smacked into the *Svenner,* hitting her amidships, inflicting a mortal wound. A geyser of black oil, like a burst artery, gouted from the stricken destroyer. Within 2 minutes it was over, the lost ship heeled over and went down. Holthe was the last to jump, from the bridge he'd so proudly commanded, and his boat had the unenviable distinction of being the Navy's only loss that morning. The proud new vessel hadn't even fired her guns and 32 of her crew were lost. Amazingly, all the other German torpedoes missed.[26]

Like a knife through butter: The Commandos

Simon Fraser, 15th Lord Lovat, who in real life even managed to upstage his later screen persona as played by Peter Lawford,[27] was piped ashore in fine Highland style by Bill Millin, a consciously staged piece of legend-building, marvellous theatre, but the enemy bullets were still real. The heroic piper was later and fittingly lauded in verse (*see* Appendix ii). 'Shimi' Lovat came from a long line of Highland scrappers and looked the part: tall and Hollywood handsome. He had moved from one conventional elite, the Scots Guards, to the rather less orthodox Commandos. He had had plenty experience of raids in Norway and a distinguished role in the Dieppe disaster when his men, with superb élan, took their difficult objectives.

Now commanding 1st Special Service Brigade, he would land on Sword Beach. They'd had a typically rough crossing, with oily sardines and no rum for breakfast even for those who had the stomach for it. Then there were the waves of Allied aircraft screaming in overhead, a blistering chorus to the symphony of naval shells engulfing the beach ahead. They were still 8 miles out. As the flotilla closed, the big guns gave way to the lesser battering of destroyers, picking up enemy muzzle flashes. It took 45 minutes to close on the beach: Lovat had divided his landing craft into waves, he didn't want his entire brigade crowding the sands and giving the enemy a splendid array of packed targets.

His commandos were going in behind 8th Infantry Brigade. Their job was to take assigned strongpoints – heavy infantry work rather than dash-and-grab raiding. One troop went ashore singing *Jerusalem* and why not, these men were latter-day crusaders come to deliver a captive France from the tyrant's jackboot. Shimi himself was going ashore in a plywood-hulled craft; the first echelon had the use of sturdier steel-hulled boats. They felt very exposed. There was a great deal of smoke but not enough to completely shroud their landmark. A damaged LCT with wounded and dead aboard limped back in front of them. Now they were among the obstacles: skeletal ribs of hedgehogs laced with mines, spiced with incoming fire. The enemy were firing armour-piercing rather than HE rounds, a bizarre blessing as these just punched through the flimsy wooden hulls and kept going; HE would have shredded them. Still, despite damage, they made it: 5 out of 22 launches were hit but most still made it ashore. Down went the bows on Lovat's boat and, as CO, like the clan chiefs of old, he led the charge. Bill Millin offered *Blue Bonnets* as a musical accompaniment. As befitted his raffish style, Lovat went ashore wearing a monogrammed white jumper beneath his battledress and carrying (allegedly) a strictly non-issue .45-70 lever-action Winchester. John Wayne couldn't have done it better.[28]

They pelted up the beach. Inevitably, men went down. Mullen, the artist, like a broken doll, lay with both legs shattered at the end of a bloody trail. He was beyond speech but out of pain; a glance showed a helpless case and that death was busy with him. David Wellesley Colley, a Downside boy with a cheerful smile, lay against the pack of a sergeant who had pulled him into shelter. He was shot through the heart. Tears were running down the NCO's face. 'Mr Colley's dead sir. He's dead. Don't you understand?'[29]

'Little' Ginger Cunningham was shot through the legs as he ran. 'Big' Murdoch McDougall yanked him up and carried the smaller man clear – Ginger loudly lamenting how the Germans managed to miss such a big bloke yet hit a far smaller one![30] Despite his wounds, Ginger, the unit medic, stayed in the game – patching up wounded and hobbling gamely with the aid of Lovat's stick. A brave *resistant* M. Lefevre had sabotaged cables powering flamethrowers on the beach. Lovat, rather snappily, felt he'd done better than 8th Brigade. Shimi was none too impressed with 3rd Division – 'muscle-bound mentally and physically, after four years training in the UK.'[31]

W. H. Jeffries served in No. 6 Commando and landed from an LCI:

After sailing, below deck we made a very special study of our maps, checked our arms and ammunition and had plenty of hot soup provided by one of the crew. June the 6th, soon after dawn, we were crouching low on the deck and to our left a battleship was firing, and above a few Spitfires to cover us in. At this point the enemy gunners were trying to get our range and shells were bursting all around us.

Soon we were heading for our part of the Normandy coast, and at once all hell seemed to break out. As the enemy machine gunners opened up, very calmly the LCI crew dropped the landing ramps down, and with good luck from the crew we started on our way through the sea. Part of our task was to reach the airborne forces who in the night had taken and were holding the bridge, now named Pegasus Bridge. After leaving the beach we made our way through open grassland, and all around the Germans had placed notice boards warning of mines. But by a careful study of the ground we found the way across a part where cattle had been grazing some days before. We moved so fast that we were onto one group of Germans drinking coffee in the edge of a field. Our instructions had to be carried out. Push on to the bridge, never mind the odds.[32]

One of Lovat's units, 1st Battalion, Royal Marines, 4th Franco-British Commando, was led by *Capitaine de Corvette* Philippe Kieffer and their job, coming ashore at Rive-Bella, was to take the former casino, no longer a gambling den but a redoubt. Born in Haiti but of Alsatian stock, Kieffer had volunteered for the French Navy in 1939. He'd escaped the fall of France in June the following year and signed up for the Free French Navy in London. A fluent English speaker, he'd been impressed by the fledgeling commando force and, despite already being 40, he set about raising a Gallic contingent, the *Fusiliers Marins et Commandos*. Blooded at Dieppe, by 6 June 1944 they were veterans of numerous raids.

Kieffer had 177 men, 21 of whom were killed and 83 wounded. His commandos, many of them Bretons, were the only all-French unit to take part in the invasion. No. 4 Commando came ashore on Queen Beach Red. Lieutenant-Colonel Dawson was wounded, so Kieffer led the survivors towards Ouistreham. Luckily, a local gendarme was able to give some pretty precise information on the mini-fortress, once the casino, (rebuilt for defence in 1942). Kieffer himself was hit twice by shrapnel as he directed the attack, which became very up close and personal – a hard, bloody fight, eventually won by the bayonet.

Despite his wounds the Frenchman refused evacuation for two days and was back in action barely a week later, taking part in the breakout battles. He was amongst the first Free French to enter Paris, a bitter victory as his 18-year-old son, serving with the *Maquis,* was killed by the Germans at almost the same time.

Lovat, storming up the beach, passed through 8th Brigade busily digging in. Commandos don't really do digging in, they go and find more enemy to biff. With No. 6 Commando as vanguard, they charged. Bombing their way through the defences, stripped down to essential fighting kit, they chucked grenades into pillboxes, scorched the defenders with flamethrowers and hosed everything in sight from Brens. This was what they'd volunteered for. Snipers lurking in bombed-out buildings were systematically stalked and dealt with. Marksmen picked off any German daft enough to raise his head.[33]

A steady trickle of dazed captured enemy were shepherded down onto the beach and into captivity. 'We were almost through the Atlantic Wall...'[34] Even Shimi was impressed by the network his commandos had punched through. The Atlantic Wall wasn't a line of static defences, 'grouse butts' as he calls them, but a meticulously constructed set of interlocking positions offering serious in-depth and all-around defence. The underwater obstacles fed onto minefields, back towards individual strongpoints, studded with ordnance and MGs behind them, infantry in trenches and reserves of armour further back.

Each pillbox was a citadel of reinforced concrete, sunk hull-down and half-buried in the ridges of the dunes. Walls, 2 feet thick, stood 6 feet above ground level, their height increased by a very solid roof that gave further feet of concrete head cover. Lovat saw that these German bunkers made ours look puny. Theirs were sited in depth, about 100 or 150 yards apart, girded with strong wire entanglements, interlaced with more mines. There was sweeping enfilade fire. There might be half a dozen defenders with a 75mm gun and automatics; the pillboxes were interspersed with MG cupolas.[35] Tremendous as this lot was, the commandos weren't going to be stopped. No. 6 Commando 'moved like a knife through enemy butter.'[36]

Elegy from a supporting wave

My Grandfather, Horace Grainger, was in a supply battalion whose job it was to resupply the troops immediately after their landing. He told us that it would always haunt him as there was no time to clear the bodies from the water, and from lots of the beaches. So they had no choice but to drive over bodies, he said that the sound of bones crunching under the vehicles would haunt him forever. He said that it should be a lesson for everyone that wars were terrible things and to be avoided at all costs.[37]

The British were ashore and had punched through the Atlantic Wall. Now they had to press on and take Caen. But, by the end of the day, the city hadn't fallen and it would be another 43 days before it did.

5

JUNO BEACH, MORNING

It was a happy world we shared together, you and I, there were joys and tears, long hours of idleness, and the zest of being young and free. To you I was no hero that day when I became a soldier. Still less was I a hero to myself. It was a war not of my making but in it I have found a cause too precious to betray. This is why one day I WILL COME BACK TO YOU.

Oh yes it might have been easy to have turned aside – I heard no call to battle – only deep down within me a conviction that was greater than myself if I had lived to love you, could I risk death to fight for you? It was a simple echo of the heart that whispers now – I WILL COME BACK TO YOU.

There is only misery in war to those who weigh life in comfort, gold and power. Those are the scales of our enemy and they have called me for your side to challenge our possession of the right to live; men call it 'freedom', but I call it – you. How simple then it seemed as I stand in line, awaiting the order that has already gone forth to thousands of my comrades. Proudly I will press on to victory because I WILL COME BACK TO YOU.

Though out on that battlefield may lie many of those who staked a claim to life, their souls triumphant will go marching on – cleansed by the fire of tribulation in the cause of right.

Shoulder to shoulder we will stand – even in death. And if my living comrades of the line should close their ranks for me, I too will be there, content. God's wish will be fulfilled – a night – a little day and I WILL COME BACK TO YOU.

Fusilier McLuckie RNF: *I Will Come Back to You*

We owe it to our self-respect as British soldiers to show ourselves really well-behaved in every way. But we, unlike the Germans, can be naturally friendly, seeing that the French are naturally our friends ...

Instructions for British Servicemen...[1]

My father, James Clifford Whiteley who'd served with 40 Royal Marine Commandos, never talked about his part in the war. Then one rainy Sunday in 1974 while the family were all together his son-in-law who was in the RAF gave him some ribbing about 'his bit' in the war. In response my dad over the next hour for the first and only time told us about his wartime experience. He had enlisted rather than be called up and was 18 years and 3 months old when D-day came along. He had been given a landing craft to take over filled with supplies for the first wave.

As everybody knows the invasion was postponed for 24hrs. My dad's LC was tied up against a section of the Mulberry harbour in Weymouth. With the waves banging the LC against the Mulberry harbour they were trying to sleep. My dad and his mate were awakened at 4am with the LC full of water and sinking! The LC was banging against a metal projection, which had holed the wooden craft. The two men jumped into the water as the craft sunk. Their cries were heard and they were picked up by a fishing boat going out to sea. They asked to be put ashore and the fisherman said first he'd pick up his lobster pots – which took three hours!

When they got back the place was like a hornets' nest with Navy divers and all sorts! The 'high ups' knew a craft had gone down, they weren't worried about the men, but what was on the LC, ammunition, bombs? Could it explode and damage the Mulberry Harbour thereby scuppering the whole Mulberry project? My dad turned up to an ear blast, I don't think the contents were dangerous so the brass were reassured but my dad, who was a Lance Corporal, was demoted on the spot for technically leaving his post and the trouble he had caused! He was given a second landing craft. This one WAS full of fuel or ammo.

They went across and hit Juno Beach (I think) and they were asked by the beach-master, who by the sound of it was the chap played by Kenneth More in *the Longest Day*, what they had. My dad listed his explosive cargo. There were large numbers of men pouring ashore and they were still under fire. The beach-master told him in no uncertain terms to get the bloody thing well away up the beach away from the men!

My dad backed the LC out and took it further up the beach where it was empty. As they were going in they hit one of Rommel's underwater obstructions and were stuck fast. Then they came under fire. My dad said it was amazing; all this tracer fire arcing down the beach. He was mesmerised and just stood there staring at the whole dramatic scene as the tracer skittered along the sand towards them. His mate had already taken the prudent course and jumped into the water and was shouting 'Jim! Jim! Get off!' Snapping out of it, he leapt into the water and swam away as the LC exploded. So two LCs both sunk with cargo and nobody hurt! What a lark it seemed.[2]

And now for Canada

Like the 51st Highland Division, the Canadians had scores to settle. Their countrymen who'd thirsted to be in the fight had been chosen to spearhead the Dieppe raid. That had gone badly, very badly. A thousand of the 2nd Canadian Division had been killed, nearly twice as many captured, and now they were back. Not quite a year after the *Jubilee* disaster, the 3rd Canadian Division had been selected for Normandy. They trained hard, nobody could afford a repeat of Dieppe, working with the RN and the British 2nd Armoured Brigade to be equipped with DD tanks.

By 26 May, the 15,000 Canadians and 9,000 Brits were concentrating and on 1 June they commenced embarkation at Southampton. They'd be hitting the beaches at 07.45 on 6 June. Now Juno beach was divided, looking from the sea, into two sectors, 'Mike' to the right and 'Nan' on the left. Two brigades would lead the charge – the 7th coming ashore at Courseulles on 'Mike' and 8th at Bernières on 'Nan'. Swimming DD tanks from 6th and 10th Armoured Regiments would support both. Fire support would come from the 107mm mortars of the Cameron Highlanders of Ottawa. Behind 8th Brigade, 4th Special Service Brigade would take care of any troublesome strongpoints then swerve east to establish contact with 3rd Division's commandos at Sword. Between them, the Special Forces would take out the enemy radar installation at Douvres-la-Délivrande. Another infantry brigade, the 9th, would form a second wave, reinforcing the success of either of those who'd gone in first.

Once they'd taken the two coastal settlements and St Aubin, the Canadians were tasked to push inland reaching a series of objectives, defined by some arboreal enthusiast as 'Yew', 'Elm' and 'Oak'. The third and final bound, 'Oak' was bounded by the railway tracks south of the N13 leading from Caen to Bayeux. At that point they'd halt, dig in and see off any attempts to dislodge them.

Prior to the beach assault, the RAF pounded the enemy defences. At dawn on 6 June, USAAF took over and kept up the relentless deluge from the bomb-laden skies; as the armada drew in, the Navy would add the fire of 11 destroyers to the tempest, (2 of them Canadian). Neptune was equally restless and the waves were so rough the actual landings had to be delayed by 10 minutes to allow some dispersed landing craft to catch up. Despite the fire and fury, the Canadians would find many of the enemy bunkers pretty much unscathed and open for business.

Getting ashore

A Canadian officer on board an LCI describes landing on Juno Beach:

> At about 8 o'clock, our craft formed line and we were going
> in. Most of the fellows were ready. I was interested in the

expressions on their faces – some looked like a wounded spaniel, some were quite nonchalant about it, others made a feeble effort at gaiety. What amused me most was a fat boy trying to whistle, but the best he could do was blow air, with a squeak now and then. Just between ourselves, I was pretty scared myself about that time. Those last few moments were awful; it was the waiting that was hard. We were coming under pretty intense small arms fire by this time. At last the gangways were run down, and it was a case of get up and get in and get down. I manoeuvred into position to be as near as possible to the front.

I wanted to be one of the first to land, not because of any heroics, but waiting your turn on the exposed ramp was much worse than going in.

Once he had landed:

Many of the troops had already crossed the beach and were fighting forward towards their objective, a ridge back from the beach a few hundred yards. If, as the radio announced later, it was an unopposed landing, God forbid that anyone should ever have to go in on an opposed one! Our beach was littered with those who had been a jump ahead of us. A captured blockhouse being used as a dressing station was literally surrounded by piles of bodies.[3]

R. Haig-Brown was serving with 93rd Light Anti-Aircraft Regiment, Royal Artillery, equipped with Crusader tanks fitted with 20mm anti-aircraft guns. His unit landed on Juno Beach:

Our job was to get eventually to two bridges, one over the Orne canal at Bénouville, and the other 100 yards to the east, over the Orne River. We were to protect them from air attack as they were the only road link between the beach and the 6th Airborne Division who had landed to the east of the river.

The bridges lay on the other side of a minefield. As I had been on the course, I was told to organise a way through for the tanks. I knew exactly what to do until I came across the first mine. I had never seen one like it before. Even if I knew all about German mines I was not prepared for this and all the others to be British, captured at Dunkirk in 1940 and used against us now. I had no idea how to handle any of them. When eventually I did clear a way through, no-one would volunteer to drive the first tank down my taped path. 'You cleared the way, Sir,' said the troop sergeant major, 'and if you don't mind,' he added with a huge grin, 'perhaps you would prove it is all right by taking No.1 tank down there yourself.'[4]

William Ruck served with 22nd Dragoons:

The craft moved slowly, I remember the white cliffs of Dover going by. The morning was dark and the sea was choppy. To my right was a small landing craft with a couple of small tanks and some marines who were soaking wet. There was no time to discuss the matter, seasick or not, we mounted the vehicles ready for the off. I stuck the tank in first gear keeping the revs up, the only thing that mattered was getting to dry land. We raced up the dunes and landed on Juno beach with the Canadians.

As we moved forward to higher ground we passed wreckage and bodies and could hear the infantry busy among the trees. Some planes came overhead and Olly, our gunner, got hold of the Browning on the turret and had go back, it was a taste of what was to come. Early the next morning, we were still only a small way from the sea and moved over to the British sector on the outskirts of Bayeux. All the while huge shells flew overhead. The Germans were sending heavy armour in the form of Tiger and Panther tanks, more than a match for our Shermans. We were camouflaged up and ready for the attack on Caen.

As the evening came I was standing with the lads watching the tracers flying by and I saw the damn thing coming. I took a dive for cover under an old tank and I felt a fair old thump in my left rear and I knew I'd been caught when my leg went numb and I could feel blood. There were those a lot worse off than me. Somehow I made it onto a stretcher; lines of stretchers filled the place, it was a harrowing time.[5]

My father was a corporal in the Royal Marines. He captained a landing craft at the first wave ferrying Canadians to Juno Beach. On his first return to the ships to collect more troops his LC was hit by a shell and sunk. The crew were safely plucked from the sea. My father didn't immediately receive another LC so that his war was more or less over early in the morning of D-Day. When, after a few days, he was given another LC the battle had moved on and he ferried material and weapons to tame beaches until a port was liberated. Then the big ships came into their own. When, in 1994, I proposed to him that he attend the celebratory bash then being planned in Normandy he looked at me as if I were mad. 'Why would I want to go and celebrate all of that?' he asked me, 'it was bloody awful.'[6]

Abraham Dufresne was born on 9 October 1920 in Rivière-au-Renard, in the Gaspé region, Quebec, Canada. Fourth oldest in a family of ten children, he also had three half-sisters. Having worked as both fisherman and lumberjack in his hometown, a single lad, he enlisted at the age of 20 in the Regiment de Chaudière and was sent to Base Camp Valcartier, a training camp established during the Great War.

His regiment was sent to England in August 1941. His initial experience was not a happy one; he was admitted to the hospital as he had a bad case of flu. He seems to have been what is politely described as 'a bit of a lad'. Abraham went AWOL seven times and was disciplined each time by being confined to barracks. For all these young men coming so far from their homes, this was a bit of a big adventure; they didn't want to miss out. An awful lot of them would be missing the rest of their lives.

On 1 June 1944, those regiments participating in the invasion began their final preparations. LRC would board *Clam Lamont* and the Landing Ship *Monowai*, which would take them from Southampton out into the Channel where they'd deploy into landing craft for the last stretch until they splashed ashore in front of Bernières-sur-Mer. As part of 9th Brigade, they waited, crammed aboard, many sick, some trying to pass the time and ease their taut nerves with dice.

The Chaudières boarded landing craft around 10:45 on 6 June. The sea was still just as rough and they hit Juno about an hour later. They were in reserve, coming ashore at Bernières-sur-Mer as part of the second wave supporting the Queen's Own Rifles of Canada. They caused quite a stir with the locals who weren't expecting to meet these Quebecois speaking French to them. The LRC were, in fact, the only French-speaking regiment taking part in Operation Overlord, aside from Kieffer and his commandos.

Abraham with his comrades would fan out on the beach and aim for the seawall. They'd be expected to mop up any opposition the first wave had overlooked. As it turned out, there were plenty of Germans still active and full of fight. Small arms fire and mortars greeted them. It was a dash of 150 feet (46 metres) across the beach to the seawall. Quite a few didn't make it and Abraham Dufresne was one of them. He is buried in Bény-sur-Mer.[7]

Ernest Stanley Pickford was born 15 September 1923. Ernest spent three years in high school. When he was 16, his father died and Ernest got a job working in a munitions factory. Two years later he joined up, just before his 18th birthday. He was 5 foot 11 inches, (1.8 metres), which at the time was considered pretty tall. He trained for another two years at Camp Borden, around 100 km north of Toronto. The army decided he'd be best suited serving as an orderly in a field ambulance unit. He was taken on strength with the No. 2 District Depot RCAMC in Toronto, then transferred to 25th Field Ambulance. He had a variety of postings before sailing from Halifax, disembarking at Liverpool on 24 February 1944. He'd do his war service with 14th Field Ambulance and boarded a transport ship in Portsmouth on 3 June bound for the shores of Normandy. He felt he was ready, his training was complete. Medics would tend the wounded from the first wave ashore, while others worked to help set up base hospitals that could hold a minimum of 22,000 casualties.

On 6 June the 14th, 22nd and 23rd Canadian Field Ambulances were the only medical units forming part of the initial landing force. Ernest, as part of the 14th, would have been on the front lines. These field ambulances units were attached to 7th, 8th, and 9th Brigades, roughly 18 medics for every 2,000 men. The supporting wave was scheduled to land 3–4 hours later once the initial assault had secured the 'crust' of the beach. On the morning of the attack they arrived a few hours later than planned. Some of the tanks supporting the first two infantry brigades sank before making it to shore.

'There were six tanks on the craft ... my tank alone got to shore, the other ones weren't so lucky,' remembered Philip John Cockburn of 1st Hussars, who arrived with Ernest. 'The landing was total chaos, bullets flying everywhere with accuracy; the Germans were wounding and killing left and right. Many soldiers were warned but nothing could have shown them what it would be like. I was warned, but that didn't help any.'[8]

In that storm of fire and confusion medics scrambled amongst the many casualties, trying to decide who was worth treating and who wasn't. Their first frantic hour was spent gathering wounded, applying first aid and dragging injured soldiers behind the wall or anywhere they could find shelter. As the day ground on, they established advanced dressing stations, (essentially make-shift hospitals intended to help the wounded and to hold casualties since none could be evacuated that first day). These were set up at Banville, 2 kilometres south, inland of Courseulles-sur-Mer, and at Pierrepoint, 5 kilometres inland. By the end of the day, more than 4,500 soldiers would receive high-quality medical attention.

Ernest Stanley Pickford was killed in action on 9 June and was buried in the Bény-sur-Mer Canadian Military Cemetery.[9]

M. G. Gale drove a Sherman tank serving with 44th Royal Tank Regiment, 4th Armoured Brigade, and landed on Juno Beach on D+1 (7 June 1944):

We had been in North Africa, Sicily and Italy, and were I suppose veterans, having taken part in two D-Day landings. We knew when we were all told to man our tanks and prepare to start engines that the time to land was close. The ship slowed to a halt, the bows opened and there before us in the morning light was the beach. Fighting was going on just off the beach. I moved the tank very slowly down the ramp and began to ease her off the end, waiting for the drop into what we had expected to be about 6 ft of water.

We were all battened down, and well waterproofed, which as it turned out was just as well, because instead of 6 ft there was 10 or 12 ft of water. Unknown to the ship's captain, we had pulled in right onto a shell hole, and there we were, well under water. Before I could decide what to do, voices were reaching us over our radio telling us not to try to move. The water as it turned out was almost to the top of our air intake, and if we had tried to pull out, the rear of the tank would have gone down and perhaps we would have all been drowned. I was told to cut the engine and wait for instructions. We sat there waiting for the tide to go out for almost two hours.

We were able to follow what was going on, on the radio, but seeing nothing except water through our periscopes, until at last as the water went down, we could see and finally with the better part of our Regiment well off the beaches we were able to rejoin them. We had not enjoyed our forced stay in the water but who knows, because of it perhaps I am alive today.[10]

Building bridges

George ('Geordie') Dunn was a Wearsider and coal miner, his birthday was on 9 June so his mates had wondered if he'd get to celebrate his 21st in France. He was the driver in a Churchill tank[11] and the radio man, Roy Manley, was his best mate. The crew was led by Sergeant Jim Ashton who, at nearly 30, seemed like an old man to the rest. Their Churchill carried a 'fascine',[12] its job was to drop its cargo of eight stout timber logs in the gap where aerial photography had shown a culvert had been blown. This was past the dunes in the wet ground heading inland.

Once they'd deposited their load and formed a crossing for the Canadian infantry coming ashore behind them, they were to advance to the road junction just a bit further on, take and hold it. If the war was bearable, and they knew exactly what they had to do and certainly weren't fazed by it, Jim Ashton's enthusiastic and never-ending renditions of popular songs delivered with gusto from the turret formed their main gripe. He sang as they came ashore, warbled as they moved inland, the warbler just couldn't stop. Geordie knew where he was going, spotted the gap he needed to find in the dunes, trying to ignore the dead and wounded littered the shrinking beach-head, narrowing rapidly as the tide climbed in.[13]

Engine trouble had delayed their LCT so they came in behind, rather than with, the first wave. Flails had already scoured for mines and a second fascine tank coming up behind performed its allotted task and filled in the tank ditch just through the gap. On they went and Jerry saw them coming, a storm of mortars and small arms peppered the dunes. The culvert though wasn't far ahead, maybe 50 yards.

Flails kept flailing and cleared a path for them. When they reached where the culvert had been, it didn't look too bad, just a stream. Their troop commander radioed they should just push on and on Geordie pushed. What had seemed nothing more than a decent sized puddle was, in fact, a significant wet gap and the realisation dawned on them as the tank slid nose first into the drink, braking didn't help and down she plunged.[14]

Geordie was lucky not to have drowned. His mates yanked him clear of the driving seat as water flooded the compartment. They scrambled clear, clinging to the turret, the only part of the tank still above water and that was sinking. Somehow they all floundered back to dry land and pelted for cover in the dunes as enemy tracer sought them out. Covered by MGs from the rest of their troop, they all made it unscathed. The tank virtually disappeared.

Almost but not completely, bizarrely Geordie's misfortune proved a bonus for the Allies. A bridge tank could lay a track 30 feet (9 metres) across. The gap Geordie had blundered into was double that, therefore, in theory, it was unbridgeable. What

Geordie had inadvertently done was solve the problem; his sunken tank became a mid-way bridge abutment for the far end of a track laying on the submerged turret. The fascine was freed and dropped into the remaining un-bridged section. More logs were brought up and the whole gap was crossed.

Meanwhile, in the dunes, Jim Ashton had started singing again. They seemed to be safe enough, though mortars were still falling, and then one fell right on top of them. Jim had sung his last ditty. Roy Manley had listened for the last time. Stunned, Geordie half-fell, half-rolled down the dune, only just registering the warning sign in German that informed him he was in a minefield. The rest were all dead. He stumbled clear before passing out. When they amputated what remained of his left leg and arm, doctors couldn't believe he'd managed to get so far on a shattered limb. He lived but would never hew coal again. Their unplanned bridge was consolidated and also survived.[15]

Tony Rubenstein's battle

As the Canadians struggled ashore at St Aubin, British Royal Marine Commandos[16] were right behind them. Not all were your hard-as-nails, salty types. One of their officers Anthony Rubenstein was only 19, from a comfortable *haute bourgeois* background, a long line of distinguished lawyers. Had it not been for the war, he'd still have been studying at Cheltenham College, looking forward to a cushy billet in Civvy Street. He'd joined up at 17 and now found himself a sub-lieutenant in 48 RMC, in charge of a section (effectively a weak platoon-sized unit). Now the Navy has its own traditions and doesn't doff its cap to any in the army, not even the Guards. *They* claim a heritage going back to Alfred the Great and that's pretty hard to beat. Yet, despite their macho image, Rubenstein, with one of his NCOs Sergeant Blyth and several of their men, shared a shameful secret; they all loved ballroom dancing![17]

Being Navy they had their own smaller, sleeker version of an infantry landing craft, each of which held a troop of about 70 marines, (the commando comprised six troops, each divided into two sections). In these craft they crossed the Channel; each had its own mini-version of the quarterdeck, a cabin space reserved for officers. Their mission was to hit Juno beach on the left or eastern flank of the Canadians near St Aubin and seize the gap, about 4 miles (6.5 kilometres) or so that would link them to the Brits on Sword. Hopefully, at the half-way point they'd shake hands with more of their number coming west.[18]

Rubenstein and his comrades had been thoroughly briefed and the toughest nut they'd have to crack was the enemy strongpoint in Langrune-sur-Mer. At the outset it ought to be easy, the infantry and tanks would be ashore and punching through the carapace of the enemy's beach defences. Sappers would have cleared the infestation of obstacles, and the preliminary bombardment from air and sea would have wrecked whatever strongpoints there were. That was the plan anyway and he'd no reason to doubt it would all be just that straightforward. He'd not been to war before.

As they cruised in half-an-hour behind the Canadians, it all seemed to be going rather well. Their vast armada seemed unstoppable, the shore quite calm. A few hundred yards out, as they coasted in towards the beach, all hell was let loose. Mortars spewed fountains around the landing craft; MG fire and lazy arcs of bright tracer clawed at them, pinging off the hull. His education continued as he watched the craft next to them shudder to a halt as it fouled one of the underwater obstacles and became a sitting target for enemy fire, which came rattling and screaming from the dunes, a vortex of noise. The bombardment hadn't been so totally crushing after all.

Their LC nudged in the few final yards and the ramps splashed down, these were your old-fashioned Gallipoli era jobs, single file only like the *Queen Mary*, not ideal when people are trying their very hardest to kill as many of you as possible. The marines formed an orderly queue while sailors hosed the shattered buildings with Vickers guns. As Rubenstein got onto the flimsy gantry, the bloke in front was shot neatly through the head. The dead man jerked back against him but, true to his training, he shoved him off and got going. Having struggled through the last billows of surf and pelted across the sand, he hurled himself behind the seawall. Behind him, half swallowed by the rushing tide, was a hell of wrecked and burning vehicles, a slew of abandoned, broken kit and lots, an awful lot, of dead.

Several of the commandos' craft were lodged on the spikes, sinking under the weight of enemy fire. Heavily laden troopers were desperately trying to swim ashore, helpless in the stiff current. He watched his friend Yates drown and saw the body of the man he'd pushed aside bobbing and flopping on the waterline, sack-like in death. He didn't have long to reflect, someone had cleared the way, gapped the minefield and they must press on.[19]

They had so many dead and missing that two troops were now barely one. In fact, it wasn't as bad as it seemed, a full LC's worth of marines had been rescued in the water but their deliverers were ordered back to Blighty and so the sullen and furious commandos went with them, not having fired a single round. Those who were ashore crept, largely unmolested, along the coast, probing along narrow Normandy lanes. Captain Perry ordered Rubenstein to exercise his best sixth-former's French when they came to a local café, doing brisk trade despite the kerfuffle. '*Ou sont les Boches?*' he began. This formal overture sparked a no-doubt helpful but otherwise unintelligible torrent of information all delivered in the strong local accent he couldn't begin to comprehend.[20]

Now they came under what is euphemistically termed 'friendly fire', although being shot at never seems all that amicable. Their own Navy comrades mistook them for the Boche they were hunting and gave them a salvo. Lieutenant Curtis, Rubenstein's troop officer, went down. There was not much they could do but pump the wounded full of morphine. Curtis handed over the baton and muttered he'd see Rubenstein back in London, a stiff upper lip and movie moment, but they both knew Curtis would never see Piccadilly again.[21]

Langrune-sur-Mer was the toughest nut of all, largely undisturbed by the Allies' best intentions. The Germans had taken a whole block of houses and turned an improvised bastion into a fortress and they were very good at this. It had the seawall to the front and cleared streets, like No-Man's-Land, on all the landward sides. The houses were no longer dwellings but strongpoints with trenches, wire, mines and pillboxes built in, each affording overlapping arcs of fire; in short, a right bastard and probably the biggest bastard of the lot. Nobody was waving any white flags.

It was now late morning and that pleasant spring light, which so characterises the Calvados coast, gilded the solid menace of the redoubt. Captain Perry led an assault team in from one landward flank and Rubenstein the other. Just beyond the main block was what had been the village crossroads. Now it was covered by a sturdy bunker that sprayed fire at the commandos as they dodged, ducking and sprinting, from doorway to doorway.

Perry dodged through the houses into their long back gardens and his men hacked a passage through yard walls to outflank the guns. If anyone had been thinking about history, this was the tactic employed by the utterly disreputable but seriously charismatic Warwick the Kingmaker to win the skirmish at St Albans in 1455 and kick-start the Wars of the Roses. Probably not many thought of that. This action brought them to the last house facing the junction.[22]

Rubenstein was left in charge of the huddle of commandos while Perry went off to scout. A sniper got him. Young Anthony, at 19, was now in charge as the last officer standing. *What do we do now sir?* Sixty-five men waited for an answer. He called his NCOs as an O group but as they debated in the porch, a mortar round came in and wounded two of them, blowing Rubenstein clear down the cellar steps. Amazingly, he was unhurt.

Time to get back into the fight and a very hard fight it was. For 9 hours the commandos looked for an opening, duelling with small arms and grenades against an unseen but omnipresent enemy, well dug in, very well armed and clearly highly motivated. They dodged from shot-up house to shot-up house, looking for a chink in the enemy's armour. But there weren't any. Fritz had really thought this one through. Every inch of open space was covered by MGs, snipers were ready for even a second's exposure, and mortars followed them like dragon's breath.

In the afternoon, Rubenstein and a handful of troopers burrowed their way into a corner of the main redoubt. Fritz had thought about that one too, building an internal blast wall and stocking up on grenades, their wooden handled 'potato-mashers'. Even a lone Sherman that had joined in the fight couldn't punch a hole through the steel and concrete barrier. Rubenstein had swapped his .38 Webley revolver for a Lee Enfield and potted a lone German pelting along one of their trenches, one of the very few they actually saw.[23]

By dark it was still a stalemate, the commandos were exhausted, thirsty and hungry, low on just about everything and the plain fact was they'd not scratched the surface of the strongpoint at Langrune-sur-Mer. Not for lack of will, courage or persistence; it was impossible for men armed only with small arms and grenades. By dusk Rubenstein got fresh orders, just mask Fritz in his bunkers and dig in on the periphery, a strong counter-attack was expected. He'd sent Sergeant Blyth off on a recce and he hadn't come back.

Rubenstein stayed while the others filed off to get digging. He wandered the eerie broken streets, now quiet, searching for his lost patrol. The sea sounded rhythmically as it hissed along the sands, the ebb and suck of timeless tides. The only gunfire was sporadic and far off. The surviving German defenders, just as tired, didn't bother him. Later on, he gave up the search and got back to his men who were bivouacking in an orchard, which was a standard feature in the Normandy landscape.

The commandos were angry and full of fight. They wanted to get stuck in again and avenge the deaths of so many comrades. Rubenstein sank into an exhausted sleep. In the morning, he led them back – and they took the place: more than 30 Germans came out of the wreckage with their hands held high and Sergeant Blyth was found, injured but alive. It had all resulted in a lot of growing up for one sixth former in a single day and night.[24]

Getting there
Juno was very tough indeed; the Canadians and Brits had hard and costly fighting to win their toehold. In spite of this, they took their objectives and moved on as far as the 'Elm' bound, while some armour did get beyond 'Oak', the third and final stop. In some

places they'd pushed 7 miles (11 kilometres) inland, the deepest penetration of any Allied troops on D-Day. On their right, they'd shaken hands with 50th Division, from Gold beach at Creully, but to the left and east, when looking to hook up with British 3rd Div on Sword, a gap remained: a vital gap and Major General Edgar Feuchtinger's *21st Panzer* from Marcks' LXXXIV Corps was ordered up to exploit the hole. This would prove tricky.

6

GOLD BEACH, MORNING

He lived, before the baleful sun
Was risen to burn the yellow sand
To which from out the seas he ran
And then, a moment later, died.
His voice, as stumbling through the surf
He shouldered friends in the khaki wave,
Was mix't with theirs, as strong and rough,
And then, no call or moan he gave,
He laughed, it mingled strangely with a sigh
His thoughts we knew, were far away
And lonely, as the sightless eyes
That saw no beauty in the bay.
Yes, lonely and quiet, as the single grave
Shallow dug beyond the clean washed sand
Safe from the curl of the grasping wave
He lies, and has passed the barren land

E. Yates: *Beach Casualty*

Don't criticise the French Army's defeat of 1940. Many Frenchmen are convinced that they had a fine but insufficiently equipped army, not very well led. Many others are themselves critical of the French Army of 1940, but they, too, will resent their own criticism coming from a foreigner ...[1]

The weather was foul, probably at its worst off Gold Beach. The wind notched up to Force 5 as the troops clambered heavily, laden with kit, into their LCAs; they were about 10,000 yards (9,100 metres) out. Even the most seasoned sailors amongst them, those who'd avoided sickness on the rough crossing, were throwing up despite bolting down their hyoscine hydrobromide seasickness pills. The idea had been to launch the DD tanks from 7,000 yards (6,400 metres) but, in fact, the Shermans only hit the waves at a tenth of that distance. Still, the Sherwood Rangers lost some tanks.

A poet at war

Living in a wide landscape are the flowers –
Rosenberg I only repeat what you were saying –
the shell and the hawk every hour
are slaying men and jerboas, slaying

the mind: but the body can fill
the hungry flowers and the dogs who cry words
at nights, the most hostile things of all.
But that is not news. Each time the night discards

draperies on the eyes and leaves the mind awake
I look each side of the door of sleep
for the little coin it will take
to buy the secret I shall not keep.

I see men as trees suffering
or confound the detail and the horizon.
Lay the coin on my tongue and I will sing
of what the others never set eyes on.

Keith Douglas: *Desert Flowers*

The poet Keith Douglas (1920–1944) came ashore with the Sherwood Rangers. He was already a seasoned warrior and his *Alamein to Zem Zem* would become a classic. Born in Tunbridge Wells he'd had an unfortunate childhood, bedevilled by his mother's chronic illness and his father's chronic impecunity. He was lucky to stay on at his prep school, luckier still with his cavalier attitude to rules and to authority in general. But even at this formative stage, his growing gift was getting noticed. His talent won him a scholarship to Merton College, reading history and English. In 1939 he rushed to join up, wanting a cavalry regiment in spite of his generally anti-militarist sentiment. In February 1941, after RMA Sandhurst, he was commissioned into 2nd Derbyshire Yeomanry, transferring that July to the Nottinghamshire (Sherwood Rangers) Yeomanry. He served with distinction in the Western Desert.

Apparently, his batman once quipped – 'you're shit or bust, you are!' and there was something of the cavalier in Douglas. *Desert Flowers* pays distinct homage to fellow-poet Rosenberg. He saw himself as being tested, 'the test' in competition not only with war but with his writing. Always rather detached, aloof even, he was distant from the men under his command yet not really part of the officer corps to which he belonged. In the Great War, a bit like his unlucky father, he'd probably have been one of those 'temporary gentlemen'.

Douglas described his poetic style as 'extrospective'—that is, focused on external impressions rather than inner emotions. The result is a poetry which, according to one's sensibilities, is either callous in the midst of war's atrocities, or powerful and unsettling, because its precise descriptiveness puts the burden of emotion on the reader.[2]

It's perhaps not surprising he identified with Isaac Rosenberg who, in his *Break of Day in the Trenches,* reaches out to engage with a passing rodent and stick a poppy behind his ear, to strive to find some human expression in the industrialised mass destruction of war. Douglas also attempts to find a corner for his humanity, in verse which is driven by a need for synthesis and harmony. He only partly belongs in the world of war, yet his poetry is both his refuge and his defiance; that old anger at authority.[3]

Douglas's own test ended on 9 June as he was advancing from Bayeux, killed by mortar fire. Interred initially close to where he fell, he now lies in the cemetery at Tilly-sur-Seulles.

The price of Gold

Monty had ordered a massive naval bombardment to support the landings – fearful of the German armour, he'd wanted to deliver a huge blow that would enable his attacking formations to break clear of the beachhead before the *panzers* could be scrambled. He couldn't know he had an ally in Hitler, whose gentlemanly sleep patterns would hamstring his armoured reserve.

Despite this enormous weight of fire, it was no picnic. The Tommies came ashore nearly bang on time and bang on target. The strongpoint at Le Hamel held out until midday and inflicted casualties with raking fire along the sands. Hobart's 'Funnies' again proved their considerable worth and many British soldiers lived because of them. General Bradley's 1st and 29th US Divisions that were splashing into the surf off Omaha, bloody Omaha, where the carnage was terrific (as depicted in the opening scenes of *Saving Private Ryan*), could certainly have done with them.

These young Allied servicemen were in the prime of their youth, prepared, trained, readied, equipped and now to be tested. Seasickness, however, is no respecter of history, as Bill Jalland and most others were discovering:

They offered us breakfast but I didn't really want any, I had to lead the way down the starboard side ramp in my new battledress. The platoon was formed up and the prow of the ship gouged into the shingle.

The LCIs were coming in with a series of tight circles, then peeling off as their turn to hit the beach came around, it worked like a charm. The US naval personnel lowered the ramps which crashed into the shingle. I was just to walk off and get up the beach ASAP. So I stepped off manfully and went straight to the bottom, the water was above my head! I was aware the prow of the boat was continually smashing into the shingle – I was afraid it would smash me. My waders were now completely full, I couldn't do a thing. I got rid of the folding bike, tore off my waders, unfastened webbing; thus

I arrived on the shore of Fortress Europe, completely soaked, unarmed and on my hands and knees.[4]

This was perhaps not quite the form of Homeric deliverance the Allies had in mind. Fortunately, some inter-Allied assistance was at hand:

Seeing me struggling a US sailor chucked me his tin hat, saying 'Here, you'll need this more than me,' which was a very nice gesture. Somebody threw a rope from the LCI – we'd not been able to get as far in as we had on exercises – but the line was secured and everybody got ashore without incident. As we went up the beach we saw frogmen dealing with the obstacles. I suppose they were from the Royal Engineers – I'd never seen frogmen before.[5]

G. Holley was serving as a wireless operator in 'B' Company 1st Battalion, Royal Hampshires. He recalls the view of Gold Beach as he approached in an LCA early on D-Day:

The long line of beach lay ahead and immediately behind hung a thick pall of smoke as far as the eye could see, with the flashes of bursting shells and rockets pock-marking it along the whole front. We had the word from the Subby [the Royal Navy Sub Lieutenant commanding their LCA] to get ready and the tension was at its peak when we hit bottom, down goes the ramp, out goes the captain with me close behind. We were in the sea to the tops of our thighs. Floundering ashore, we were in the thick of it. To the right and left the other assault platoons were hitting the beach.

Mortar bombs and shells erupting the sand and the 'breep-brurp' of Spandau machineguns cutting through the din; there were no shouts, everyone knew his job and was doing it without saying a word. There was only the occasional cry of despair as men were hit and went down. The beach was filled with half-bent running figures – from experience, we knew that the safest place was as near to Jerry as we could get. A near one blasts sand all over me and my radio set goes dead (during a quiet period later on, I find that shrapnel has riddled my set, and that also a part of my tunic collar has gone). A sweet rancid smell is everywhere, never forgotten by those who smell it – burnt explosives, torn flesh and ruptured earth.[6]

Captain Eric Hooper, transport officer with 9th Battalion DLI, was experiencing problems of his own:

As I was standing on top of the ramp, we hit a buried mine that exploded and blew the ramp up and made a hole in the sand. They'd issued us with oilskin trousers, which came right up to your chest, which you tied up with a string. When I got into the water, I couldn't touch the bottom and started to float. Air was trapped in the trousers and the bubble rose up to my chest and I became buoyant and I started turning over. Just then the waders burst and I sank back into the water.[7]

Eric Broadhead, also with 9th Battalion came ashore from an American craft:

The sea was rough. This in itself complicated the landing. Around 7am we were ordered to dress with all kit. We were below decks, wondering what was going on. Heavy naval gunfire could be heard. 501 had landing ramps which dropped down from her side into the sea, or the beach where it was possible for her to nose far enough in. It was when these ramps dropped we knew the voyage was over. We scrambled on deck. The kit we had was terrific – waterproof jackets that came up to one's chest from one's feet, these I tore as I struggled on deck.

Ahead only a matter of yards away was the French coast, but it was too far away to keep dry. Naval personnel were shouting 'Get ashore', ships were everywhere like a traffic jam. Down the ramps we went, but this only led into the ship in front, across its decks, then came 10 horrible yards between ship and shore with water in between. Over the ship's side, still dizzy from seasickness, and into water 4 ft deep. Each one of us let out a gasp as the water swirled around, and we struggled for shore. It was the hardest ten yards I ever did, but we all got ashore. It became apparent that the enemy had been taken by surprise, at least on our particular section of the attack. After five minutes re-grouping as a battalion, I saw a real life German soldier for the first time; he was being brought in as a prisoner by the lads who beat us ashore.[8]

Another DLI officer recalled the scene on Gold Beach:

Away to the east, about 800 yards from where our craft was due to beach, I could see a Sherman tank fitted with flails crashing its way through a minefield on a green slope just off the beach. What a Wellsian [as in H.G. Wells] picture! It looked like a gigantic crab and as it crawled forward. There was, every now and then, a burst of flame as it flailed a mine. Further to the right I could see orderly lines of men filing out of beached landing-craft and then converging into thicker lines as they made their pre-arranged beach exits. From that distance they resembled a nice, orderly football crowd until into their midst fell one or two mortar bombs and the resemblance ended. Yet the flow of men was in no way halted or dispersed. They looked, as indeed they were, inexorable and irresistible.[9]

A sergeant in the Royal Signals describes boarding an LCA:

Blimey! This is where you need your seasick tablets. The little LCA is being tossed about all over the place. We are packed in like sardines, all standing, all thinking that any moment now it will capsize! Except those being sick and I don't imagine they care very much. Off we go, I am rather thrilled, and my confidence and spirits are quite high now. About 100 yards from the beach, the bloke in charge of the LCA called out 'Sorry lads, this is the best I can do. Mind how you go off the ramp as it might crush your feet.'

Well, off we went, bedroll on shoulder, kit on back, rifle slung around neck, and fingers crossed! Although the water probably wasn't more than four foot deep, the shell holes and bomb craters made it eight feet deep in places. The beach itself was a shambles, guns, tanks, landing craft and scores of vehicles; either floating around, stuck in the sand or burnt out. Houses and factories just inland bombed or burned, rows of bodies covered with coats or blankets, Jerry prisoners, insolent as ever, marching down to the beach as we staggered up. It looked just like the main road to Hell![10]

Flailing

Of all of Hobo's creations, the flail tank must be one of the most ingenious. How to clear a minefield quickly? Detectors will take time and sweat always saves blood but a tank with chains extended on a boom that thrashes the deadly ground like a giant's carpet-beater can do it so far more quickly and there's less risk to the personnel inside, pure genius.

Captain Roger Bell was training as an accountant in 1939 but joined up and spent the next four years, and more, UK-based and undergoing training, on top of training, and then a bit more training. While others fought beneath blazing desert sun or chattering jungle canopy, he trained. D-Day would change all that and his regiment, the Westminster Dragoons, would be called upon, at last, to do their patriotic chore, finally for real, on Gold Beach. The Dragoons and their iron steeds embarked from Southampton Water on 5 June, a troop of six tanks and Roger was 2I/C. Citizen soldiers were going to war.[11] Rather queasily as it happened, the choppy seas soon sent most heaving to the rails. Roger Bell didn't suffer from sea-sickness, or from nerves either, he was quietly excited in a kind of *Boy's Own* way – no fears of fear came yet. He slept blissfully through the night passage. Next morning, refreshed and stepping out onto the rolling deck, he beheld the vast spectacle of that great armada spread out around, crowding the white-capped waves. A sight no soldier had seen before and probably never will again, Operation *Neptune*. The Dragoons were no longer spectators, they'd be centre-stage and that stage, a smudge on the grey horizon, was getting closer by the minute.

It wasn't only Bell himself but his men, with the prospect of the dismal crossing nearly over, who were lively and chatting, gulping down a strong brew, a breakfast for those who felt they could take it and all the last-minute things a tanker needs to do. Roger had brought a bottle of spirits in case his nerves needed a stiffener, they didn't so the cork stayed in.[12]

He now had a grandstand view of the beach as they cruised closer. It was around 3 miles (4.8 kilometres) across, Le Hamel marking the western flank and La Rivière the east. Past the first of these, a ridge of uneven hills butts into the coast and creates jutting cliffs that separate Le Hamel from Arromanches. At the other extremity, a high seawall, topped by a roadway, formed an equally tricky man-made obstacle. These features neatly framed Gold Beach. It was dotted with holiday villas, now steadily being reduced to matchwood, and linked to a parallel road with wetlands beyond. Past the wet gap, the coastal hills rose in a shallow curve.

Roger Bell would bring his tank ashore near La Rivière on the east, and his personal target was a gun emplacement housing an 88-mm built into the seawall. This could neatly enfilade the whole landing beach, a sure-thing killer if it wasn't taken out, ideally quickly.[13] Those German defenders crouching in their claustrophobic bunkers were presently experiencing a *Gotterdammerung* all of their own as shell upon shell crashed down on them, as rocket salvos screamed in and the RAF did their bit with a full six squadrons of 'heavies', history's loudest ever wake-up call.

It all seemed to go like clockwork; the Navy got them almost to the door. Nearly anyway and you can't blame the RN when your tank's engine refuses to start, now that's a real bugger, especially when there are four in the queue directly behind you. Fortunately, the RE Bobbin tank[14] ahead did start up and Roger begged a tow. The sappers were none too happy, and you can't really blame them, but as soon as the tow was taut and the vehicles lurched forward, Bell's engine manned up and started.

He was aware of the deadly obstacles left and right but was still fixated on his mechanics; tanks were churning and lumbering up the beach. Several were hit, an RE Petard[15] spectacularly brewed up, hit by enemy guns and immobilised, almost in front of them. Worse, his own vehicle shuddered and flames gouted up behind the turret. This wasn't good, Shermans weren't called 'Tommy-cookers' for nothing. 'Out, out,' he yelled, then almost in the same moment he realised they had not been directly hit, it was just a piece of sheared-off metal spinning across the beach. He soon realised what was doing the damage, his very own 88-mm. Whatever damage the hurricane of HE had done, it had completely missed this one. Four-and-a-half years of training hadn't, as it turned out, been wasted. Bell drove full tilt into the gun's line of fire, marked by the cluster of burning victims. He could see the barrel quite plainly, shielded by a heavy steel shutter. He was around 100 yards (91 metres) west of the emplacement and his first two HE rounds seemed to have no effect whatsoever. Next he banged off three AP shells. Had he got the bloody thing? Another tank lumbered past between him and the gun, no more than 50 yards and nothing happened; result![16]

That job attended to, it was time for the mines. His Sherman bulldozed the wire and thrashed the minefield beyond, the wild dervish dance of chains flogging the soft ground. He remembered he had to chuck out a green smoke grenade for the benefit of those following. As he struck the striker to ignite, the Sherman wobbled and he dropped the grenade which, true to function, soon shrouded him in a cloying green blanket, his very own *Babes in the Wood* show. Cursing, he scrambled to find the canister and dump it overboard. With equilibrium at least temporarily restored he realised that while the flail was thumping away like a champion, there were no resulting explosions. The ground was very wet, alarmingly so, but nothing in it was going bang.[17]

Inadvertently, he'd steered into deep mud; even the tank's tracks were unequal to the task. They were well and truly bogged. Another pair of tanks, coming up behind, avoided the mud-bath, swarmed up the bank and clattered off through what little was left of La Rivière. Out he got and down he climbed to see what might be done, perhaps not quite realising he was a fair facsimile of a jolly green giant. Still fully verdant, he went back to the beach to find some help.

The sanatorium

Behind the tanks came infantry, 1st Hampshires as part of 50th Div and with them C. S. M Harry Bowers, MM, MiD. Unlike Roger Bell, Bowers, a Cornishman, had seen a great deal of action.

At 36 years old, he was a veteran of four amphibious landings and was someone who had indeed suffered from pre-op nerves; he knew what he was in for. On a more material plane, his boots were too tight and causing him severe discomfort. Dodgy boots come high on a foot soldier's list of complaints.

Even as seasoned a hand as he was couldn't fail to be impressed by the sheer scale of the enterprise, the noise growing like distant thunder until, when they hit the beach, it drowned out everything else, numbing the senses, shrinking the periphery. Much of the noise was enemy fire sweeping the beaches as Bowers pelted up the sand towards the wire. Bangalore torpedoes were thrust under the heaped coils and they burst through. Next he was crouching by the very temporary shelter of the low seawall. When he drew breath to look about him, Bowers realised their casualties were mounting. Only when Major Warren, his company commander, scrambled up did the pair of them spot the enemy pillbox doing all the damage.[18]

It was cunningly built into the seaward end of the local sanatorium and was neatly enfilading the beach. It has to be one of war's deadly ironies that an institution built to improve people's health is used as a platform for killing. Bowers probably didn't get the irony just at that moment as only he, the officer, one squaddie and the W/O were in any position to take on the MGs – and that position was none too good. For a while, as they crawled nearer, the stubby wall gave cover but then it ended, with another 100 yards of fire-swept nowhere-to-hide ground still to go. The place was studded with several MGs and a single 88-mm.

Over the wireless, a message came through recalling Warren, now in charge of the whole battalion. The W/O died a minute later and the other man decided he also needed to be elsewhere. Bowers was now very much on his own and there really wasn't much he could do. He too gingerly retraced his steps and came across the colonel of the battalion who been shot up and had a bad arm wound. The officer was lucid still and understood Bowers' message about the pillbox. 'Go and see what you can do about it,' was the curt order. An injured colonel is still the colonel and Bowers certainly didn't relish the task any more than he had done a short while ago, but it seemed he had no choice.[19]

Orders are orders, of course, but the good news was that their supporting armour was punching holes in the defences. This hadn't come cheap, the tankers CO had already gone down to a sniper's bullet and other tanks had brewed up. The armour had, in fact, penetrated into the village but he was dangerously exposed as their supporting infantry was still bogged down on the beach. If nothing else, however, the Shermans had distracted the Axis gunners and Bowers was now very much on their case.

He had his Sten and a haversack full of Italian grenades, souvenirs from earlier landings, besides which he far preferred them. Back he went along the seawall, now breached by the Allied tanks, back to the dead ground in front on the strongpoint. There he found two Royal marine commandos already swapping shots with the defenders. They were 'Paddy' and 'Taffy' – he'd shared a landing craft with these lads. This pair was up for a scrap and both carried Thompson SMGs.

Together they began their deadly crawl across that bare No-Man's-Land, trying to outflank the pillbox and get behind. German infantry who had made a sally were equally determined to stop them. Inch by lethal inch they moved forward till they got into cover in the ruins of what had been the sanatorium building. Jerry hadn't forgotten them and grenades came showering down. One landed perilously close but didn't detonate as the seconds ticked by. It's OK, Bowers breathed, only a dud.

It wasn't, and it went off. 'Paddy' ended up with a leg full of shrapnel. Once bandaged he still had plenty fight left in him and Harry got them to lay down covering fire while he worked closer to the strongpoint. He scrambled through a canyon of ruined masonry, jumped through a blasted window opening, and onto the roof of the pillbox. Flat on his belly, overhanging the edge he was directly above the aperture. And they knew it; a white flag now timorously emerged from the slit. 'Not bloody likely,' he exhaled, and in went several of his prized Italian specials.

That was it, moments after the boom of detonations, the survivors came out, hands held high. Harry knew a bit of German and this lot didn't look, sound or smell like Jerries. Indeed they weren't, just more Russian *Hiwis* – nice boots though.[20]

Stan Hollis wins the VC

Stanley Elton Hollis was born on Teesside in 1912, so he was in his 30s when he landed on Gold Beach with 6th Battalion Green Howards. He'd begun his career as a navigational officer in the Merchant Navy but that ended with a serious bout of fever. Before the war, he'd worked locally as a lorry driver, and joined the TA, 4th Battalion, transferring to the 6th on mobisation. He'd had an active war, he'd been very busy, in fact: promoted to sergeant at Dunkirk, he'd served in North Africa and Sicily, then was wounded during the savage fight for Primosole Bridge. Just as well, he'd never be more severely tested than on D-Day at Gold Beach.

His battalion had trained hard, up near Inveraray on Scotland's rugged north-west coast. Reveille on 6 June for the Green Howards was around 02.30 with a decent breakfast for those who had the stomach for it. They had then transferred from their transport *Empire Lance* to landing craft, which they had loaded up with kit and ammo beforehand. They were about 6 miles out, on a grey, choppy and gusty morning, in the cold hour before action on a sour belly. Stan was passed a box of condoms by his CO Major Ronnie Lofthouse and told to give them out. Very likely sex wasn't much on their minds, except for the more ardent and those not prone to sea-sickness. Company Sergeant-Major Hollis's earthy response was: 'Sir, are we going to fight them or fuck them?'[21] In fact, the contraceptives were intended as waterproof tompions to keep their rifles dry!

Getting down via the nets into the landing craft wasn't easy; the violent pitching of both vessels and the ungainly weight of kit wasn't conducive to smoothness. If the motion of the ship was bad, this was much worse and the laden bobbing craft had to cruise around in circles until, like a line of ducks, they set off in line abreast, 'A' Company on the left and 'B' on the right. As they chugged steadily if not speedily (around 5 kph) towards the hostile shore, which took a good hour or so, the whole Allied bombardment provided a deafening chorus, the thump of those big naval guns, crack of 25-pounders, bright salvos of streaming rockets, rounds spurting sand from the beach. He profoundly hoped this might do for the mines.[22]

Stan identified a German strongpoint dead ahead as they cruised in to land (in fact it was a railway shelter), and grabbing a Lewis gun he rattled off a full pan of ammo (the marks were there for years apparently).[23] The gun was stripped of its water cooling jacket and, as he hefted it clear of the bracket, forgetting it would be red hot by now, he badly blistered his hand.

They plunged into the surf. Just ahead of Hollis another old sweat, Sergeant Hill, slipped in a shell hole and went under, dragged down by his kit. The craft's propellers chopped him to bits. As they got to the shore, their beach-master went down. Mortar rounds were coming down at a depressingly high rate, though they weren't getting any small arms fire. The plan called for Stan to lead mortar-men and Bren gunners from each platoon to charge ahead and set up at the high water mark, providing smoke and covering fire to get the rest through the belt of mines ahead. On their right, a tank brewed up and the turret hatch bowled along the sand; it was a lethal projectile but no-one was hurt.[24]

One enemy plane swooped down overhead but they got away with that too. Up the beach, they went and onto a low ridge of dunes festooned with thick wire entanglements. Birds were sitting, apparently unconcerned, on the coils. One wag suggested they had no choice as there wasn't any room left in the sky. Ahead now was a dense belt of mines. 'D' company were first through after their assault engineers had gapped it, Stan and the others followed the reassuring lines of white tape. Beyond the minefield lay Meuvaines Ridge and Mont Fleury Batteries.

Once through the hedge beyond the belt of mines, the Green Howards were fully exposed to the attention of the German defenders dug in on the higher ground and a storm of fire descended as they struggled forward; it turned out Private Mullally, the wag, had told his last joke. Inch by fire-swept inch they crawled forward; Major Lofthouse had spotted the pillbox that was doing most of the damage. Hollis saw it too and stormed forward, his Sten chattering. He made it and lobbed a grenade in, killing two defenders and persuading the rest to give up – 'they were quite willing to forget all about the war.'[25]

He barged ahead, up a shallow communications trench aiming for a larger bunker whose inhabitants went into the bag: 'about eighteen or twenty'. A pretty decent haul and it turned out these were the fire control team for the battery up ahead. As the battalion advanced up the hill, Stan looked back just for an instant and saw, from his higher position, the whole vast teeming armada laid out – 'it gave us a great feeling of confidence.' It was only 09.30 and they could see enemy bolting from their positions but not that far, falling back behind a sheltering wall and firing. Hollis saw one German crazily loping along the top of the wall. Swapping his Sten for an Enfield rifle, he brought the fellow down first shot but was lightly wounded in the face just after, 'not a lot of damage – a lot of blood, it looked a lot worse than it was.'[26]

On they went into the village of Crépon. With Lieutenant Patrick now dead, Stan was commanding 16 Platoon and the major ordered the company to check/clear the several farmhouses lining the approach road. Stan broke and entered one of the silent steadings; it seemed deserted except for one terrified boy of perhaps 10 or 11. The effect of seeing this ferocious, blood-garnished veteran bursting in must have been utterly terrifying. As Stan came out to check the rear, an enemy round smacked off the backyard wall, fragments whizzing. Aside from a pair of excited local canines, he could just about make out an enemy gun.

After reporting back to Lofthouse, Hollis detailed half a squad to start shooting up the hedge in front of the enemy. This drew a sharp response and most of the group were killed straight off. Another approach was needed and the major ordered Hollis to get hold of a PIAT[27] with a brace of Brens and creep forward through an extensive rhubarb patch, which gave out onto a line of trees. They got forward without drawing fire and Stan blasted off a round from the unwieldy PIAT. It missed and the German gun shot up the farmhouse in retaliation; stone, timber, plaster and dust erupted. Stan crawled back to report but intensive bursts of fire, from both sides, told him his two Bren-gunners were in trouble.

Stan grabbed a Bren himself and started crawling back, sheltered briefly behind what was left of one of the walls then, in a lull, charged forward spraying the distant hedge. Under cover of this dramatic diversion, the other two blokes made it back unscathed. A tank arrived and moved ahead of what was now a general advance, 'C' Company on the left, 'A' and 'B' on the right; Stan's platoon was left of HQ, sheltering behind the tank. It was raining.

The tracks chewed through mud and then stopped; small arms fire all around them. More men were going down.

Stan could see a lively pair of Germans firing down the narrow lane, one shooting, one covering/re-loading; the Tommies were very exposed and getting shot up. Stan decided he'd deal with this duo and felt in his pouch for a grenade. While he'd seen to it earlier that everyone else had plenty of ammo and bombs, he'd forgotten his own supply.[28] Hastily borrowing one, he chucked it, 'I used to throw them like a cricket ball', and then dashed out under the cover of what he hoped would be the blast. Second mistake: he had forgotten to pull the pin but the Germans were still heads down, waiting for the blast, so he was able to do for them both.

His platoon was down to just over a dozen but now they'd reached the enemy-held hedge, there was another just beyond, so the sunken ditch between meant Stan & Co could crawl in relative safety if in acute, wet, discomfort, between the two. As they slopped through the mire, it was obvious they'd not been seen, so they effectively came on the flank of those Germans still holding out. Bringing up whatever automatic weapons they still had, Hollis got them to spray the far hedge and beyond. Enemy fire immediately slackened and then stopped.[29]

By now more armour had appeared and Stan, with Sergeant Major Moffat from 'B' Company, was able to get a badly wounded officer, Captain Young, hoisted onto the hull and casevaced. Stan Hollis won the VC for his actions, the only one to be awarded on D-Day. His citation reads:

In Normandy on 6 June 1944 Company Sergeant-Major Hollis went with his company commander to investigate two German pill-boxes which had been by-passed as the company moved inland from the beaches. Hollis instantly rushed straight at the pillbox, firing his Sten gun into the first pill-box. He jumped on top of the pillbox, re-charged his magazine, threw a grenade in through the door and fired his Sten gun into it, killing two Germans and taking the remainder prisoners.

Later the same day... C.S.M. Hollis pushed right forward to engage the [field] gun with a PIAT [anti-tank weapon]

from a house at 50 yards range... He later found that two
of his men had stayed behind in the house... In full view
of, the enemy who were continually firing at him, he went
forward alone ... to distract their attention from the other
men. Under cover of his diversion, the two men were able
to get back.

Wherever the fighting was heaviest [he] appeared, displaying
the utmost gallantry... It was largely through his heroism and
resource that the Company's objectives were gained and
casualties were not heavier. .... He saved the lives of many of
his men.[30]

Heading for Bayeux

Meanwhile, Bill Jalland and his comrades passed up the beach
unscathed:

As we moved inland there was, I remember, some shelling and
the MO, Dr Thornton, was one of the first casualties; there
was a fair bit of pandemonium but the beach, at this stage,
wasn't all that crowded with supplies. We went in through
La Riviere; we didn't pass much evidence of fighting, no
knocked-out tanks or whatever, not much small arms either,
though I know they had a rough time over at Le Hamel.

There was some evidence of the heavy bombing and some
houses had suffered damage. We had orders to keep moving,
we had to reach Bayeux. We knew it wouldn't be long before
heavy shelling started. Ian and his cyclists went off – it was
harvest time, corn standing in the fields, we saw some German
infantry moving in the distance but they didn't bother us and
we didn't bother them![31]

Despite high drama, the day was not entirely devoid of lighter
touches:

Captain Phil Hampson rode along bareback on a horse he'd
acquired and we took some prisoners; these were Russians
and they came in yelling 'Russki, Russki'. They had their
hands high and, though some of the chaps viewed them

just as traitors, none was actually shot. We treated them as POWs. They didn't seem to have any prepared positions. The landing had been very accurate and we could find our way around, we'd seen aerial photographs and could recognise landmarks, such as churches. Our job was to press on to Bayeux; we saw the odd enemy tank, they stalked us and we stalked them.[32]

Sergeant Brown was amongst the gallant throng of cyclists:

When we were at last off the beach, we met up in a 'hide' where we had a self-inflicted wound in 'D' Company. I heard a rifle shot. An old fellow of 40, a bundle of nerves, had shot himself in the hand. I said, 'You shot yourself, bastard!' He said, 'I'm sorry Sergeant-Major. I can't go on.' 'It's alright,' I replied, 'leave your rifle here and get yourself back. You've been hit in the hand." I wasn't going to court-martial him.[33]

Lieutenant Jalland and his platoon had by now advanced some distance inland, though still a way short of Bayeux itself:

As we dug in I was sent for by Battalion HQ, the Brigadier [Senior] had disappeared and we had to go and look for him. I took half a dozen men and bikes from Ian English's Company. The passwords were 'Bread' and 'Cheese'. Well, we searched copse after copse; every time we murmured 'Bread' and we got plenty 'Cheese' in reply, there was engineers, pioneers, all sorts mixed up but no sign of the Brigadier.

He'd been ambushed, his signaller and driver killed, he was saved by the 'red' hat! Half a dozen Germans under a corporal held him. The men just wanted to kill him. The corporal wanted him kept alive, (he spoke German), as anybody in a red hat was important and would have lots of important intelligence. Anyway, the Germans trussed him up but, at nightfall, he wriggled into a ditch; the Jerries panicked, ran and he escaped. Meanwhile the rest of us got no sleep and someone else took Bayeux.[34]

All in all, Gold Beach had been a resounding success. Resistance had been tough; soldiers of German 352nd Division were no pushover but the defences had been breached and supporting waves successfully got ashore. By dusk on 6 June, the bridgehead was 6 miles by 6. Fortress Europe had been truly penetrated. Bayeux wasn't yet in Allied hands but Tommy was close and probes had reached the suburbs. By noon on D-Day+1, 7 June, elements of 56th Brigade with supporting armour were breaking into the city. It had been badly knocked about but all of its treasures, the marvellous cathedral and, above all, the Tapestry, survived (then concealed in the Château de Sources near Le Mans).

Perhaps it's fitting that this ancient and lovely city, so connected to the warp of English history, should be the first major urban settlement to be liberated. General Dietrich Kraiss commanding German 915th Regiment put up a pretty poor showing, so the *Tricolores* were soon flying from rooftops and balconies in the battered streets, streaming symbols of liberty and hope, the four-year curse of occupation finally lifted. A week later, in the afternoon, drowsy in spring warmth, a British vehicle drove through Bayeux, proclaiming by loudspeaker that not only was De Gaulle in France he'd be speaking to the people of the historic Normandy city in an hour in the Place de Chateau, that precious hour the citizens had spent the dark winters of oppression dreaming of.

7

GETTING A GRIP, THE AFTERNOON AND AFTER

I am forever haunted by one dread
That I may suddenly be swept away,
Nor have the leave to see you and to say
Goodbye; then this is what I should have said
I have loved summer and the longest day
The leaves of trees, the slumberous film of heat
The bees, the swallows and the waving wheat,
The whistling of mowers in the hay.

I have loved words which left the soul with wings
Words that are windows to eternal things
I have loved souls that to themselves are true
Who cannot stoop and know not how to fear
Yet hold the talisman of pity's tear:
I have loved these because I have loved you.

Anon: Vale

Don't give your food, clothing or other supplies to civilians or others. The Civil Affairs personnel will distribute supplies as soon as they become available. Giving your supplies away not only encourages further requests from civilians which cannot be satisfied, but puts an additional burden on the already over-burdened supply system.[1]

Group Captain P. W. Stansfield flew over the fighting in Normandy on D-Day in his Spitfire:

On the 6th June 1944 I was second-in-command of 34 Wing, a 2nd Tactical Air Force Photographic Wing based at Northolt. Flying a Spitfire XI of 16 Squadron, I was detailed for a flight over the beachhead at 3pm, to photograph the Airborne HQ at Ouistreham, where ground signals were to be displayed in case of a failure by the Airborne HQ radio equipment. So great was the procession of ships and craft in convoys crossing the Channel as far as the eye could see that it was unnecessary for me to fly a compass course. I merely flew in the general direction of the convoys. Except for some German flak batteries to the landward side of the Airborne HQ, who fired some rather unpleasant-looking orange tracer shells at me (and missed).

I think I only saw what I thought was one German fighter, which I avoided by popping into the cloud, doing a turn and coming out in a different direction. After two or three runs over the target to ensure I had identified and photographed the Airborne HQ, I climbed out to sea and set course for Northolt.

- Airborne HQ = the headquarters of the British 6th Airborne Division, which had landed by air to protect the east side of the main beach landings.

- Flak batteries = groups of German anti-aircraft guns.[2]

After the Normandy battle, Monty would claim he'd intended all along to draw the bulk of German forces against the British and Canadians in the east to allow General Bradley's US forces to build up in the west and then break out. This was indeed what happened, but whether Montgomery intended this before it occurred or subsequently adapted to the realities, is unclear. It was definitely part of his plan that 3rd Division coming ashore on Sword Beach should take Caen on 6 June. This was wildly ambitious and disregarded several key German strongpoints such as 'Hillman' and 'Morris', which slowed the advance sufficiently to allow the *panzers* to deploy and block the approach. The fight for the city was a long one, brutally attritional and several armoured thrusts foundered at considerable cost. The proud and lovely Normandy city was pounded into rubble.[3]

The 'Wyvern' (43rd Wessex Division) came ashore on 23/24 June and, barely two days later, went into action as part of VIII Corps' River Odon offensive. This would directly threaten Caen and the bridgehead soon drew a sharp riposte with three *panzer* divisions thrown into the fight. This was from 25 to 29 June and Caen didn't fall for another 10 days. *Operation Jupiter*, the fight for the high ground between the Orne and Odon rivers (Hill 112) was an attritional slog, reminiscent of conditions during the Great War. The Wyverns suffered 2,000 casualties. Sydney Jary, then a 2nd Lieutenant, was sent out as one of the replacements:

I was a reinforcement officer for either 1st Hampshires in 50th Division, or the 7th as part of 43rd Division. As events turned out, I joined neither. The 43rd Wessex Division's first major battle had been Hill 112 and due to their high rate of officer casualties I was sent away from my own regiment for the following twelve months. The 1st Battalion Somerset Light Infantry was a close-knit unit which had been almost decimated within a period of 48 hours.

On 5th July three officers and 62 ORs were needed as reinforcements. Between 14th–18th July, a further twelve officers and 479 ORs arrived and even then the battalion was still below its full strength of thirty-six officers and nearly 700 NCOs and men. Because I had previous experience of the 6-pounder A/T gun, the CO, 'Lippy' Lipscombe, posted me as 2 I/C to the battalion's A/T platoon, consisting of six guns.[4]

Hanging on and digging in

Towards sunset we saw an unforgettably moving and impressive spectacle as the reserve brigade of the 6th Airborne Division, glider-borne, came in low from the sea and landed in the open country immediately to the east. Supply parachutes of all colours came drifting down from the escorting heavies [heavy bombers], as the gliders drew away from the planes and swooped down into the corn.[5]

After their initial drop the paras, by morning on 6 June, were digging in. In spite of the mishaps and confusion, all their principal objectives had been taken. While the galloping major was blasting through the darkened streets of Troarn, 1st Canadian Parachute Battalion had come down in the vicinity of Varaville and Robehomme. Despite being scattered, they managed to biff both bridges there and start digging in around Bois de Bavent. Captain A. J. Jack, who'd been the one to blow the span at Robehomme, treated his blokes to a fry-up in the meadows, despite warnings from locals that there were plenty of the enemy about. The French were suitably impressed by such cheerful sang-froid.[6]

Some of the sappers had landed close to Ranville and gone straight into the bag. They were soon straight out of it; Sergeant Jones succeeded in relieving one of their guards of an MP40 and shot all eight of them.[7] Sapper Thomas, despite wounds, took exception to an enemy trio who'd been using him as target practice and killed all three with grenades.[8] Around Ranville, the engineers got to work demolishing obstacles and marking out landing grounds.

One company officer, an unnamed captain, found the River Dives straight off, he landed in it. As well as being very wet, he was very alone but picked up a quartet of troopers at the first farm he came to, as well as a young French lad who volunteered to guide. Their objective was Varreville and they got there in the small hours. There was plenty of shooting and yelling but no actual sign of any more Brits. Bizarrely they did encounter a middle-aged Englishwoman, obviously a resident, who gave the lads directions for Le Mesnil and, hopefully, Brigade HQ. So far so good, but then they stumbled into a confused firefight with an enemy patrol in woods, losing their guide, who was killed by a grenade.

Adrift, they struggled on over vile, swampy ground, picking up odd stragglers until the captain had a weak platoon behind him. Local farmers provided much-needed bread and milk and they slogged on through the maze of Bois de Bavent. Battling

1. The Green Howards on the beach. (By kind courtesy of the Green Howards Museum Trust)

2. Aerial view (1). (By kind courtesy of the Green Howards Museum Trust)

3. Aerial view (2). (By kind courtesy of the Green Howards Museum Trust)

4. Aerial view (3). (By kind courtesy of the Green Howards Museum Trust)

5. A Mark V Panzer, the Panther, arguably the best all-round tank of the war, they stayed in use with the French until the 1960s. (Author)

6. The Green Howards begin marching inland. (By kind courtesy of the Green Howards Museum Trust)

7. A US M2 Howitzer, 2.3 tonnes weight with a six-man crew. (Author)

8. A US Ford M8 Greyhound Armoured Car, 8 tonnes with a four-man crew and 37mm cannon, capable of 55 mph. (Author)

9. The ubiquitous ¼-ton Jeep, a real game changer, first appeared in the Western Desert but was used in very large numbers by British and US forces in Normandy. (Author)

10. The M4 Sherman, weighing 30 tonnes, with five crew and a 75mm gun. Though they were known as 'Tommy cookers', over 50,000 were built and they continued in service with world armies long after the war. (Author)

11. German 75mm PAK 40 anti-tank gun. (Author)

12. British 17-pounder anti-tank gun. (Author)

13. The US M3 White half-track weighed in at 9 tonnes. It was a very adaptable and versatile vehicle, able to carry twelve troops and capable of 45 mph. (Author)

14. German Sd.Kfz.251 Hanomag half-track, slightly faster, with a top speed of 52 mph. (Author)

Above: 15. View from the sea; British landing craft comes in.

Left: 16. Churchill Petard tank, one of Hobart's 'Funnies'.

Below left: 17. Troops move up off the beaches.

18. An impromptu graveside service.

19. Another track-laying 'Funny' in action.

20. British paras check timings for Operation Tonga.

Above left: 21. Admiral Sir Bertram Ramsay.

Left: 22. Air Chief Marshal Arthur Tedder.

Below left: 23. CO of 21st Army Group Lt Gen. J. T. Crocker photographed near Caen.

Below: 24. French civilians showing ID cards to an RASC Captain, 6 June 1944.

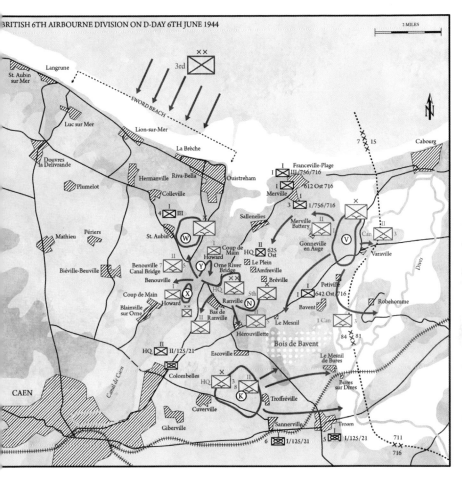

Map 1. 6th Airborne Division area of operations 5/6 June 1944.

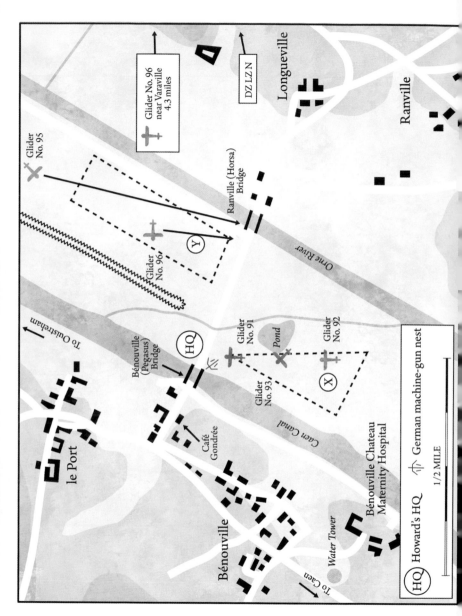

Map 2. Pegasus Bridge operations 5/6 June 1944.

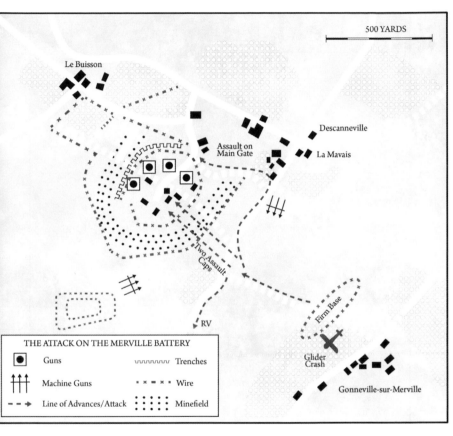

Map 3. The attack on Merville Battery 5/6 June 1944.

THE ATTACK ON THE MERVILLE BATTERY

- Guns
- Machine Guns
- Line of Advances/Attack
- Trenches
- Wire
- Minefield

Le Buisson

Descanneville

Assault on Main Gate

La Mavais

Two Assault Caps

Firm Base

RV

Glider Crash

Gonneville-sur-Merville

500 YARDS

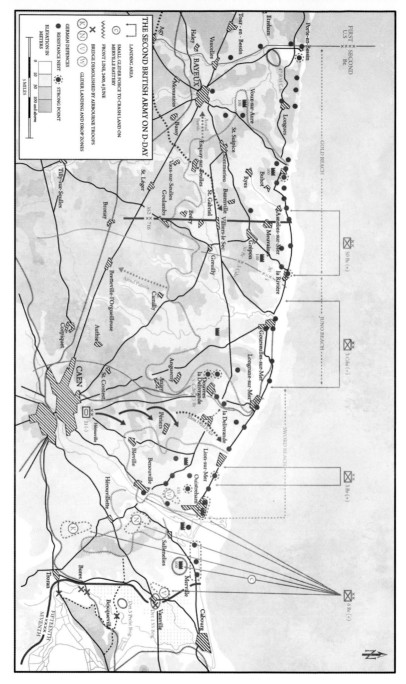

Map 4. Sword, Juno and Gold Beaches, 6 June 1944.

over swollen canals, hacking through brush, they pushed on, increasingly tired. They did witness the exhilarating spectacle of a brace of Spitfires bringing down two ME109s, and the serene flotilla of their glider-borne comrades come sailing in. It was 22.00 on D-Day when they finally got on the right road for Le Mesnil, helped by another local who'd already clearly been celebrating his deliverance but at least he got them on the right road.[9]

Though the gliders fared better than the parachutists, some were still scattered and 14 were lost, 3 ditched in the Channel and 5 never made it past the white cliffs; but all in all, the skilled pilots accomplished prodigious feats of accuracy. Members of the Glider Pilot Regiment are some of the often unsung heroes of breaking into Fortress Europe. In the wake of Axis successes with airborne operations in 1940, the Allies had to race to catch up. The initial Glider Pilot Squadron recruited some suitably raffish characters, many of whom seemed to dodge such tedious recruitment processes as medicals. Expanded into a full regiment, the glider-boys became part of the Army Air Corps.

Each recruit underwent a 12-week flying course, followed by another 12 on gliders, then a final six to train on Horsas. Once they'd landed and hopefully delivered their passengers safe and sound, they were expected to fight on as ordinary infantrymen.[10] One, Captain B. Murdoch, found himself manning a 6-pounder A/T gun under attack from a troop of *panzers*. Though the gun-layer was killed, Murdoch and the surviving crew took out four of the attacking tanks.[11]

Major Lyne had not had a good evening on 5 June. Flak had bust his tow as they came in over the coast and another round caught them as they sailed in. Though their jeep cargo was damaged, none of the paras was hit. They came down into an orchard, rough but not too destructive, though Lyne broke his ankle. There were only seven of them and they'd no idea where they were. It seemed the Germans did though, and they had to lie up till dawn.

An obliging farmer showed them the line of the River Dives, all good except they were on the wrong bank and had to swim for it. Finally, they teamed up with some Canadians by Robehomme. The enemy was still on their case and it took a full three days to fight their way through to Ranville. They survived in no small part because locals were prepared to risk their own lives to help – one family proudly showed their cherished portrait of Queen Victoria, no idea if she'd have been in any way amused.[12] Despite their tiredness, Lyne's scratch force, soaked, bruised and filthy from stumbling through the inhospitable Bois de Bavent, were still full of fight and took on an enemy convoy on the road to Ranville; two truckloads of enemy infantry and a staff car bearing a quartet of officers were summarily dealt with.

While it may not have played out exactly as a textbook operation, the initial landings had been successful, the bridges were taken, as was Merville battery, (even though it had to be stormed a second time as the Germans re-occupied the site), the Dives' bridges were gone and a perimeter established. All 6th Airborne had to do now was hold it, but more gliders including the heavier Hamilcars[13] were coming down on the cleared landing grounds.

If the Hussars had tanks that could swim, the Armoured Reconnaissance Regiment possessed armour that could fly![14] Their bridgehead was still vulnerable, the paras held a salient around the settlements at Ranville, Le Mariquet and Herouvillette; 1st Special Service Brigade was holding part of the perimeter around Le Plein and Bréville. Some men were still lost and straggling, 800 had become casualties.[15] The Germans had been surprised but they wouldn't be staying that way for long.

Bréville, a small and unremarkable hamlet, a mere 12 kilometres from Caen, had been taken by 9th Parachute Battalion on the 6th. It sits on the high ground of Le Plein, and Otway's survivors had marched there from the smoking shell of Merville Battery. At Hauger, Fortunately warned in advance by an observant local, they took on an enemy strongpoint defended by a couple of companies. Dawn had broken and the defenders, mainly Russians, fought stubbornly for their Nazi masters. It had taken the added firepower of 1st Special Service Brigade to finally break in, but the place was never fully taken and offered the enemy a balcony for a counter-attack, (*see* below). The Germans' objective was to burst through the thin cordon and drive a wedge to the coast. The crust was thin and the defence even thinner.

By 10 June, the enemy was getting dangerously close to succeeding; both commandos and paras had taken heavy losses. It became the job of 51st Highland Division[16] to push them back. The Black Watch were first into the breach and paid a heavy price, though the Canadian paratroopers managed, at considerable cost, to close the gap. Both sides were near exhaustion, but 'Windy' Gale decided on a final push. He could commit the depleted remnant of 12th Parachute Battalion, just one company from 12th Devons, a single squadron of Shermans and whatever artillery support he could scrape together. Concentrated in and around the church at Amfreville, 12th Para was barely 300 strong.

The fight for Bréville was desperate, a classic soldier's battle and the Germans weren't planning on giving up. Paras stormed the village, suffering heavily from mortar fire, but battled through and dug in on the far side. The Devons were badly hit but those Shermans proved their worth and the place was taken, though winkling out diehard snipers went on through most of the night, flames from buildings leaping into the summer's darkness.[17]

The bloody road to Caen

Having spent their afternoon without a lot happening, the KOSBs finished digging in, opened up their rations and got Tommy cookers on the go. They enjoyed a quiet night but the next morning brought orders to move out, their objective was to be Cazelle on the Caen to La Delivrande road and the Germans had marksmen in the church tower at Hermanville. It needed the big guns to quiet them. The *Luftwaffe* was also keen to do their bit: 'six Heinkels appeared, ready to pounce but were shot up and driven off by Allied fighters before they could do any damage.' Cazelle fell without a fight, bar some long-range stonking.[18]

Less than half-a-mile further on, the mortaring became more insistent and more accurate, men were hit and the KOSB bunkered down in Le Mesnil Wood. Their second night in France was enlivened by a virtuoso display of night firing, the steady rattle of small arms, lit with firefly tracer and with an ominous undertone of moving armour. They had to be surrounded. Next morning the CO announced they'd break out, charging to the tune of *Blue Bonnets* on the pipes. Fortunately, there was no enemy; their night-time chorus had been provided by Allied tanks who'd thought *they* were the enemy. Returning beneath the trees, the battalion stayed put till 9 June.[19]

It was a fairly short respite; the KOSB would fight for the woodland and village of Cambes as an element in winning the brigade's object, Saint-Contest, strategically important as it overlooked Caen. With 2nd Suffolks they'd establish an initial forward line, allowing 2nd Royal Ulster Rifles to pass through. Cambes proved tough. A few ME109s ventured up to strafe them and the Ulstermen struggled through the deadly bocage. The Borderers moved up in support after the guns had softened up the village. Between the tree line and the buildings, there was a steady incline over open fields. They didn't yet know it but they were up against *12th SS Panzer*. These Hitler Youth fanatics put up savage resistance and the advance over open ground was bloody. But by dusk, they'd cleared the village and were dug in on the far side, with newly arrived A/T guns at the ready to see off the expected counter-attack, though none came.

Cambes was one of the less pleasant sights of the campaign. Trees had been stripped and shredded by the furious bombardment, paths and lanes were littered with fallen branches. The chateau was blasted and gutted, the village wrecked and emptied except for a few old women who still crept about in the ruins. The gardens and orchards were dishevelled and torn up. Over everything hung the sickening odour of rotting bodies, bloated cattle and horses lay on their backs, with legs stiffly and awkwardly pointing skywards. Our own and enemy dead lay where they'd fallen, sprawling and grotesque. Trenches and dugouts were choked with the usual depressing litter of battle – helmets, scraps of equipment, broken rifles, burst open ammo boxes with long entrails of bullets ...[20]

Meanwhile, Lance-Corporal Hennessey and his un-horsed Hussar comrades were finding fresh mounts:

At Hermanville we re-organised and found that most of us had got through the assault somehow. Next morning

I managed to get hold of a parachutist's collapsible bicycle and set off back to the beach to see what could be salvaged from our tank. I recall being roundly cursed by an RASC truck driver for cycling on the left of the road. The beach at Lion-sur-Mer was crowded. There were dead and wounded, POWs, reinforcements arriving with parties of sappers searching for and clearing mines. I found our forlorn tank as the tide had receded but someone had been there before me and it was pretty well stripped.

In the days that followed, we based ourselves in Hermanville. We learnt that the East Riding Yeomanry had had an unfortunate encounter with a *Panzer* Regiment and we saw our first evidence of what an 88mm round could do to a Sherman.[21] Before long, replacement tanks arrived for us and we weren't sorry to be remounted. About then we heard that our CO, Colonel Harrap, had been killed along with his driver.

One of our first forays thereafter was a mopping up operation in Breville, supporting airborne forces that were still in the area of Ranville. I remember seeing the many crashed gliders and marvelling at their density on the ground. One, I knew, still had its full complement on board – all dead.

There was a sharp fight at Breville, [the same battle fought by the paras and Devons as described above]. We were in the area of a crossroads and were kept very busy for quite a time. I raked a hedgerow with my Browning [MG] in reply to MG fire from there and learned later from a paratrooper friend I must have accounted for the twenty-two bodies which were found there. That was quite a day and we weren't sorry to be withdrawn.

Some time later we were ordered back to Luc-sur-Mer on the coast to refit and clean up. I have the impression it was then that we ceased to be 27th Armoured Brigade and changed our sea-horses for the fox's mask of 8th Brigade. The weather was beautiful. We were introduced to mobile bath units, so we brought ourselves and our tanks back to 13th/18th standards of cleanliness. One day while on maintenance we saw a veritable host of aircraft crossing the sea and heading inland for Caen. Wave after wave of bombers sailed over and from where we sat we had a grandstand view of the destruction of the city.

In the days that followed we were engaged in a number of skirmishes in the difficult bocage country, much movement through sunken lanes, harbouring in orchards and winkling Germans out of fields of standing corn. We became familiar with the smell of death and the sight of bloated, dead cows.[22]

There's not much of the old bocage left, modern agriculture has completed the job of destruction. Where you do find survivals, it is so easy to see how difficult this ground was in '44. The fields are tiny, medieval, possibly prehistoric, in origin, hemmed in by high hedges, linked by sunken lanes, and there are stone farmhouses, solid as bunkers. It's a landscape out of time; in war, a defender's dream – close, compressed, claustrophobic and disorientating. It is one of the oddities of the Normandy campaign that Monty, whose planning for the beaches was so totally meticulous, seemed to have missed this. An awful lot of Allied soldiers would die as a result.

We were based in one particular orchard which seemed to be the favourite target for some German mortars who, two or three times a day, would send over a stonk which began to take its toll of our crews and echelons [supply personnel]. From there we used to make frequent trips to an area of high ground from which we'd spend hours in observation of the factory chimney district of Colombelles.

All was not plain sailing by any means. The Germans put up some stiff resistance from time to time and we began to develop a healthy respect for their A/T weapons. Our great advantage was air supremacy, although even this could have its dangers. One day, in a clearing, we were attacked by a couple of Spitfires who luckily must have seen the yellow smoke grenades I frantically threw out because they flew off without causing any damage.

Mistaken identity worked in the other direction too. We had a tank rigged up with multiple .50 cal Brownings for

AA defence, known popularly as the Lulworth Piano. The only time I can remember it going into action, it succeeded in bringing down a low-flying aircraft. Shortly afterwards we were visited by a furious flight-lieutenant who demanded to know who's side we were on! After the US breakout in the west, Operation *Cobra*, the Brits were tasked in late July to take the strategic crossroads on the high ground of Mont Pincon (Operation *Bluecoat*). This was a tough, bloody and often confused fight; the Hussars would more than do their bit.

It must have been late July that we found ourselves in support of infantry at the foot of a large hill. We were told this was a key point and had to be taken at all costs. There was a certain amount of small arms and automatic fire coming from scrub lining the approach roads. 'A' squadron was given the task of assaulting, 45 Troop leading. Our infantry followed closely behind the tanks, they were very vulnerable to the bullets sweeping the tracks as we forced our way forwards. We attempted several of these before we found one which seemed to lead directly to the summit. By now the mist was coming down, which gave us a certain amount of cover but also complicated our navigation of these unknown lanes.

Nonetheless we went with all possible speed to reach the top (someone had said there was a wireless station up there manned by German WAAFs!). On the way up Sergeant Rattle's tank came off the track and very nearly turned over but the orders were 'press on' and we did just that. We approached the summit, still in fog and took up position in all-round defence. There was still some fighting and ominous noises in the gloom but gradually others arrived and eventually the infantry would consolidate and the hill was captured; we learnt, with some pride, that this was an important victory.[23]

It was.

On D-Day morning 'Shimi' Lovat and his commandos, having sliced and diced Hitler's Atlantic Wall, now had the equally strenuous task of breaking out inland to link with the Ox and Bucks at Pegasus. They'd punched a 300-yard (275-metre) hole in the coastal defences. Beyond lay relatively open country, fields and wetland slashed with deep irrigation ditches, not at all inviting. According to their timetable, they had 2½ hours to get to the Orne Crossings. It would be tough going but the men were up for it. This was what they'd trained for; getting ashore and through the beach positions had taken 11 minutes.[24]

Each company leap-frogged forward aiming to get across the dismal plain and up the slope a couple of miles ahead – the total distance to Pegasus was around 4 miles (6.4 kilometres) pretty much due south-east. There was plenty of opposition and the commandos had to fight for every yard but on they went, overcoming more enemy positions and taking prisoners. Just after the hamlet of St Aubin d'Arquenay, an artillery battery manned by Italian troops was captured and a team spiked the guns. Commandos stormed up the long, single village street, though not until after they'd been stonked by those fearsome 'Moaning Minnies'.[25]

It was exhausting and very dangerous work, a tree-lined hedgerow hid German machine-gunners but Lovat and his men, with some Royal Marine Commandos they'd swept up, made it into St Aubin with supporting fire from a couple of maverick Shermans.[26] There was sporadic resistance from buildings in the straggling settlement but nothing concerted, no counter-attack and, mercifully, no *panzers*. Snipers were still a potent menace and Lovat was lucky when he turned to assist a gaggle of civilians, stone chips showered him as a round thumped the wall behind.[27]

One of the commandos swiftly dealt with the offending sharpshooter (who was dressed in civvies) but more Germans were approaching, infantry coming in by horse and cart, deploying for the attack. Lovat decided to ambush the enemy, a platoon-sized unit, clearly lacking in fieldcraft. The fire order whispered down the ambushing party is not one to be found in training manuals. 'Pick the officers and NCOs and let them come right in.' The ragged volley caused a surprise; dust flew off the back of the fair-haired platoon commander as he spun around and fell; half-a-dozen others, who had bunched in the centre on reaching the buildings, went down in a heap.[28]

Providentially, a Sherman clanked up at this point and the fight was over. It turned out these were Russian *Osttruppen*, (eastern troops) officered by now-deceased Germans, and it was clear from the general atmosphere pervading that personal hygiene wasn't among their priorities. They were, however, very happy to become POWs. Their wagons and horses proved very useful too. Bénouville was only half-a-mile ahead and it was obvious a far stiffer fight was raging up there. Howard's paras at the bridges were facing a far more determined counter-attack.

With tremendous, even reckless, élan worthy of his Highland ancestors, Lovat marched his men straight up the road with scouts and flankers ranging among the bright red poppies. The lane dipped into a hollow with the bridges at the base and then climbed again towards Caen. Wrecked vehicles, hastily dug slit trenches with dead and wounded from both sides cluttered the shallow valley. Several attacks had been seen off and the surviving A/T gun, one of two landed earlier by glider, was swapping rounds with German SP guns.

> I ran across with Piper Millin, [Private] Salisbury and a handful of fighting men. There was a fair amount of mortaring, and a machine-gun up the water pinged bullets off the steel struts, but no one noticed and brave fellows from the gliders were cheering from their fox-holes at the other end.[29]

Now, this is the stuff of legend and so it's remained. The commandos had reached the bridges and teamed up with Howard's weary survivors. The fight wasn't over, far from it. Naturally, Lovat apologised for being a full two minutes late.

The Special Service Brigade would be thrown into the desperate fight for Bréville (*see* above), on D-Day+6 and Lovat was badly wounded by a shell fragment. His part in the battle for Normandy was over.[30]

To Bayeux and beyond

Eric Broadhead and his comrades had made it inland from Gold Beach:

> The surrounding scenery in Normandy was famous for its narrow country lanes, small villages and cornfields, which were waving in a sea breeze as we pushed along a lane leading from the beaches inland, our bikes being very useful. I'm afraid a lot of us had a cowboy complex as we rode along armed to the teeth. We reached the high ground without incident, and from here one could see a perfect view of the bay with its vast array of ships of all shapes and sizes.
>
> It was just after this that we came under fire in earnest for the first time. Strangely enough, it was not enemy fire. We were pushing along down the lane, all keyed up and expecting almost anything except what happened. Overhead came a flight of fighter planes, from the Channel and heading over France – RAF fighters. As they zoomed overhead, they peeled off one by one and machine-gunned the column. This was far from pleasant, and we dived in all directions, as bits of dirt were flying everywhere. It was over as quick as it started, and we pushed on with nerves that had been somewhat stirred. It was later that we learned that we hadn't come through without loss. The price of victory had been paid and a little cross sprang up in Normandy.[31]

Sergeant William Sinton was from Byker in Newcastle's industrial east end. Though only 8 stone 7 pounds in his socks, he stood just over 6 foot 2 inches. In September 1939, as war was declared, he was having his tea at home with his wife. Bill was a reservist with 12 years' service in the regulars behind him. At 17.25 the radio broadcast a call for all reservists to report to their local depot. Within the hour, he arrived at Fenham Barracks.

Back in uniform with the Northumberland, he witnessed first-hand the horror of Coventry as his troop train passed through the blasted streets. This was Tommy's introduction to strategic bombing, terror from the skies, a deadly phenomenon Britons would soon be getting acclimatised to. He volunteered for the fledgeling paras but the training major, while admiring his courage, did say that with his height and weight the parachute was more likely to go up than down! Bill was destined to spend his war in the PBI.[32]

He became an NCO in the Fusiliers, now an MG battalion, equipped with carriers and they landed at Arromanches on D-Day + 10 as part of 59th Division and were first blooded at Annessey:

> Now this was a real sticker, the Jerries hit us with everything they had, and we were pinned down for three days; the only thing we could do was night shoots and, believe me, we gave them just as much as they gave us in daylight.[33] Each village and hamlet they passed through was laid waste, dead soldiers, civilians and animals everywhere, a regular abattoir; 'this,' I thought, 'is the price of war.'
>
> We arrived at a farm on a hilltop which had been cleared by the infantry (the South Staffordshires), and we got behind a hedge and dug out gun pits and cleared the way so we had a clear view into the valley. The night was rough, they hammered us with everything. We were glad when daylight came. The infantry were to advance through us but were held up by mortar and MG fire. We were ordered to fire directly on the Germans in an orchard, so we moved up in carriers. The brown smears of German trenches were visible beyond the orchard. We fired over open sights, clay flying up as we hammered their trenches.[34]

The infantry continued their now untroubled advance.

Moving up through yet another wrecked settlement, they caught their first glimpse of a knocked-out Tiger tank, the Mark VI *Panzer*, the Nazis' feared armoured leviathan with its tremendous 88mm gun. 'They'd blown the muzzle off the gun and lying alongside it was the biggest German I ever saw, he must have been six foot eleven and 18 stone, lying on his stomach, dead as a doornail.'[35]

Much of their ammunition was used up in continuous bursts of night firing, 'belt after belt, the condenser cans[36] were jumping'.

Such heavy bursts of indirect fire didn't go unpunished and salvos from 'moaning Minnies' sought them out. One evening the rockets were getting uncomfortably near so they loaded up and headed elsewhere in their carrier, only for the vehicle to run onto a wire entanglement and get stuck. They jumped out and hid in what they thought was a shallow trench. In fact, as dawn rose, they realised they were in a cemetery in a freshly dug grave. It took half-an-hour with cutters to free the carrier.[37]

Inexorably, as the vice around Caen tightened, they moved closer to the tormented city. Evidence of war was everywhere, an ancient pastoral landscape seemingly torn by giants' hands. They passed long columns of Allied casualties before setting the guns up about 100 yards from a farmhouse. The place was intact and handy for a brew. Jerry had noticed this too and stonked the place, Fortunately, the Fusiliers all got out safely. 'The battle for Caen was the worst we'd had up to this stage ... we fought day and night, no time for a shave or a wash; we were in a terrible state. The smell was terrible, twenty-four hours a day even when you were eating or drinking, the stench was unbearable.' In the warm, dark night, as they hammered out burst after burst, tracer flying, they could hear a great armoured scrap going on, grinding and clanking of tracks and brilliant bursts of shells.[38]

Next morning at dawn we looked through the hedge, we could not believe our eyes. There were about a hundred and fifty broken, shattered and burning tanks, British Shermans and German Tigers. The little Shermans we could see had rammed the Tigers and, at the same time, fired at point blank range. I said 'what a way to die.' My gun team all said 'we don't know how lucky we are.' Caen was followed eventually by the fresh carnage at Falaise – I've never seen so many vehicles burnt out.[39]

Joseph Bell was another Fusilier machine gunner, serving with No. 1 Independent MG Company who'd supported the Guards Armoured Division since September 1943. On 18 June they were ordered to Normandy, embarking on a US Liberty ship the next day. They had a rough crossing and didn't disembark till the 23rd. During the next couple of days they mustered at Bayeux but the Guards' armour still hadn't appeared. So they were sent forward into the fight for Carpiquet Aerodrome, relieving 8th Middlesex. This fight had already raged for some time as 15th Division sought to wrest the airfield from a very determined defence. Everyone knew how vital the place was, Joe found that there'd been 'a hard battle a few days before and the smell and sight of the dead gave plenty evidence of this'.[40]

The Fusiliers found themselves part of this desperate struggle, incessant heavy shelling, mortars and continuous fire erupting from their Vickers. Withdrawn to draw breath at Bayeux, they were soon back in action when the Guards and their tanks finally arrived. They fought through then from 17 July until the final battle at Falaise.

Sergeant T. C. Dixon, also with the Northumberland Fusiliers, landed on 28 June. They were in jeeps, which were handier than carriers and remarkably agile as well as very robust. They'd got there just in time to witness the great flying armada heading for Caen:

... a terrific aerial assault on Caen by 450 Halifaxes, Lancasters and Liberators. About 21.30 hours, the first wave of bombers came over our heads and made for the target ... we watched through glasses [binoculars] and could see the bombs leaving the racks and hurtle down on Caen ... we saw one [bomber] make a forced landing about half-a-mile away but no-one was injured. The sky was soon filled with clouds of smoke rising from the bombing; the most concentrated attack I've ever witnessed.[41]

On 8 July, the Navy added its own spectacular show of firepower provided courtesy of HMS *Warspite* and *Rodney*, whose great 16-inch guns, firing from the Seine Estuary, sent shell after massive shell roaring over the infantrymen's heads. More or less yard by yard, the British clawed their way into what was left of Caen:

9th July: The battle was of a very confused nature and went by no means according to plan. Galamanche, the initial objective was reported as captured several times over, the trouble being that we were up against Hitler Youth from *12th SS Panzer* who had a nasty habit of infiltrating back into their positions at night, while snipers were regularly left behind to bump off as many Brits as possible before dying themselves.[42]

10th July: The battle still in progress, those few Jerries taken looked very young, tough, vicious and of no further use to Europe after the war. A considerable number were gratified in their desire to die for the Fuhrer. Eventually we took and, what is more important, properly mopped up Galamanche, Bi Jade, Epron and St Contest and the Hun pulled out of La Folie and Coure-Chef.

11th July: Still the battle rages, the casualty clearing station in the next field has had a busy time ever since the fight began. We ourselves did not suffer as badly as the infantry battalions. Our losses were two men killed, one officer and twenty-four men wounded; some however were only slight and were soon back with the battalion.[43]

Fred Hart was a signaller with the Green Howards, part of 6th and 7th Battalions, waiting to cross over to Europe as reinforcements:

We heard that our lads had landed on French soil and that they were having a tough time of it and wondered just what we were going to run into when it came to our turn to land in the same spot. None of us really guessed what it was going to be like and in some cases, this was a good job.

No crowds cheered us as we moved down the country lanes and through to the seaport town, the few civilians we saw just looked at us with large, sympathetic eyes as we went slowly by. The sight of the White Cliffs of Dover fading in the distance affected us all in different ways. Some saw us then thro' eyes that were misty white, others had a curious lump in their throats.[44]

Unloading on the Normandy side went pretty well till one jeep and its officer passengers got a severe ducking in an unnoticed shell hole: 'The funniest part of this incident was caused by the jeep driver "Timmo". His completely bald head rising out of the waves brought forth huge roars of mirth both from those left on the ship and those nearby.'[45]

Once ashore they swiftly found themselves the target of the *Luftwaffe*. Goering's mighty air force nowhere near as potent as it had been but it could still bite and, for Tommy on the ground, attack from the air was still bloody terrifying: 'never has the earth been so well loved as it was on that night.' Dig as they might, some men were still wounded by shrapnel and the experience blooded those war virgins who had not seen action before.

As the battalion passed through Creully they got their first real glimpse of what the realities of war meant for this quiet rural backwater, the scale and totality of devastation, the insensate and random cruelties of long-range shelling and mortars. The blasted town was jammed with vehicles, the ancient church tower, miraculously undamaged, still standing serene. Despite the horrors, local wine shops and bars were doing a roaring trade!

They were headed for the mincer of Caen:

Early on the morning of the attack these lads had to run a line from a cutting to the signal office and to take it across a field which, to quote the major's own words 'might or might not be mined'! These words accounted for Timmo being at least a hundred yards ahead of the other three all the time and in a bit of a sweat. If this wasn't enough, they got strafed as well. As the *Luftwaffe* left off they got a brew on but then, typically, Jerry came back for another run![46]

That damn bocage

Mr R. M. S. Maude was a Major in the Royal Engineers, with 246 Field Company, 3rd Division, and 12 AGRE. In a letter to a relative, he described life behind the lines in Normandy:

You have entirely the wrong impression of what a battle is like! I will try and explain. You see you are only actually fighting for a very small part of the time, then you don't get much time to sleep or eat. But most of the time both sides just sit and look at each other and nothing happens except sporadic shelling and patrolling at nights.

And a Field Company does not sit in the front line, but two or three miles back if it has any sense. When I was with 246 there were periods when we sat in our orchards in the sun and there was literally nothing to do, and we were bored. But apart from D-Day we were never involved in any heavy fighting except very sporadically, and most of the time it was quite peaceful and I used to play with the children next door and visit the doc in the evenings for a cup of tea and a chat. Our work consisted of road mending and mine clearance or tidying up, which was done as though we were in England except that there was always a risk of shells, but they are alright provided you get warning of the first one.

The French seem extraordinarily unconcerned about the battle and the swarms of troops in their orchards and villages. They just carry on their normal lives; they're always friendly and helpful if you approach them directly, but they don't go out of their way to help or take notice of you.[47]

James Whiteley again:

Some days later as the allies pushed inland my dad went on patrol with his squad or troop. As they went down the country lanes my dad had to answer a call of nature. He asked permission and was told to catch them up. He was finishing up using the toilet paper that was provided in the little pack of sundries that came with the rations when there was a long burst of firing. He nipped through the hedge. The entire patrol and all his mates were dead (presumably, his mate that had called him off the LC as well); a machine gun ambush, caught between the hedgerows by the Germans they had nowhere to go and were mown down.[48]

In the summer of 1944, my father served with the REME. His role was to recover and repair broken-down or battle-damaged tanks, not as glamorous perhaps as the combat troops, but dangerous and technically demanding work. One day some time after the landings, his unit was passing through a small town in Normandy some way behind the advancing front. There was a holdup and they had been halted for some time.

The town had been liberated some days earlier, and rather than the well-known scenes of jubilant citizens embracing and feting the troops, there was just a single woman whose affections were most definitely for sale. An NCO decided to accept what was on offer and went into a house in the street where the column was stopped. A large number of soldiers sought distraction from the tedious delay and clambered atop a truck loaded with welding rods, there to view through a window the spectacle of the khaki-clad rump of their comrade completing his transaction with the local lady.

Unfortunately, the additional weight imposed on the already grossly overloaded truck – bundles of welding rods weigh almost as much as steel ingots – caused the truck's suspension to collapse. The spectators disappeared back to their allotted transport, leaving a couple of puzzled officers trying to fathom out why the truck, having successfully negotiated miles of war-torn, shell-pocked roads, should choose to collapse while completely stationary![49]

Victor Hyams served with 44th Royal Tank Regiment:

We drove our tank on the landing craft, which took fifteen tanks. We chained the tanks down. I saw what seemed to be thousands of ships laying off the coast of France and the *Belfast* was there with all guns blazing. It was an encouraging sight. We got in our tanks and the boat crew sealed us in. The crew wished us good luck and we were left with our thoughts. The ramp came down and we drove off. The beach had already been taken and our troops were a mile in by that time …

After a wait of several days the tanks then bombarded and obliterated two villages before moving into the bocage:

I can't forget the Bocage area – that was a deadly place because of the undergrowth and very high hedges which lined the road and which even a tank found it impossible to get through … It was all hard going. The Allied commanders had planned to take Caen on the first day, but by 29 June we found ourselves on the high ground overlooking Caen, with the Germans still giving fierce resistance. We advanced and everything happened in a short period. I was the co-driver and was responsible for the Browning machine gun. I was looking through my telescope and saw armoured piercing shells coming towards us – they are white hot streaks and don't look very dangerous.

As I turned my periscope, I saw many of the other tanks being hit and brewing up. The turret opened on one tank and a burning man emerged who hit the ground and tried to roll in the corn. My instinct was to get out and help him. The squadron was being decimated. We continued forward and then the wireless operator dropped down behind me screaming, 'I can't stand it anymore.' He had left us defenceless, as he was the loader for the gun. I turned around and said: 'Don't worry. It's going to be alright.' The order came through to retreat and we turned the tank around to go back to our original position. I shouted at the driver, 'Zig zag, Wally. Zig zag.' And sure enough, he zig-zagged all the way back. When we turned round, I could see our tanks burning and lots of smoke, where smoke shells had been fired to cover our retreat.

We stayed there and I even got out of the tank to have a pee. After about two hours, we got a message that the Germans had broken through on our flank. Lieutenant Rogers turned the turret towards where the attack was coming and told Wally to start up. Nothing happened. We were static in a very bad position. Our gun fired and then we were hit in the turret. Fortunately, it didn't go through. There was a terrific bang and some pieces sheared off the inside of the tank, blinding the gunner, who didn't wear goggles because he had to keep his eye to the periscope. Then, there was another bang as we were hit in the rear, which could have been 'game up', as our tank was petrol driven.

The commander gave the order to abandon the tank.
There was a plate behind me which I had looked after
carefully, as this was an escape hatch and I had practised
this manoeuvre in my mind many times. I got out very
quickly and dropped to the ground and almost immediately,
we must have been hit again, as I felt a terrific blow to my
head, as if I had been hit with a stick. I was blinded. I lay
there for a moment, feeling for blood. I decided to crawl
through the corn, towards where I thought our troops
were, as I wanted to avoid any German troops who may
have been advancing.

I heard the sounds of war around me and I crawled and
crawled until a feeling overcame me where I decided to
abandon life and stood up and started to walk. I was happy
that all the pain and the dreadful events I had witnessed
would come to an end. A voice shouted at me, 'What the
fuck are you doing?' I was dragged into a half-track where
there were other wounded. We were taken to a forward
casualty station. The doctor told me I had burns across my
eyes, as he tied a bandage around my head. The battle went
on all night ...

The padre came in the morning and told me he was going
to lead me out. I put my hands on his shoulders and he led
me to an ambulance. As we walked, I remember infantrymen
marching in the opposite direction and I remember the sound
of their kit banging on their bodies, I felt sorry for them
walking into this inferno which I had just left.[50]

Mr Mackenzie was a Sergeant in the Royal Signals, attached to a
headquarters unit rather than frontline troops.

It was learnt that a couple of Tiger tanks along with
approximately 100 infantry had been bypassed by our
forward troops, and were dug in in a wood a few hundred
yards up the road. The three tanks attached to our HQ had
got up, but two of them were 'brewed up'. Apart from our
own personal arms, we had nothing! We expected them to
attack us that night, so every man slept with his weapon

and ammunition, ready for a do! I didn't mind the infantry, but tanks! You can't knock them out with personal arms fire. Went to bed resigned to the fact that we would be for it! Woke up surprised to find we were OK! An hour later, twelve rocket-firing Typhoons came over, the first time we had seen them in action! What a sight, what a terror. They got those tanks alright.[51]

My mother was a Qualified Ordnance Wren on duty on D-Day. She had to go out to the boats and repair their guns as they came in to harbour after action. Her own words say it all, and I read her account instead of a eulogy at her funeral last year. She had no medals: 'I had been in the WRNS for two years and I was a Q.O (Qualified Ordnance) That means it was my job to look after the guns in our flotilla of small ships, gunboats, torpedo boats and motor launches, (G.B.s, T.B.s and M.L.s for short). There were about 30 boats in our flotilla and we used to travel around the coast of Britain and go out on gun trials, torpedo trials and raids.

'There were just four WRNS with our flotilla, two Q.O.s, plus one torpedo Wren and one radar (it was called Asdic then). We were stationed at H.M.S. *Hornet* in Gosport near Portsmouth for the six months leading unto D-Day. We all knew something was going on because leave was cancelled and we were put on permanent night shifts. We had orders to go aboard all the boats and check all the guns torpedoes and equipment to make sure they were all working and there was plenty of ammo. It seems that one morning, very early, we went to breakfast and there were no boats in the harbour at all. We knew then that this was the day – D-Day.

'We grabbed a few hours sleep and then were called to duty. The little ships were coming in gradually. We tried to count them but were too busy. Some of them were very shot up and the guns were damaged and very dirty and in many cases, bloodstained. It wasn't very pleasant but the boats had to sail again very quickly so we didn't have time to brood. First we got the guns off their mountings and back to the workshop to strip them down, repair them and clean them, re-arm them then get them back on board. The bigger guns we had to do our best with on board. There were point 5s, machine guns, rifles, pistols, Vickers twin machine guns, Tommy guns etc, about 14 types altogether.

'The seas were very choppy and we somehow had to climb up the rope ladder with armfuls of guns, (or down from the boat if the tide was out). From the jetty to the boats was a line of cats (floating rafts) attached to each other by ropes. To get from one to the other we had to wait till the one in front was high and step on it before it dropped! Not easy, but I was young and sprightly, just 21 years old. I couldn't do it now. We tried to see who was missing from the crews, we knew them all quite well and several faces were gone! When we had time to think it was awful, especially as I had been to the ship's dance with them only a couple of weeks before. They were also young, my age and younger.

'The little ships were very vulnerable; one enemy torpedo was enough to sink her. They were tough little ships as well. They could go very fast, zig-zag between the mines and torpedoes. The whole operation of D-day for us lasted about a month, then things eased up a bit and we could see who was missing and which boats didn't come back. One particular one was M.G.B 133. One of the chaps on board had a picture of me pinned to the wall above his bunk. We just called him Ginger. I never did see him again, I hope he survived.'[51]

On the morning of 8 July 1944 my Dad, William Patrick (Bill) Power, wrote a letter to Mum, and my brother Max (then nearly five), dated 8th July 1944. He wrote: 'It won't be long before we are together again, if Jerry was a decent sport he would know he was beaten and pack in now. I'm still feeling fine and getting along alright, don't worry about me this job isn't so difficult after all, I've had much tougher times on schemes. Well, darling, I must close now, look after yourself and keep happy, all my love to my own two darlings.'

Later that day he was killed in action in the battle that liberated Caen:

> I was born three months later, so I never knew my Dad. But on 8th July this year at 11am my brother and I will be laying a poppy wreath at the Cenotaph in Whitehall in proud memory of our Dad's sacrifice. Some family members will read from his letters, we will conclude by singing John Lennon's song *Imagine* – led by the wonderful singer Carol Grimes.[52]

8

THE BATTLE FOR NORMANDY

Hitler has only got one ball,
Goering's got two but very small,
Himmler is very similar,
And poor old Goebbels' got no balls at all.

Frankfurt has only one beer hall
Stuttgart, die Munchen all on call,
Munich, vee lift up our tunich,
To show vee 'Chermans' have no balls at all
    Anon; *Hitler Has Only Got One Ball* (sung to the tune of
               Colonel Bogey)

There is another kind of thoughtlessness, which some of us
may have to watch, though it is commoner among British
peace-time visitors abroad than among British soldiers. It
consists of airing the opinion that such and such a foreign
country or town or village is very lucky to have chaps like us
passing through …[1]

The battle went on, *materialschlacht*, grinding attrition.

A phase without spectacle or glitter: in a week of difficult
fighting which had yielded no great gains measured in
distance, the 50th Division had slowly ground the enemy into

impotence. From becoming incapable of effective counter-attack he passed to the stage where he could no longer hold his line. And back he went, not in a rout but carefully and steadily with the usual array of booby traps and mines in his wake. We followed, pressing him.[2]

Montgomery, as we've seen, in his strategic plan had envisaged the capture of Caen as a 6 June objective. This was not only too ambitious, but it was also seriously impractical. The strength of the German defensive posts at 'Hillman' and 'Morris' was underestimated and the attack stalled short of the city and its vital aerodrome. After the success of D-Day, the campaign of bitter attrition that followed caused mounting frustration, both with politicians and Monty's fellow commanders.

His personality was not endearing: he would always maintain the battle unfolded entirely according to plan and that the British and Canadians drew onto themselves German reserves, so permitting the Americans to build up and finally break out in the west. In the event, this is precisely what occurred but it was not the textbook fight Monty chose to describe. A series of British tactical initiatives to break the deadlock around and west of Caen generally foundered.

For Bill Jalland and others, fighting in the close country of the 'bocage' became a dreadful, sapping ordeal:

We were to attack a place called St Pierre in the 'bocage' country. I was briefed by Tommy Clapton, the company commander. He said this was a 'little trip' – the place was defended only by cadets armed with pistols and maybe 'the odd tank or armoured car or two'. I was a little bit sceptical, especially as we had a full tank brigade in support. The 'cadets' of course were the Hitler Youth supported by *panzers*. We were attacking the join between *10th SS* and *Panzer Lehr*, all crack troops.

We rode forward over ploughed fields on the hulls of the tanks. Some of the chaps with bikes who couldn't keep up would just stick their bikes under the treads so they were crushed and then clamber up! The bikes were a waste of time really. We leaguered up at Point 103, the village was maybe one-and-a-half miles away over open fields down a gentle slope. We went in with two companies forward and two in reserve. I was with my platoon towards the rear, on the east side, I think. The road was lined with poplars I recall.[3] English and Leybourne were commanding the forward companies, Chris Beatty the other with us.[4]

Sergeant Brown had also found the bikes more of a hindrance and had taken similar action:

Cycling at marching pace was pretty hard work. So when we stopped, I attracted the attention of a passing tank commander and asked him to do me a favour. 'What do you want?' he asked. 'Run over them bloody bikes with your tracks,' I said. 'Run them over?' he said. 'Aye,' I said, so he just ran them over. And then I said to my officer 'The bikes have gone, sir!' 'The bikes have gone?' 'Aye, the bloody tanks have run them over,' and he said, 'Oh well, if you haven't got a bike, you haven't got a bike.'[5]

Bill Jalland and the rest of 8th Battalion were soon facing a strong counter-attack:

Next morning we were subjected to heavy shelling and mortaring, fire was coming from enemy tanks, rounds bursting in the trees and showering us with shrapnel. We pulled out of the village but the two forward companies had some sections overrun. Sergeant Wallbank took on a tank coming down the main street and halted it, blew off a track. Johnnie Wheatley, an old friend, was killed there by a blast, not a mark on his body; we suffered horrible casualties. We fell back to the edge of the village but it was all open country behind us, a perfect killing zone, we had no choice but to stand.[6]

A crisis point had now arrived.

Johnnie Walker the adjutant was in charge; we had a rather odd collection of people, cooks, stretcher-bearers and all sorts;

the RSM was dropping off boxes of ammo and Johnnie told us to stay quiet till the Germans appeared. Their infantry started infiltrating through the village, jumping over walls and coming through the gardens, moving very quickly. We waited till we got the order then opened up on them with rapid fire – they were no more than 50 yards away. I saw 40–50 of them coming at us, well equipped, fully cammo'd up with nets etc. At some point one of their tanks was amongst us, I recall. Now, our tanks came forward from Point 103; they charged just like the US cavalry but they were butchered by 88s knocking them out like Aunt Sallies – the sky was full of dense black smoke when they 'brewed up'. We lost heavily. We never heard from our own guns, too far out on a limb I suppose.[7]

The fight was by no means over:

Most of the tank crews escaped and some of them got mixed up with us; they carried their revolvers strapped low around the leg. That afternoon we were attacked by German tanks, perhaps three or four only on the eastern flanks, not nearly as numerous as our Shermans. Ian English was marvellously heroic, he and a sergeant tried to manhandle a six-pounder anti-tank gun into action; he wasn't a gunner of course, not sure if he succeeded. We were ordered to pull out the next night, back to Point 103 then back to Bayeux where we rested up in a field and slept for most of the next day.[8]

And now they would find themselves in the heart of the bocage:

After a few days out of the line, we were ordered up again towards Villars-en-Bocage[9]. It was strange country, unlike anything we'd encountered before, ideal for the defensive. Pocket-handkerchief-sized fields, as small as 50 yards across, very high banks topped with dense hedges; the fighting was at very close quarters with the enemy no more than grenade-throwing distance.

We and the Germans sited our Brens and their MGs to provide enfilade fire; they tended not to use their tanks at night but theirs were fitted with rubber treads which sometimes made them very difficult to hear. They had a tank leaguer in the Chateau de Cordillon near us, featured in Dumas' *Three Musketeers* I recall. Sometimes they would bring one up, using the cover of those high banks, get to about 50 yards from us unheard, then open up with their cannon and machine-guns, gave us a real fright![10]

This fighting in the dense Norman bocage left a vivid, searing memory with all who experienced it. The country was narrow and enclosed. Overwhelming Allied advantages in weight of guns and armour were nullified by the ground, ideal for defence. And the Brits were up against a ruthless, experienced and highly skilled enemy whose years of murderous fighting in the east had taught him much. Some, indeed many, of the Allied soldiers were raw, their baptism a harsh and bloody one.

Not untypical was 6th DLI's experience when attacking towards the Hottot-Juvigny road. The advance, on 14 July, made some ground but was halted by intense MG fire from well-dug enemy positions. Despite a furious barrage, it required 5 hours of costly attrition to win the ground.[11] The 9th Battalion met with similar dogged resistance in its projected advance on Lingevres. A recce carried out by 'B' Company the day before had resulted in the loss of every single officer.[12]

The Germans held a belt of dense woodland directly astride the line of advance. As ever, the attack was heralded by a ripping barrage and hurricane of rockets from 25-pounders and Typhoons:

The wood literally danced in front of our eyes, and not 300 yards away. The Typhoons each did one dive and released two bombs and 10 rockets, straddling and plastering the wood... For what seemed a long time nothing happened, and then an enemy tank in the left-hand corner of the wood fired and set on fire one of our Shermans. The fire was returned with good effect by the remaining two. Another Hun tank opened up from the right-hand of the wood, and then the wood came to life. Our leading troops were now in the middle of the stubble and were caught there by a withering fire from Spandaus (MG34/42) and snipers, but they still kept going. A dash and we were in the wood, but the Hun had his plentiful Spandaus sited well back inside the edge of it.[13]

The Germans had dubbed the battle for Normandy as *materialschlacht* – attrition warfare. The Allies had massive superiority in firepower and in overall numbers. The quality of certain Allied units was heavily criticised by the Axis and by ourselves. Equally, many of their units were low-grade ersatz formations made up of renegades from the Eastern Front and even some Indian Army deserters, left over from the Desert War. Their veteran and Hitler Youth units fought superbly and exacted a high toll for every yard of ground won. Their tanks – Mark IV, V (Panther) and VI (Tiger) – if less plentiful, were infinitely better in qualitative terms, and their commanders, 'aces' like Michael Wittman,[14] were experienced and daring. Allied armoured units might expect to lose about five or six Shermans for every *panzer* knocked out.

Like most engaged in this fighting, Lieutenant Jalland and his platoon, immured in the close and deadly ground of the bocage, saw only what occurred in their immediate sector. That was bad enough:

My chaps spotted an armoured car or what looked like an armoured car; it was quite a way away, difficult to get messages back as the wretched radios were so unreliable, we had to send runners. We did have a six-pounder with us but the sergeant wasn't prepared to shoot as he felt the gun was too exposed.

Suddenly someone yelled, 'it's coming!' It came down the lane, its turret traversing; we thought we'd have to get behind it to stop it but suddenly a loud bang and it stopped dead, Hawke's grenades had blown a track off. It was a Tiger after all! The crew thought it was going to catch fire so they bailed out and pelted along the hedge fronting our line. Some of our chaps thought it was an attack and got up running ahead of them but then others came out chasing the Germans, we had quite a race! Still, we captured them and were rather pleased at having knocked out a Tiger. We had a pioneer officer, a Lieutenant Pugh, he thought we should set the tank on fire and he duly did; it created a dense column of smoke. The Germans must have thought we were about to attack, subjected us to a massive barrage that seemed to go on for ages – Lieutenant Pugh wasn't very popular![15]

Some of the more esoteric Allied innovations were not necessarily welcomed by the infantry:

We did get visits from our psychological warfare people, they used loudspeakers and microphones, we didn't think much of them and, as soon as they started, Jerry opened up with shells and mortars. We did approve of 'artificial moonlight' though. We shone searchlights from behind which reflected off the clouds above Jerry, illuminated the whole area to our front and blinded him just about completely, almost like theatre footlights!

We always had good support from 74 Field Artillery; we'd known them for years, of course, but they'd lay down a barrage anywhere, really plaster the place. The same went for the Cheshires who gave us support with their Vickers HMGs. The 2nd Tactical Air Force kept Typhoons in the air, like a taxi rank, we had an air-link and could call them down. They'd peel off and were so accurate they could target an individual enemy tank with rockets. We carried fluorescent panels in our battledress which we could spread out to mark our own positions.[16]

Though bogged down, this deadly attritional warfare was never completely static:

Both sides patrolled. I went out many times towards Park de la Mer and Hottot, never actually got into the place but did tread on a tripwire once; thankfully it was only tied to a flare. We did get into the grounds of the chateau through a hole in the wall; Jerry was using it as a tank repair workshop. We were in the same location for several weeks and Jerry patrols would get as near as the hedge, we could have touched them, we could smell them – German officers always seemed to wear eau de cologne, they smelt different to us. There was lots of sniping, from both sides; I remember one of our chaps came through saying he'd just shot someone on the lavatory, caused great amusement. Another shot some Germans queuing for food, it really wasn't very pleasant.[17]

We both used mines, though the positions, slit trenches mainly, weren't wired; the Germans made a form of mine out of packets of gun cotton and a detonator, very nasty. We dug our trenches into the bank-side and bored through like loopholes for firing; Jerry did the same but he always ensured he had a groundsheet over the rear of the trenches he dug so you couldn't see through the aperture and shoot.

A Captain Myers, who'd been to battle school, decided MG positions could be stormed frontally with the bayonet. So we laid down smoke and covering fire from the Brens, ridiculous idea, he was badly wounded as were several men with him. We used captured German *panzerfausts*[18] and they were very effective as well. Most of the time they were very close and we shouted at each other, pretty ribald as you can imagine. We did maintain our sense of humour – I remember the platoon next to mine was being heavily mortared; after a long time Jerry stopped firing and we imagined they were adjusting the range to mortar us. A corporal jumped up and in broad Geordie shouted to Jerry, 'Same range, same target'![19]

Even at local level, tactical initiatives could come unstuck through poor planning, faulty or non-existent scouting:

We were attacking Hottot and 213 Brigade were putting in the attack but the last five minutes of the bombardment was directly on our positions and we were suddenly overrun by wild Devons, Dorsets and Hampshires. Had they troubled to do a preliminary recce this would never have happened.

We got on well with them, of course, but it was still a complete cock-up! We'd been in the bocage for weeks now, we didn't get much information, there was a real lack of communication, we used to hear snippets from various officers in the support or carrier platoons. Finally 6th DLI passed through us during a big attack on Villars-en-Bocage. We later motored through what was left in lorries, we were now to be fully motorised; the place was flattened, nothing above six feet was left standing; both 6th DLI and the Hampshires caught a packet.[20]

The process that led to the final capitulation of Germany began as the Axis position in Normandy began to collapse. Whether it was intentional or accidental, Montgomery's battle of attrition in the eastern sector facilitated *Operation Cobra*,[21] the US breakout in the west. The Wehrmacht simply did not have sufficient available resources to counter both. In the east, a great Soviet offensive, *Bagration*,[22] was threatening to, and did, smash Army Group Centre, a blow from which Hitler's forces could never fully recover.

On 20 July, a group of army officers had attempted to remove the Führer with a bomb placed in the conference room at Rastenburg, his East Prussian HQ. *Valkyrie* was a failure with unfortunate consequences for the plotters, including Erwin Rommel, whose legendary career ended with self-administered poison. Hitler's suspicions over the loyalty of his officer elite multiplied as Axis fortunes waned. His orders in the west, to hold ground regardless and fritter away scarce reserves in pointless counter-attacks, contributed substantially to the destruction of his forces there which, in August, found themselves hemmed into what became known as the Falaise 'Pocket'. What resulted was like a Norse *Ragnarök* of epic proportions as the might of Allied firepower winnowed the fleeing Wehrmacht, burdened with its accumulated loot.

Bill Jalland takes up the story of the fight as the Allied pressure finally began to tell:

We attacked Mt. Pincon supported by tanks, a set-piece battle, brilliantly executed though I don't remember much detail, lost in the fog of war, we did take some casualties. I remember strong opposition and the enemy were firing a big naval gun from some distance, huge great shells, you could hear them coming, sounded like a kitbag turning over and over, you had time to get into a trench or some other form of cover.

After that battle we were fully motorised and we crossed the Falaise Pocket over to the northern flank. We were appalled, the German columns had been completely destroyed, a carpet of dead men and horses, the Typhoons and artillery had been dreadfully effective. We also came across dead Germans hanging in an orchard – they'd been lynching their own deserters, first time we'd seen that, the SS were responsible – the dead men were just a few inches above the ground, all swaying in the breeze. We had no time to stop so we left them, pushed on. We'd not much time for deserters, our own ran the risk of being shot. It's one thing when people get bomb happy, you can understand that, I've seen people sitting helpless in trenches and crying for days, that happens, but those who just run away, well you just had to stick it out regardless, we had a job to do.[23]

The Falaise Pocket was truly a scene from the Apocalypse; a modern parallel would be the wreck of Saddam Hussein's army, annihilated as they streamed out of Kuwait during the denouement of the first Gulf War:

The Germans moved along the roads till they were choked with dead horses and men and burning wreckage. Then they took to the fields, across which they moved in columns of five or six abreast. At bottlenecks such as gateways and stream crossing-places, the traffic piled up and was then destroyed by shells and rocket-firing planes. Swiftly destruction would spread across the entire field until it was impossible for anything on wheels or tracks to move across it. In a day or two many fields became like the roads – simply impassable owing to the carnage and destruction. It was a battlefield that decided the fate of France.[24]

This was the shattered wake of a defeated army:

Both sides and often the middle of the roads were jammed with wrecked lorries, guns, horses and tanks; dead men and horses lay about in grotesque attitudes, and here and there a truck or gun limber, which had been set on fire and was still smouldering. Abandoned staff cars and many other vehicles were packed with loot: field glasses, typewriters, pistols and small arms by the hundred, cases of wine and boxes of ladies' clothing. Many of the vehicles were untouched and could have been driven away, but no one had the time.[25]

Paris was now about to be liberated as the Germans, those who'd fought so hard and bled so freely in Normandy, appeared to collapse. It almost seemed as though the war in the west might even be ending:

> We reached Vernon on the Seine and Archie Bark, the IO, and I went forward in a jeep, his I think. Paris was literally just down the road and we could even get a glimpse of the Eiffel Tower. We thought we'd be the ones to liberate Paris but it had to be done by De Gaulle and the Free French. We were held back but the Parisian Resistance rose against the Germans and were dealt with very harshly, perhaps it was Archie and I who started the excitement! We were sent on towards Arras and Amiens, the V1s[26] and V2s[27] were creating havoc in the south of England. We went back along the route the battalion had retreated over in 1940, on the way to Dunkirk. Every town and village we passed through was lined with flags and the people pressed us with flowers and wine, they made us feel like heroes.[28]

Increasingly, and whilst there were many vicious and sudden skirmishes ahead, the advance was turning into a victory march:

> All this while we met very little resistance and we were taking a fair number of prisoners – not the quality of troops we'd met in Normandy, older men and young boys of 15/16, they were demoralised and pretty confused, generally would not stand.
> Though we were following the Dunkirk route, most of those in the battalion now were still at school in 1940, our

officers were virtually all under 25. Then in one village we went into we found the people had stored all of the battalion's musical instruments, abandoned by the bandsmen in 1940. Everyone had saved and cherished one of these, kept them clean and polished. There was a handing-over ceremony, quite emotional except none of the chaps now could play and as not all the replacements were light infantry and could do the quick march, the guard of honour was a right shambles![29]

We were driving east going hell-for-leather; you could see the V1 and V2 trails in the sky and we even drove in two columns on each side of the highway, there was no civilian traffic and you weren't likely to meet anyone coming the other way. We were in three-tonners plus a whole selection of captured German vehicles, trucks, half-tracks and VW cars. We looked so Germanised an entire field battery of 88s followed us, thinking we were all Germans retreating; they followed us all day and at night we took them prisoner, they didn't see the funny side at all.[30]

One of the major difficulties the Allies encountered was that of resupply, particularly of fuel. Despite success in Normandy, they had yet to capture a functioning deep-water harbour; Cherbourg was still being cleared. By September these mounting difficulties and the speed of German recovery under Von Rundstedt[31] would greatly slow the advance, which would bog down in the Low Countries.

This did not, however, impede 151 Brigade's (6th, 8th and 9th DLI) wild career across northern France:

We were kept supplied with fuel, coming in through PLUTO ('Pipe Line Under the Ocean'), and we got ours either in jerry-cans or disposable tins; you just created a hole in the top, poured in the fuel and threw it away. Even when we stopped at night we didn't set up a full tactical perimeter, there was some probing but nothing serious, we didn't find any of the usual mines or booby traps.

Our morale was very high, bolstered by the reception we got from the civilian population. We saw how the French dealt with their own collaborators – girls were whipped or had their heads shaven in the squares; our chaps had very little sympathy for them and it was their business anyway. We did encounter groups of the Resistance, they had Sten guns dropped by the RAF and were always asking if we had spare 9mm ammunition but we needed all of ours. Occasionally we'd run into ambushes and there was some shelling and mortaring, mainly just isolated groups trying to escape eastwards.[32]

Sergeant Tom Myers from 6 DLI and his comrades were doing their bit.

We got in about seven at night with no sign of Germans, so we went into a café and had a beer and got talking to two pretty girls. The barman said to me in broken English, 'They've been collaborating with the Germans.' I said, 'They can collaborate with whoever they want – I'm going to have that blonde tonight,' and my mate said, 'I'll have the other one.' We spent 24 hours there and then it became a mad rush. Jerry had started his real pull-out and it was on the trucks and away.[33]

The Durhams were not yet out into those broad, sunlit uplands Churchill had earlier promised; the formidable obstacle of the Albert Canal remained, as Bill Brown discovered:

... we were about to have three days' rest when we were ordered to cross the Albert Canal that night. Assault boats were there to meet us. These were collapsible wood and canvas boats and heavy to carry down the bank. We could see boats sinking and blokes getting shot by German machine-guns. Later, I was standing, talking to a section commander in a sunken road, when the enemy opened up with a machine-gun.

It looked like flashing lights going past me. I fell into the sunken road. About three men were killed and my guts were oozing out. I said to a young officer, 'Give us your hand. Grip it as tight as you can.' He took my hand. I was conscious all the time; I thought, 'If I lose consciousness, I will die.' Stretcher-bearers came and they put about four field dressings on me and carried me down the road. The German machine-guns could have opened up on us but they didn't.[34]

For Bill Brown his wound was definitely a 'Blighty' one.

One who had cause to remember his 21st birthday in August, as the battle for Normandy reached its denouement with the near annihilation of German forces meshed into the Falaise Pocket, was W. R. 'Nobby' Noblett serving with the 15th/19th Hussars:

The task of 'R' Squadron 15/19th was to support the [43rd] Division across the Seine at Vernon while RECCE Squadron were given the task of finding an un-blown bridge across by one of those many villages which bordered the river. Anything less like a RECCE would be unimaginable. The road towards the villages on our side of the river was totally exposed to the opposite bank. As we had no cover whatsoever we made a s**t or bust dash down the cart track of a road, a tactic we were to employ time and again. The first village we came to – 'bridge blown', as was the next and then, bingo, we found one intact. I don't know who decided it but a newly-appointed lance-corporal by the name of Alquist was volunteered to go over the bridge first, a decidedly risky operation in view of the fact it was almost certainly ready to be blown.

After many attempts at trying to put our hero at his ease, he and his driver slowly mounted the ramp in their Daimler Scout Car and 'Boo-oom' up went the bridge in a cloud of splinters. I think the calmest person of all, who took it in his stride, was lance-corporal Alquist. On the evening of the 27th [August], we crossed a bailey bridge at Vernon, put across by the divisional engineers. Because the bridge was under enemy observation and artillery fire we did another Formula One gallop. At dusk, we pulled up in a line [of scout and armoured cars] by the side of a road covered by a hedge. We laid up there until the morning – according to Ken Butler's diary, it rained all night.

I was awakened next morning by Lieutenant Neville Fellows with the words – 'come on Nobby, wake up and Happy Birthday, you mother's sent you a cake and it's your turn for guard duty!' It was my 21st birthday and it was a beautiful summer's morning as we advanced in line up the road. The tanks had passed us sometime during the night and were now engaging the enemy further up the road. They had received some sporadic fire from the field on our right, just off the road. There was no intelligence as to the strength of the enemy so RECCE was ordered forward to suss the place out. It was hard to picture a more peaceful scene than a harvested cornfield with the corn stacked in stooks all over the field.

We advanced about 500 yards off the road onto the edge of the field – all quiet then, suddenly, we came under rifle and MG fire. I saw Ozzy Spanton charging down one side of the field to our right, throwing hand grenades with great abandon, a sight to see. Suddenly, there was silence then, three enemy infantry appeared with a white flag. It was all so innocuous, like watching a film in the cinema.

I remember thinking that wasn't very hard. I saw Captain Bill Robb climb down out of his Humber Scout Car, (a vehicle I never liked, it could not reverse fast enough for my liking), to accept the surrender. Then, all hell broke loose, the whole field erupted with enemy small arms and he was severely wounded. Lieutenant Dickie jumped out to help. Bill Robb, died of his wounds, 'Slapper' Drake and Tommy Dakin were also killed.

Everyone was firing back at the enemy who could not be seen, they were dug in behind the corn stooks. So we withdrew to regroup. Ken Butler was to lead us from now on. The lesson to be learnt – this was an operation totally unsuitable for our resources. The Colonel sent tanks in to set fires and destroy the field. We rounded up and took 200 prisoners. My last memory was of Ben Johnson shepherding a shocked group of prisoners by shoving them forward with his scout car.

I will always remember my 21st Birthday...[35]

During the years of occupation, resistance to the invader had taken on some quixotic guises:

Mon Colonel,

At Lannoy, chief administrative point of the counties, comprising the north and the smallest town of France, the 5th Northumberland Fusiliers Regiment accompanied by their band, had established their HQ in May 1940 at the Chateau of Prevost, belonging to Mr. Requillart. The German attack in Belgium witnessed the departure of the regiment and their leaving with me, on the spot, a small number of men to guard the material and the musical instruments belonging to the regiment.

Following the hasty retreat, the robbery and stealing of May 1940, the arrival of the Germans at Lannoy, then the occupation of the chateau by these savages, as they were – the first Nazis broke up or destroyed all the materials of every kind, going so far as to put their bayonets through the drum. It is this drum that I, Maurice Wanin, manager and tenant of the Hotel de Vie, Café du Lannoy, was charged to look after. I had taken it into the chateau with the intention of hiding it from these brutes. I hid it very carefully until Liberation Day. I informed three British officers who were visiting our district who, in turn, informed the officer commanding their regiment.

This was, Mon Colonel, the story of the drum.

Please accept, Colonel, from an old soldier of the war of 1914–1918, the assurance of my sincerity and respect...

M. Wanin[36]

After further adventures and some bureaucratic meddling, the drum was re-united with the Fusiliers and safely returned home.

Though the terrible Battle for Normandy had ended in a resounding Allied victory, both key and decisive, the war was far from over. Pressure upon the Allied coalition was growing, partly due to supply difficulties and partly due to Montgomery's general boorishness. If Eisenhower was not a general of the first rank, he was a constant diplomat whose intemperate subordinate taxed his capacities to the very limit and increasingly beyond. Antwerp had been liberated but was not yet usable, the Scheldt Estuary remaining un-cleared. Monty came up with his masterstroke to end the war with a single massive thrust aimed at Germany's industrial heartland, the Ruhr. Operation *Market Garden* was breathtakingly audacious and ultimately seriously flawed.

For the Durhams of 151 Brigade, they would have their hour. They might have been denied Paris but they would have the honour of entering Brussels:

> We were moved north to take part in the liberation of Brussels, led by Guards Armoured Division, we went in on the back of their tanks. I'll never forget our reception, every building was bedecked, thousands of people waving, laughing and singing, it was a very emotional experience, we were very conscious these people regarded us as their personal liberators and personal heroes.[37]

Nobody could deny that the men of Durham, and from all those other British cities, towns and counties, had more than done their bit.

9

AND NOW

Call from Monty, 7pm, the Germans are surrendering, North and West Germany, Holland, Denmark and Norway – the news of the surrender was announced at 8pm on the BBC.

Eisenhower, diary entry, 4th May 1945

The French are our friends. The Germans are our enemies and the enemies of France. Remember that the Germans individually often behaved well in France. We have got to behave better ...[1]

William the Conqueror's great castle still dominates Caen, a delightful Normandy city. The twin abbeys holding, or which held, the mortal traces of the Bastard and his tiny, feisty consort, also survive. Much of the ancient city did not; it was flattened by Allied bombing and hard fighting. It's been rebuilt – just about everything that was devastated, and there was an awful lot of damage, has been reconstructed.

Normandy is almost back to what it was. The rolling rural and coastal region has small, solid villages; the beaches are languorous in summer and filled by holiday-makers; hotels, pensions and camping grounds abound. What has mainly gone is the bocage, that graveyard-shift network of ancient fields and hedges that the Allies, so very oddly, did not seem to have thought about or certainly not thought about enough. It all looks a lot easier today.

It's often hard to understand just how wasted this ground was by the time the Battle of Normandy reached its grand denouement in the *Ragnarök* at Falaise – another town where the great bulk of one of Duke William's citadels looms grandly over the pleasant streets. If you want to know what the whole area looked like just after D-Day, there's a wonderful 360 Degree Cinema above Arromanches, which uses a 'Circorama' presentation to create an immersive experience that fully reveals the extent of destruction.[2] It should be said that when visiting Normandy, Major and Mrs Holt's map and guide to the battlefields are invaluable; they combine succinct accounts of the build-up, all the action, with a comprehensive gazetteer.

I've been to Normandy many times conducting groups of all ages around the battlefield, including schools and MoD parties, who may have been enthralled or just mightily bored. Bayeux with its splendid Romanesque cathedral and busy thoroughfares, oddly reminiscent of 1960s English high streets, houses the great Tapestry, a wonderfully evocative reminder of an earlier, equally successful invasion; this time going the other way but every bit as much a game-changer. It's odd to think when walking the charming lanes and alleyways that thousands of young men from the north of England had this as their D-Day objective and how many of them left their bones along the road. The DVD presentation in the museum echoes the inscription on the war memorial that it was William's descendants who came back to liberate their ancient homeland.

It's best to avoid the anniversaries. The big ones are hard work. Coach-loads of increasingly frail veterans were there for the 65th in 2009; every year obviously there are fewer of them. On that occasion, there was a big re-creation of the landing at Arromanches, a re-enactors' Valhalla of vehicles and landing craft crowding the beaches. Jeeps and Harley-Davidsons blasted across the sand and belted along the narrow roads in sufficient numbers almost to rival the originals, driven lovingly by anoraks of varying ages, in full, pristine kit.

Getting down to the port on the day was a tour-guide's worst nightmare. The French police fully vindicated their reputation for sloth, inefficiency and indifference. It was one thing getting military traffic up away from the beach, getting the same men back down the hill sixty-five years later proved nearly as big a trial. A bus-load of assorted British Bobbies could finally endure no more and took over traffic management beneath the bemused, bored stares of the gendarmes and, from that point, matters improved. The then UK Prime Minister gave a speech in the harbour about as passionate as a school-day sermon, read in such a monotone it was as if Gordon Brown already knew the result of the next year's election.

The group of DLI and Light Infantry/Rifles veterans I was guiding enjoyed a more uplifting experience the day before, 5 June, at Omaha Cemetery, familiar to tens of thousands who've never actually been to one thanks to Steven Spielberg's *Saving Private Ryan*. The place is immaculate, a superb and mellow garden of remembrance with a state-of-the-art visitor centre that probably cost more than all the British memorials in Normandy combined. It's not as slushy as you'd expect; there's a bit but it's not Hollywood. On the day, our Brit veterans encountered President Obama preparing for a big address on the 6th. The place was heaving with Secret Service types in dark glasses, all fearful nobody would recognise their disguises, but the President took time to talk to our old soldiers and that was impressive.

Just west of Arromanches is Port-en-Bessin, the hinge of the US/UK offensives on 6 June 1944. Fortified by Vauban in 1694 as a defence against the English, it was the job of 47 (RM) Commando to take the port on D-Day+1. The place was well defended with gun pits and bunkers. The commandos had worked their way along the coast from Le Hamel, heavily weighed down with 90 pounds (41 kilos) of kit. It was a tough fight, helped by big guns from HMS *Emerald*. The marines secured their objectives and held on against determined counter-attacks, which claimed the life of their CO Captain T. F. Cousins.

What remains of those bunkers still straddles the rising ground east of the town and I have taken several school groups there. The enthusiastic pupils were ranging through the emplacements, trenches and strongpoints, unimpeded by Health and Safety warnings, hard hats, petty officials in fluorescent jackets armed with radios, sealed-off areas, or any of those modern restrictions.

As well as the vital hinge, Port-en-Bessin became the nodal point for the Petrol-Line Under-the-Ocean (PLUTO), one of the Allies' really good ideas. Mountbatten was credited with the idea and work had begun two years before. The flexible pipe laid at sea was towed over from Southampton in great 70-mile sections on vast 'cotton reels' named CONUNDRUMS. Fully wound, each of these weighed in at 1,600 tons which, as Major and Mrs Holt point out, was equal to the average weight of a destroyer.[3]

One of those who came ashore on the Calvados Coast was Maurice Pinkney who, after pre-war service with the Durham Militia, enlisted in the 7th Green Howards in July 1939. Maurice was to see much hard fighting, firstly in North Africa and then with 50th Division on Gold Beach. His experiences are recorded, in part at least, in verse:

In an English bay at peace we lay, on the second day in June,
And to fore and aft, there are thousands of craft. We'll be
    heading to France pretty soon.

The heart and soul of movement control lay in getting us
    down to the shore.
And the organisation and administration is better than ever
    before.
Here a naval Rover, our welfare takes over. He gives us our
    loading orders,
While up in the sky the RAF boys fly high and guard us from
    Jerry's marauders.
The troops are on board. Our vehicles are stored, and the
    captain yells 'Anchors aweigh.'

Then gently we slide with the outgoing tide, to take up our
    place in the bay.
Our orders we know. We wait the word, 'Go' then the world's
    biggest battle begins.
It will not be in vain. France must live again, and the Nazis
    must pay for their sins.

Maurice Pinkney: On the Way – June 1944

Though the cause was just, Maurice was not a great admirer of the sea or at least not of crossings in crowded troop ships:

Who longs for the sea? I can tell you, not me,
My experience has not just begun.
I've done many trips on various ships.
As a soldier it isn't much fun.

Now a sailor be frank, on landing ship tank,
As far as the Tommy's concerned,
Things are a bit flat. You'll agree about that.
And I'll swear something better we've earned.

As a typical sample, take this for example.
More than five hundred troops are on board.
The proverbial cat – no room to swing that.
You can't say one lives like a lord.

The accommodation and bed situation
Is six to one bed, 'tis quite true.
And the food that they right isn't fit for a pig.
No wonder the sailors wear blue.

At the signal for rally we dash to the galley
For biscuits and bully-beef stew,
Diced carrots and spuds, with a dash of soap suds,
And cold tea from yesterday's brew.

The next meal we get, the coffee is wet.
Our spirits are too but why worry.
We oft' wait for hours in hail, wind and showers.
But what of it. We ain't in no hurry.

The NAAFI – there's none, ship's library – no bon.
There isn't a book in the place.
Understand why I'm blue. There's nothing to do.
I'd sleep but I can't find a place.

But we'll probably grumble when onshore we stumble,
And wish we could move in reverse.
For we're landing in France and there's every chance
That conditions there will be worse.

The going is tough but we're made of the stuff
Of which all British soldiers are made of.
Though we grumble and rile in true British style,
There's not a damned thing we're afraid of.

So let's get at the Hun, Let's get the war won,
And let's get back to our loved ones at home.
Forget about war, have peace evermore,
So that never again need we roam.
Maurice Pinkney: *A Soldier's Cribb*

Like most soldiers, Maurice was not reflecting on grand strategy. His
thoughts were with Mary, his future wife; then serving as a nurse:

My heart is still in Winchester though I left there long ago.
I can still see the trees as they sway in the breeze, and the river
    so graceful and slow.
I can picture the blossoms blooming as I stroll in the cool
    twilight,
Inhaling perfume of the lilac in bloom and the scent of the
    flowers so bright.

There is also another attraction, a girl by the name of Mary.
She is lovely, attractive and twenty, and graceful as any fairy.
In a sheltered spot on the rolling downs we would sit and
    admire the view,
While deep in the woods a thrush would sing and the cuckoo
    would chant his 'cuckoo'.

Yes I saw it in sunny springtime, the happiest time of the year
When mating birds build their nests for two and romance was
    in the air.

But I'm sure had I seen it in autumn or under a cloak white
    as pearl
I would love it. If I could but stay there, stay always with
    Mary, my girl.
Maurice Pinkney: Looking Back – June 1944

France proved less congenial. Maurice recorded his experience of Normandy for his local newspaper the *Northern Echo* in 1994 for the 50th anniversary of D-Day:

> I felt it was an honour going back to France that day. Apart from the excitement I can't honestly say what our thoughts were that murky morning. Everything seemed to be such a mix-up yet order was automatic. Getting ashore was not so difficult, as it seemed Jerry was caught on the hop. The most anxious part was getting off the beach up a steep incline. We had to get forward, because there were thousands of people behind us – jostling and shoving like a football crowd. Once the defending forces got over the initial shock, they threw everything they had at the Allies, while thousands of Royal Navy shells screamed overhead in reply. I felt very vulnerable. It seemed that every bit of shrapnel, every bullet, every hand grenade or mine was meant for me. Being in a Bren gun carrier, I did at least have an inch of steel around me. The hardest part of any adventure of this kind was seeing a pal knocked over and not being able to help. One was drilled not to stop but let others following up deal with the casualties.

Maurice, tactfully for one who was courting a nurse, found time to pen an ode praising their contribution:

Folks say, 'Salute our Soldiers' who battle in the war.
They do not seek for glory but peace for evermore.

Why not, 'Salute our Nurses', now that we are well,
Who nursed our tortured bodies back from a living hell?

Let us speak in admiration of their mercy, faith and love.
Pray then in your heart of hearts, 'God bless them from above'.

This is just the humble thanks of a soldier once in your care.
I forever will remember to salute our nurses everywhere.
                    Maurice Pinkney: *Salute our Nurses – July 1944*

Maurice came safely home and married Mary. He died in
December 2003.[4]

After the German collapse and the mincer of the Falaise
Pocket, the whole of occupied France seemed to open up like a
ripe cheese. The Free French liberated Paris, whether Eisenhower
wished them to or not, and you can hardly blame Leclerc: who
wouldn't want to free Europe's most civilised city from the most
barbarous of occupiers? The war might be over by Christmas,
but it wasn't. Von Rundstedt, re-instated by a desperate Fuhrer,
pulled off the 'Miracle in the West'. Monty's great big idea to
launch a lightning thrust across the rivers to break into the
Reich by the underbelly of the industrial Ruhr proved just one
bridge too far. Hitler wasn't quite done and launched the great
Ardennes counter-offensive in December. The Battle of the Bulge
proved a chimera, a costly failure and in the spring Monty
crossed the Rhine.

Dresden had already been swallowed by the flames of the
firestorm, though the controversy keeps on igniting. In April,
the Brits liberated Belsen; in the West, news-reel audiences saw,
for the first time, the hideous depths of inhumanity they'd been
fighting against. That helped the case for bombing Dresden but
it was the Russians who took Berlin and flew their flag from the
scarred shell of the Reichstag. The Second World War in Europe
was over and the next one could get started.

It could be said D-Day and the Battle for Normandy were key
to Allied victory in the war. If the Germans had been able to throw
the British, Canadians, Americans, Poles and Free French back into
the sea, it would have been a long time, a very long time perhaps,
before a second attempt, and that gap would have given Hitler
time to massively upgrade the Atlantic Wall. Without Normandy,
the Germans could have moved forces east to counter the Russian
offensive and maybe have even held the line there. But that didn't
happen; the Allied airborne, infantry, commandos and all forces

who took part made sure it didn't. By their courage and sacrifice they made the plan work, not perfectly for sure but in the end it did work; they cleared Normandy and opened the road to Paris and beyond, the road to Berlin. Our indebtedness to them all is immeasurable.

I wanted to beg you to stay; instead I smoothed my apron and watched you walk away.

I wanted to fall down on my knees and cry and scream and plead and plead and plead,

Instead I boiled water, made tea while you fastened braces, polished boots, shone buttons.

'I'm more likely to die down that bloody pit' you said, we both knew it wasn't true.

'This is our way out, our chance to get away, from the grime and the dirt and the same places/faces day after day.'

You always thought you were better than our little town, where we grew up side by side,

Always the tallest, strongest, fastest and bravest lad at school, born for better things.

I knew you all my life, loved you since we were fifteen, and now I had to say goodbye.

'It's not for long love' you said 'we will all be home by Christmas love' you kissed me, held my gaze with those blue, blue eyes and turned and walked away.

I held that image in my mind till this day, you striding down the street, proud to be in khaki, prouder still of the red cap covering your sandy blond hair.

Played it over and over in my mind over the years, wondered if I could have changed things in any way.

Seventy-five years to the day I watched you stroll down our street round the corner, gone.

I'm old now Johnny, and now at last, I hope, soon, to see you again.

Samantha Kelly; *Waiting*

GLOSSARY

AA – Anti-aircraft

AFV – Armoured Fighting Vehicle

ANCEF – Allied Naval Commander Expeditionary Force

AP – Armour Piercing

AA - Anti-aircraft

AT – Anti-tank

AWOL – Absent Without Leave

Bde – Brigade

BEF – British Expeditionary Force

Bivvy – Bivouac

Bocage – typical Norman small, enclosed, high-banked fields

GIGS – Chief of the Imperial General Staff

C-in-C – Commander in Chief

CO – Commanding Officer

COSSAC – Chief of Staff to Supreme Allied Commander

Coy – Company

CP – Command Post

CSM – Company Sergeant-Major

CWGC – Commonwealth War Graves Commission

DCM – Distinguished Conduct Medal

DD – Duplex Drive – 'swimming' tanks

Defilade – protection by or shielding from hostile ground, observation and flat projecting fire offered by any artificial or natural obstacle, such as a hill or rise

'Delousing' – minefield clearance
Div – Division
DLI – Durham Light Infantry
DSO – Distinguished Service Order
DUKW – amphibious vehicle
Enfilade – gunfire directed along a line from end to end
ENSA – Entertainments National Service Association
FANY – First Aid Nursing Yeomanry
FAP – Forward Aid Post
Flak – anti-aircraft fire
FOO – Forward Observation Officer
GOC – General Officer Commanding
HE – High Explosive
HQ – Headquarters
IO – Intelligence Officer
Kamerad – a shout of surrender, used by German soldiers; *kamerad*
    means comrade.
KOSB – King's Own Scottish Borderers
LCA – Landing Craft Assault
LCF – Landing Craft Flak
LCG – Landing Craft Gun
LCI (large or small) – Landing Craft Infantry
LCM – Landing Craft Mechanised
LCR – Landing Craft Rocket
LCT – Landing Craft Tank
LCVP – Landing Craft Vehicle and Personnel
LOOB – Left out of battle
LRC – Regiment de Chaudiere
LST – Landing Craft Tank
Luftwaffe – German Air Force
MC – Military Cross
MG – Machine gun
MiD – Mentioned in Dispatches
MM – Military Medal
MO – Medical Officer
MP – Military Police
NAAFI/EFI – Navy, Army and Air Force Institutes/Expeditionary
    Forces Institute

NCO – Non-commissioned Officer
O Group – Orders Group
OB West – *Oberkommando West* – Supreme Command West
OH – Official History
OKH – *Oberkommand des Heeres*
OKW – *Oberkommand der Wehrmacht*
OP – Observation Post
Ost – Scratch battalions formed from Russian POWs
Panzerfaust – German style of bazooka
PIAT – Projector Infantry Anti-tank
QM – Quartermaster
RA – Royal Artillery
RAF – Royal Air Force
RAP – Regimental Aid Post
RAC – Royal Armoured Corps
RAOC – Royal Army Ordnance Corps
RASC – Royal Army Service Corps
RCAMC – Royal Canadian Army Medical Corps
RE – Royal Engineers
Regt – Regiment
REME – Royal Engineers Mechanical Engineers
RMC – Royal Marine Commando
RN – Royal Navy
RNF – Royal Northumberland Fusiliers
RSM – Regimental Sergeant-Major
RTR – Royal Tank Regiment
Scarper – Disorganised and precipitate retreat; verging on rout
Schnellboot – German motor torpedo boat
SIW – Self-inflicted Wound
SOE – Special Operations Executive
SP – Self-propelled; refers to artillery, effectively as field gun
    housed in a tank-like hull
TA – Territorial Army
USAAF – United States Army Air Force
WD – War Department
WO – Warrant Officer
W/T – Wireless telegraphy
VC – Victoria Cross

APPENDICES

i. Orders of Battle, British Airborne Operations; Orders of Battle, Sword Beach; Orders of Battle, Juno Beach; Orders of Battle Gold Beach

Airborne
GOC: Major-General R. N. Gale, 6th Airborne Division
3rd Parachute Brigade
5th Parachute Brigade

Sword
GOC: Major-General T. G. Rennie, 3rd British Division
8th Infantry Brigade Group
13th/18th Hussars DD Tanks
1st South Lancashire Regiment
2nd East Yorkshire Regiment
Bombarding Force D: Battleships HMS *Warspite, Ramillies* and *Roberts*; Cruisers HMS *Mauritius, Arethusa, Frobisher, Danal* and *Dragon* (Polish); 13 destroyers including HNMS *Svenner* (Norwegian).

Juno
GOC: Major-General R. F. L. Keller, 3rd Canadian Division
6th Armoured Regiment (1st Hussars) DD Tanks
The Royal Winnipeg Rifles
The Regina Rifle Regiment

10th Armoured Regiment (Fort Gary Horse) DD Tanks
The Queen's Own Rifles of Canada
The North Shore (New Brunswick) Regiment
Bombarding Force E: Cruisers HMS *Belfast* and *Diadem*;
11 destroyers including FFS *Combattante*

Gold
GOC: Major-General D. A. H. Graham, 50th (Northumbrian)
Division
8th Armoured Brigade DD Tanks
6th Battalion The Green Howards
5th Battalion East Yorkshire Regiment
1st Battalion Dorset Regiment
1st Battalion Royal Hampshire Regiment
Bombarding Force K: Cruisers HMS *Orion, Ajax, Argonaut,
Emerald,* HNMS *Flores* (Dutch); 13 destroyers including
Krakowiak (Polish)

ii. The legend of Bill Millin

The sighing surf on sand abounds, and seabirds call, the only
    sounds
At break of summers day, and yet, within the hour men will
    have met
Their destiny as war's shrill chatter ends this tranquil scene.
    The clatter
Of machine guns spit their hate, as landing craft nose in to
    grate
Against the shingle to disgorge their human load who wait
    to charge
Into oncoming deathly hail, but never faltering, nerves taut,
    pale
Faced, leaping down into the cold wet breakers, seeking firm
    foothold.

Struggling forward, arms raised clear to gain refuge ahead,
    so near
And yet seeming so far away as spiteful guns traverse and spray

The killing ground that lies ahead, already littered with the
    dead
And dying who would never see this bitter, bloody victory.
Then faintly, through the deafening din, an alien sound is
    heard, the thin
Melodious wailing cry of Highland pipes, though bullets fly
Around him, he is unscathed still. Thus starts the tale of
    Piper Bill.

Bill, who piped for Brigadier Lord Lovat, raised a special
    cheer
When, leaving on the previous day, took up his pipes, began
    to play
Road to the Isles, as, leaving Hamble River for this costly
    gamble,
Lifting spirits of the men, calling, cheered and cheered again,
Who as the Solent slipped away, all knew that on the
    following day
They'd face their own worst fears and doubts, prayed that
    when it came about.

They would stand firm and conquer fear to face the perils that
    appeared.
And now, amid the smoke and roar of high explosives, Bill
    endures
The hail of death, which all around leaves him untouched,
    while yet the sound
Of *Highland Laddie* fills the air as fingers on the chanter dare
To still defy the lethal storm, this awesome hell in all its forms.
Yet death and wholesale demolition, backdrop to this
    exhibition
Of the art of Scottish piping, even with the bullets sniping,
Will not quiet this hardy Scot, surviving mortar shell and shot.

He marches at the water's edge, still playing, able still to
    dredge
From deep within his mortal soul the courage to maintain
    and hold

Himself upright despite the urge to run for safety, then emerge
When all is still and quiet again, escape the trauma and the
     pain.
But Bill is made of sterner stuff, clutching his pipes he starts
     to puff
And fill the bag, then with a squeeze, his hands again with
     practiced ease
Launch into yet another air, lifting spirits everywhere.

And so the legend now is born, as Bill continues to perform
Beyond this strip of golden sand known as Sword Beach,
     where many men
Have fallen, sacrificed their all in answering their country's
     call,
But in this page of history this part of France will always be
Where Highland Bagpipes did their part with inspiration, and
     gave heart
To all who witnessed Bill that day, who, when he crossed that
     beach to play,
With all his great panache and poise, gave the Highland Pipes
     their voice.

     Tony Church; *the Legend of Bill Millin – D-Day Piper.*
This poem was written in 2011. Millin had, in fact, died the
year before.

iii. *Combined Operations Staff Study – period 2nd–14th October 1944; Operations* Neptune *and* Overlord – *an account of the Operations of Force 'G' and 50(N) Division in the Assault on Normandy – June 1944 (by kind courtesy of the Green Howards Museum Trust)*

This remarkable document was compiled by the Green Howards
and was, in fact, rescued from a skip by the regimental museum
curator! Fortunately, it survives now in the museum archives.

The object of Operation *Overlord* was to secure a lodgement on
the Continent of Europe from which further operations could
be developed. The general intention of the operation was:

(a)   To carry out airborne landings during the night of
      D -1 & D-day

(b)   To assault a five divisional front with three British and
      two US Divisions in landing ships between Varreville
      and Ouistreham in the bay of the Seine, early on D-day.

(c)   To land two follow-up divisions, one British and one US,
      later on D-day and D-day+1.

(d)   Thereafter to build up our forces at the average rate of
      one and a third divisions per day

The task of securing a bridgehead on the Continent was
entrusted to 21st Army Group who assaulted with 1st US
Army on the right and 2nd British Army on the left. C in C
21st Army Group worked with ANCEF at a combined HQ
established on the south coast of England. In the Eastern
Task Force area, 2nd British Army assaulted with 30 Corps
on the right and 1st Corps on the left. The divisions actually
carrying out the assault were 50th Division under 30 Corps
and 3rd British and 3rd Canadian under 1st Corps.

Defences of 'King' Sector

As an example of the problems facing the [50th] Division,
the following is a detailed description of the defended
localities in King Sector area of La Riviere, which was to be
assaulted by 69th Infantry brigade. It was decided that these
nine localities required destroying or neutralising prior to
the landing:

(a)   A section post on the right edge of King Sector centring
      on a 5cm A/T gun in a concrete shelter. This gun was
      sited to fire along the beaches in either direction. The
      seaward face of the concrete shelter was blanked off.

(b)   An MG position was located in the centre of King Sector
      at the junction of 'Red' & 'Green' Beaches.

(c)   At the western end of the village of La Riviere, there
      was a very strongly defended position well-sited and
      including an 88mm gun, a 5cm gun and several MGs.
      The 88mm gun was in a very heavily constructed

concrete casemate. It was sited so as to fire along the beaches with a traverse of not more than 25 degrees to seaward and was so placed as to be invisible from seaward, and this offered no aiming point to the assaulting artillery.

(d)   The central sector of the village was defended by infantry but not heavily.

(e)   A MG position at the eastern end of the seafront at La Riviere.

(f)   Normal field fortifications not considered to be occupied but bombarded as a safety precaution.

(g)   Mont Fleury Battery – 4 x 155mm guns.

(h)   A well constructed and well sited infantry position 600 yards (550 metres) behind the western edge of the village.

(i)   Ver-sur-Mer Battery – 4 x 155mm guns.

A similar set of defences existed in the 'Jig' Sector to be assaulted by 231 Infantry Brigade.

Conclusions

The following statements can be made:

(a)   The degree of surprise achieved more than offset the disadvantage of carrying out the passage and the landing in rough weather.

(b)   The heavy preliminary bombardment, although it did not effect a great deal of material damage, achieved the desired result of neutralising the enemy batteries by the effects on the defenders.

(c)   Although un-cleared and causing fairly extensive damage to incoming craft, the underwater obstacles were not so dense or effective as to jeopardise the operation.

(d)   The system of naval control of the beaches and of the repair and recovery of damaged are points of major importance in the planning of combined operations.

iv. The Green Howards on D-Day – 6th June 1944 (by kind courtesy of the Green Howards Museum Trust)

THE GREEN HOWARDS ON D DAY – 6th June 1944

The Longest Day – The Invasion of France, hour by hour

June 5th
1800 hrs A seaborne invasion force of five Allied assault groups, consisting of 130,000 men, leaves the English coast travelling through prepared channels cleared by minesweepers.

June 6th
0005 hrs German coastal batteries between Le Havre and Cherbourg are bombed by Allied aircraft as part of the deception plan.

0020 hrs British airborne troops secure Pegasus Bridge, over the Caen canal and other bridges over the River Orne.

0430 hrs US airborne troops capture St Mere Eglise and secure roads leading up to Utah beach.

0500 hrs 9th Parachute Regiment destroy guns at Merville Battery thus protecting troops who will be landing at Sword Beach.

0530 hrs Allied warships begin bombardment of the Normandy coastline and landing craft leave mother ships bound for the shore.

0600 hrs Allied bombers pound the German shore defences. More than 5,300 tons of bombs dropped.

0630 hrs American troops begin landing on Omaha beach and face devastating German fire, which pins them down until 1100 hrs. Americans begin landing at Utah beach.

0730 hrs British troops land at Gold Beach (including 6th and 7th Green Howards) and Sword Beach.

0735 hrs Canadian troops land at Juno Beach.

0900 **hrs** General Eisenhower the Supreme Commander of *Operation Overlord* authorises a communiqué announcing that the invasion of France has begun.

1100 **hrs** The British and Canadian troops secure the beachhead on Gold, Juno and Sword beaches.

1200 **hrs** Winston Churchill, the Prime Minister, speaks to the House of Commons about the landings.

1330 **hrs** Troops on Utah and Omaha beaches begin to secure the beachhead.

1430 **hrs** The German *21st Panzer Division* unleashes a counterattack towards the coast.

1600 **hrs** The British secure the coastal town of Arromanches so that the Mulberry Harbour can be laid to facilitate rapid disembarkation.

1800 **hrs** Leading elements of 69 Brigade (7th Green Howards) approach the Caen-Bayeaux Road to the south; their objective for the day.

2000 **hrs** Allied patrols at the outskirts of Bayeux.

2300 **hrs** All the beaches are secure. By the end of the day the Allies had disembarked 135,000 men and had bridgeheads of varying depths along the Normandy coastline. By sunset a total of 10,000 men had been killed, wounded or reported missing.

WAR DIARY   *Unit:* 6 Bn The Green Howards
Month and Year: June 1944

Place	Date	Hour	Summary of Events and Information
Southampton	1&2		A, B, C and D Companies safely aboard L.S.I's (Landing Ship Infantry) in SOUTHAMPTON WATER. A/Tk and Carrier Platoons still in marshalling area near ROMSEY awaiting embarkation
Southampton	3	2300	A/Tk and Carrier Platoons moved to SOUTHAMPTON from Camp 13 arriving at dawn to embark.
Southampton	4	1000	Specialists Platoons and personnel embarked on L.C.Ts. (Landing Craft Tanks) The weather is not too good and the sea 'choppy'.

This rather laconic report in the war diary of the 6th Green Howards hides the story of the build-up of a massive invasion fleet, consisting of more than 6,300 ships and landing craft, along the south coast of England. It also hides the fact that the 6th Battalion was just a small part of a 130,000 strong invasion force about to assault the coast of Normandy in France. But for the men cramped aboard the waiting ships, it was the appalling weather and choppy seas that mattered most, causing seasickness, delay, boredom and anti-climax.

It was an unhappy culmination of months of combined operation training alongside 7th Green Howards and 5th East Yorkshires, as part of 69 Brigade of the 38,000 strong 50 (Northumbrian) Division, initially in Inverary, Scotland, in February, then in Boscombe Bay in March and around Winchester and Romsey during April and May, which had reached fever-pitch, with brigade live-firing exercises on Salisbury Plain.

Since mid-May the men had been closeted in Camp C13 and 14 just to the north-east of Romsey, which meant that, for security reasons, no one was allowed in or out. Barbed wire, several coils thick, surrounded the camp, which was entirely under canvas. American military policemen patrolled outside the wire with orders to shoot first and ask questions afterwards. It had been a difficult time for all the troops.

> During the last two weeks in May, briefing commenced with sand table models, maps and aerial photographs being used but with bogus place names. Each German slit trench was marked with the weapons that fired from it and its arc of fire. Minefield data was similarly comprehensive, including the number of rows and number of mines in each row. To compensate for being confined to camp, an extensive cinema and entertainment bill was organised which was very popular.
>
> *Captain J. B. E. Franklyn*
> *C Company, 6th Battalion*

Although initially the men were rather disgruntled to be chosen to be in the invasion after two-and-a-half years' fighting through the Western Desert and Sicily, they were now rather proud to belong to the only English county regiment to have two battalions in the assault wave.

On 5 June, the War Diary reported:

Today should have been 'D' Day with 'H' Hour at 0735 hrs, but owing to adverse weather conditions, the landing has been postponed for 24 hrs.

At 04.15 hours on 4 June, General Dwight D. Eisenhower – the Supreme Commander of *Operation Overlord* – based at SHAEF (Supreme Headquarters Allied Expeditionary Force) in Southwick House, some 5 miles to the north of Portsmouth, had made the decision to postpone the invasion for 24 hours. He had already decreed 5 June as 'D' Day and sent out his final message to the 'Soldiers, Sailors and Airman of the Allied Expeditionary Force' (*see* below). His meteorological team had informed him that the weather was deteriorating and that the rough seas in the English Channel would last a further few days before any hope of clearance.

Postponing the invasion carried many risks. The 130,000 soldiers in the first two waves of the assault risked losing their edge; for five days they were cramped in the invasion ships. The possibility of German reconnaissance flights sighting the invasion fleet and bringing in heavy bombers would increase, therefore, secrecy was paramount. The deception plan to make the Germans believe the invasion would take place between Ostend and Boulogne might also be compromised. All depended on a break in the weather in the English Channel and the coast of Normandy. If conditions did not improve, the tides and moonlight would be wrong and the invasion would have to be postponed for two weeks. Any hope of total surprise and complete success would be lost.

It was another setback and disappointment for the soldiers of the 6th Battalion crammed aboard the 10,000 ton LSI (Landing Ship Infantry) *Empire Lance*. This American-built ship was brand new and well fitted, with a crew who could not have been kinder and more helpful to the men about to face the most critical moment of their lives. Slung from her davits were two tiers of 14 LCAs (Landing Craft Assault) for the infantry to be despatched to the invasion shore. Green Howards had repeatedly practised climbing down scrambling nets hung down the side of the ship to enter the LSAs in preparation for the assault on the beaches. However, in high seas this manoeuvre would be highly dangerous to men loaded with their assault weapon, ammunition and equipment.

Group Captain Stagg, the chief meteorologist at SHAEF, again reported to the Supreme Commander on the afternoon of Monday 5 June. There could well be an improvement in the weather on the following day. Eisenhower, under immense pressure, gave the decision to go ahead. On board the *Empire Lance*, the Senior Naval Transport Officer spoke on the ship's tannoy at 1700 hours and announced:

> At 1745 hours this ship will weigh anchor and, in passage with the remainder of the armada, will sail for the coast of France.

The largest sea-borne invasion in history had begun.

> We started off at dusk on the 5th, in the throes of a howling gale, and I must say the sight of the rest of our convoy seemed most disappointing. The invasion of Sicily had shown an immense display of sea-might and now all I saw was perhaps 12 troop ships, a few tank landing craft and a destroyer or two amid the mounting waves.
>
> Captain G. M. Wilson
> Signals Officer, 7th Battalion.

Just before midnight, the roar of aircraft could be heard by the soldiers and sailors in the armada as more than 1,200 aircraft flew overhead. Three airborne divisions, including the 12th (Yorkshire) Parachute Battalion recently formed from the 10th Green Howards in May 1943, were heading to the east of the River Orne. They were to drop by parachute to secure the left flank of General Bernard Montgomery's 2nd Army, which was now en route for Gold, Juno and Sword beaches on the coast of Normandy.

As dawn broke, the whole Battalion had already breakfasted as a result of an early reveille at 0315 hours. Few men had slept during the night because of the heavy swell and anticipation of what lay ahead. When they went on deck to their muster stations, they could see a vast armada of ships on each side of them and ahead were aware of flashes on the horizon, where Allied bombers were engaging enemy coastal batteries. Until the time they had set sail, few knew the exact destination of the invasion force, nor the names of their individual objectives.

Maps had been issued down to platoon commander level and now the objectives on the sand models at the various briefings began to make sense. For 50 Division, it was to be 'Jig' and 'King' Sectors of Gold Beach between the hamlet of Le Hamel to the west and the small village of La Riviere to the east. In 'King' Sector, the 5th East Yorkshires were to take La Riviere whilst the 6th Battalion were to cross the beaches and capture the Mont Fleury battery. These large series of concrete bunkers guarding German artillery were situated to the immediate west of La Riviere, almost half-a-mile inland from the shore, beyond a house with a circular drive in front of it. 7th Green Howards were to be in reserve and land at 0815 hours, then follow through the 6th Battalion's position once they had captured the small hamlet of Ver-sur-Mer (*see* map). From there, the battalions of 69 Brigade were to advance on Crépon, Creully and reach the main Bayeux to Caen road some 9 miles inland. It was hoped they would reach this road by dusk, but that all depended on getting safely across the beaches onto higher ground and destroying the coastal defences.

The enemy defences consisted roughly of a strongpoint of five to seven pillboxes with machine guns and one with a 105 mm gun on the right of the battalion front, a coastal battery of four 150mm guns and its own local defences on the left, with about 600 yards inland, a line of shelters and fire trenches from which machine guns could fire ... there were a number of beach obstacles including floating mines and mines on stakes to be negotiated by the navy. The battalion front was about 900 yards long and the depth of our initial attack was rather under

2000 yards, although arrangements had to be made to attack a position believed to be a rocket site about 3000 yards inland.

Lt Col R. H. W. S. Hastings
Commanding, 6th Green Howards

The *Empire Lance* reached her lowering position for the assault craft at 0500 hours, approximately 7 miles from the shore. The LCAs were then lowered from their derricks into the heavy swell. Landing craft do not stand much buffeting against the side of a rolling ship and occasionally the ropes got tangled and some craft took more than 20 minutes to reach the turbulent surface of the sea below. This caused delay.

Well, we had to go down scrambling nets into the landing craft and the sea was rough and the landing craft coming up and down. It was a bit awkward getting down with our equipment. We had big Bren pouches sticking out and rifle butts and Sten gun butts, and I can remember going down those nets and thinking to myself 'There must be easier ways of earning a living than this.' However we got in the landing craft – about 18 to 20 men to a boat – and cast off from our transport: 'The Empire Lance', and we cruised round and round in circles until the whole company was afloat and then we set off in line abreast for the shore

CSM S. E. Hollis
D Company, 6th Battalion

The soldiers of both the 6th and 7th Green Howards then had to spend two very uncomfortable hours in their landing craft as the marines and sailors, steering the LCAs, got them into formation for the landing on the coast. Most got very wet and some were horribly seasick. It was a misty morning and it was difficult to see the objectives on the shore as the landing craft rose and fell in the swell, and buffeting waves sent spumes of water over the metal ramps in front of the vessels.

Leading the assault were teams of Royal Engineers who were to dismantle the mines and lay tape for safe passage for the two squadrons of amphibious Sherman tanks from the 4th/7th Dragoon

Guards. They were to be closely followed by LCTs carrying tanks with flails to smash onto enemy mines dug into the beach and some tanks carrying fascine rolls to drop into shell holes or tank trenches. The landing craft of the leading elements of the 5th East Yorkshires were to the immediate left of A and D Companies, which had B and C Companies behind them (*see* diagram).

The naval bombardment was excellent. HMS *Warspite*, standing a mile out at sea, sent salvoes that sounded more like an express train thundering over our heads. Cruisers and destroyers joined in the bombardment. Landing Craft Guns (LCGs) carrying 25 pounders fired all the while as they steamed ashore. Rocket ships, which came within 100 yards of the shore, sent off four salvos a minute of 90 rockets each. Preceding the leading waves of assault troops came the DD (Duplex Drive) Tanks in their hundreds. These tanks had air-inflated cushions attached to them and propellers to drive them ashore, the tanks firing as they did so.

Captain J. B. E. Franklyn
C Company, 6th Battalion

At Sea	6	0535	As the great armada of ships approach the French Coast in the dull mist of the dawn, many flashes can be seen from the coastline as Allied bombers and fighter-bombers fly in to engage enemy shore batteries
Area Map Ref 9186		0710	A, B, C, D Companies and Bn HQ safely aboard the LCAs made their hazardous dash for the mainland in a sea that did not favour such an important landing, whilst Allied cruisers and destroyers heavily engaged enemy shore batteries.
France sheet7/E/S 1:50,000		0735	'H' Hour

CSM Stan Hollis later recorded that during the previous evening on board the *Empire Lance*, his Company Commander, Major Ronnie Lofthouse, had given him a square box and said 'Give one of these each to the men, Sergeant Major.' When Stan opened the box, he saw it was full of condoms. 'Well,' I said, 'What are we going to do? Are we going to fight them or fuck them?' The condoms were to cover and waterproof the muzzles of the rifles, Bren and Sten guns. In the water-lashed landing craft and in the waist deep water off the shore, they proved their worth.

It took us about an hour and a quarter to get to the shore – the LCAs doing about 5 knots. After we had been in the landing craft for about half-an-hour everything in the world opened up behind us. Twenty-five pounders firing off loading platforms, other floating platforms firing thousands of rockets in one salvo and cruisers and destroyers firing, everything opened up.

As we were coming in, I was standing in front of the vessel and saw this shelter ... I thought it was a pillbox. As we were coming in I lifted a stripped Lewis gun off the floor of the landing craft and belted the thing with a full pan of ammunition. It was then that I received the most painful wound of the war. As I lifted the barrel off, it was white hot and I got a bloody great blister right across my hand. It was as big as a finger and was very painful. On reaching the high water mark we lost one of our very important officers. We lost Major Jackson, the Beach-master. He was the man that was supposed to say: 'Right, you go that way, and you go this way.' So we dashed over the beach. We ran up to the top were there was just rolled wire and believe it or not there were two or three birds sat on the wire. An Irishman, Mullally, alongside me said 'No bloody wonder they are there, Sergeant Major, there's no room in the air for them.' He was killed a few minutes later.

CSM S. E. Hollis
D Company, 6th Battalion

One of the leading officers ashore was the Beach-master, whose task was to direct the men and later the transport in the right direction, as well as report back progress to higher authorities. Major Richard Jackson, Support Company Commander, had been selected by the Commanding Officer for this important role.

When we jumped out there were no bullets. The beach was apparently still deserted. The water was only about a foot deep and I quickly advanced up the beach, flanked by a radio operator and a regimental policeman carrying a Sten gun. At every step, we were expected to be fired at but were not. The lack of opposition became eerie. Then after about 200 yards, we must have reached a German fixed line. Suddenly they threw everything at us. The mortars took us first and I was badly hit in the leg. My radio operator and the policeman were both killed outright by the same explosion. The radio was intact and for a while I helped troop movements. Two waves of infantry passed me by. After a time the field of fire receded. The tide came in, icy cold. Badly wounded, it seemed absurd to die in inch of water. An RMP sergeant from my home town saved me and carried me to a sand dune where I lay all day.

Major R .J. L. Jackson
Beach-master, 6th Battalion

Not all the men in landing craft had such a smooth landing. Some mistakenly lowered their ramps too soon before reaching the sand on the beach.

The doors of the craft opened, the ramp went down ... this was it. Sergeant William Hill (nicknamed Rufty), my best mate, was first to go followed by two privates, whose names I can't recall. This was the last I saw of them. The landing craft had not run aground and they were sucked under and drowned. Rufty had got out at Dunkirk a few years earlier and had been through all the battles in the western desert and Sicily, now he was dead without even getting ashore.

Private J. Williams
Bren Gunner, A Company, 6th Battalion

A Company, under the inspirational leadership of Major Freddie Honeyman, had landed just to the west of La Riviere – the objective of 5th East Yorkshires. Their task was to destroy seven small pillboxes, which were covering the beaches with machine guns and 105mm gunfire. Supported by tanks from the 4/7th Dragoon Guards, A Company took them, one by one, but were held up by the enemy, who threw grenades at them over a 6 foot wall and fired Spandaus at them from the flank. Major Honeyman, although wounded in both arms and legs from mortar shrapnel, with Lance Corporal Joyce and Sergeant Prenty, jumped over the wall and by using grenades and Sten guns destroyed the enemy, thus clearing the beach of small arms fire.

> When we touched down, we had had about 60 yard of wading to do before reaching the sand. The assaulting Companies were almost clear of the beach. The enemy, who by this time had really woken up to what was afoot, threw everything they had at the high water mark. My Company came in for a very sticky time of it. Our Company Commander, Captain Jack Linn, was hit in the leg halfway up the beach but continued to direct operations from the sitting position until hit again and killed. A very great loss to us all; he was an exceptionally gallant and popular Company Commander. Our 2ic, Captain Chambers, assumed command, even though he had been hit heavily in the back of the head and was bleeding profusely.
>
> Once we reached the cover of the dunes at the top end of the beach, we were immune from fire. A check of the Company showed fairly heavy casualties. In my Platoon, I had lost 12 out of 33. This was rather shattering at so early a stage. Fortunately, the other platoons were not so heavily hit.
>
> Captain J. B. E. Franklyn
> C Company, 6th Battalion

As the second wave landed, D Company was assaulting the Mont Fleury battery. Two of the pillboxes, in front of the battery, had been captured single-handedly by CSM Hollis in the first of two actions (described elsewhere in the magazine) of supreme gallantry which earned him the only VC awarded for bravery on D-Day.

We were landed at exactly the right place and we had hit no obstacles. We were very, very lucky. When the ramp went down we saw the house with the circular drive ahead of us – just where we were supposed to be – and we went slightly to the left of this; D Company having gone straight for it. On the beach we saw huge signs in German about the mines but we just had to go through there. No one struck a mine, so whether the signs were untrue or we were dead lucky, I don't know. Yes, there had been flail tanks there but we couldn't literally follow their tracks inland off the beach, we could only move up a lane across a road leading to the house with the circular drive. It seemed to me that there was no confusion; there were so few of us, our other companies being ahead. There were just tanks, flail tanks and us. We went round the side of the neutralised pillbox and saw wounded Germans gasping for water and the temptation was to stop, but, of course, there was a fear they might put a gun on you or a bayonet. But, anyway, we didn't have the time to stop.

2nd Lieutenant J. Milton
B Company, 6th Battalion

The four assault companies had landed exactly on time, at 0735 hours and 0750 hours, at the correct locations, thanks to the skill of the marines and sailors driving the LCAs. The 7th Battalion in reserve, who were to follow-up and were to land 45 minutes later, were still some way out at sea. They were not so lucky, as the tide turned and the sailors had difficulty in maintaining their positions as the current took them further to the west. They could see the progress of A and D Companies in the first wave, which landed some 5 minutes after the tanks had touched down at H Hour (0730 hrs). They also saw B and C Companies in the second wave, which had landed 15 minutes later. But, soon, the two guide markers of La Riviere to the left, and the house with the circular drive, to the right, were being obscured by smoke and explosions.

Major Claude Macdonald-Hull MC, who was second-in-command of the 6th Battalion, with two signallers and a runner, was aboard the main signal ship. This was a small craft carrying nothing but high-powered wireless sets, some 600 yards from the shore. On this craft, he was in direct communication with the higher military and naval commanders, both afloat and in England; the RAF above; and with the Battalion ashore on the assault beaches. It fell to Major Macdonald-Hull's lot to report that the 6th Battalion had taken its first objectives 48 minutes after landing. 'I doubt whether the Green Howards have ever received such heartfelt congratulations from the Navy, as when this piece of news came through,' he reported. This news was received in London a few minutes later. Shortly after this, Major Macdonald-Hull and his small party landed and soon rejoined the battalion, now almost a mile inland.

As he landed, the 7th Battalion, who had been in reserve, were making their way onto the beaches, but not quite in the right location as the current had swept them further to the west.

The Battalion landed about 400 yards to the right of the intended beach. We moved along the water's edge to the correct position and many men were still being sick or trying to find their 'land legs'. What a war! We moved inland beyond La Riviere and were shot at from close range and then, from some high ground, we could clearly see some German soldiers dismantling a machine gun. Dispersed them quickly with the excellent Bren and passed on. The sun came out – it was warmer weather than we had experienced for some time. My battle dress was drying nicely and steaming. My cigarettes, although in a tin carried safely through North Africa and Sicily, were ruined; brown and ugh! We came to a farm – roses climbing over the buildings. Cattle dead, legs stiff and pointing skywards. Farm searched and six German soldiers found cowering in the outhouse.

Major R. H. E. Hudson
OC B Company, 7th Green Howards

It merely remained to jump off into four feet of water and wade ashore, a task none too easy with full kit. It rather reminded me of surf bathing in north Cornwall, though I would say it was not quite so enjoyable as that popular pastime. In getting ashore, I slipped on a small rock and fell onto a mined pole. Either it was a dud or the frogmen had dealt with it and saved my life, as all I received was a cut on the hand from a completely dead mine of the Teller family. I was on French soil at last. Our task was to clear the beaches and proceed as far as the main Bayeaux to Caen road and the Brest to Paris railway, parallel to the road, about seven to eight miles inland.

Captain G. M. Wilson
Signals Officer, 7th Battalion.

Soon the two leading companies of the 7th Battalion, B and C, were in Ver-sur-Mer. They found the coastal battery there had already been knocked out and that all C Company had to do was to round up about 50 prisoners, whom they sent back to the beaches under escort. The Battalion then pushed on to Crépon, supported by 4/7th Dragoon Guards and 68th Field Battery R.A. By that time 5 carriers, the mortar platoon and 6 anti-tank guns had joined the Battalion. They had been the last of the Battalion to land on the beach. D Company were given the task of clearing the enemy out of Crépon, (where CSM Hollis of the 6th Battalion had previously performed the second act of gallantry that won him the award of the VC) as the rest of the Battalion, under Lt Col P. H. Richardson DSO, OBE, skirted the village and continued the advance toward Creully without them.

We were ordered to make good a bridge north of Creuilly, but there was no opposition. The enemy had withdrawn. Shot at in Creuilly by the Winnipeg Rifles entering from the east, who mistook us for enemy. We made friends and waited for the rest of the battalion to come up. Sent off in the lead to the south. Skirmish around Fresné-le-Crotteur where we were so far ahead that we were shelled by a supporting cruiser. Frantic signals stopped it after three salvos. On to south of Coulombs, a few hundred yards south of the Bayeaux to Caen road and our D Day objective. At 2200 hours we were ordered to dig in for the night. It had been a very long day.

Captain D. Warriner
OC C Company, 7th Green Howards

By now the 7th Green Howards were well ahead of the rest of the other infantry battalions in 69 Brigade and were told to withdraw for the night to a position just north of Coulombs to allow the others to catch up. They were indeed congratulated as the British unit that had advanced the furthest south from the beaches on D-Day in the whole of 2nd Army.

On the first day, the 6th Battalion, had advanced more than 6 miles south from the beachhead, just 3 miles short of their objective on the Bayeaux to Caen road. Surprisingly, they had suffered only about 90 casualties, which was a comparatively low figure from what had been expected by the planners back in England, but it consisted of two company commanders, one carrier commander, several subalterns and some of the best and most experienced NCOs.

The 7th Battalion, as the reserve battalion in 69 Brigade, had lost far less than the 6th Battalion. Some, alas, were the result of friendly naval gunfire because they had not been expected to advance so far south from the beach by that time. In all probability, the naval gunfire had been called for by an air spotter who, not realising that British troops had advanced so far, mistook them for the enemy. This was one of the hazards of mobile warfare in densely packed fields and orchards bounded by sunken lanes, rocky banks and thick hedges – typical bocage country.

There were many heroic actions on D-Day by men from the 6th and 7th Green Howards. In recognition of outstanding bravery on that day, gallantry medals were awarded to the following:

VC (CSM Hollis),
DSO (Lt Col Hastings)
2 MCs (Majors Honeyman and Lofthouse) and
5 MMs (Sgt Potterton, L/Sgt Prenty, Lcpl Joyce, Pte Addis and Pte Thompson).

In the centre of the Normandy village of Crépon, there is a memorial to the men of the Green Howards who landed on D-Day and later fought in the Normandy campaign. On a stone plinth is a life-sized bronze statue of a typical Green Howard soldier at the end of D-Day. He is seated looking exhausted yet still determined, holding his bayoneted rifle in his left hand and dangling his helmet by the strap from his right. It is a fine tribute to all those Green Howards who fought for the freedom of Western Europe on that longest day.

Appendix v: *The Diary of J. O. Downey*

What follows are selected extracts from a previously unpublished diary written by Lieutenant J. D. Downer of the 13th/18th Hussars (included by kind permission of the Light Dragoons, 'Charge' – the Story of England's Northern Cavalry, Discovery Museum, Newcastle upon Tyne), which offers a detailed narrative account of tanks in the conflict, complete with logistical detail, so very important, indeed vital, to modern warfare.

The unit was very much in the tradition of the light cavalry, created in November 1922 as a result of post Great War cutbacks as an amalgamation of the 13th and 18th Hussars, both of which had distinguished histories and named as the 13th/18th (Queen Mary's Own). In December 1935 the unit was transferred into the Royal Armoured Corps. After 1939 during the battle for France it served as a recce formation within 1st Armoured Reconnaissance Brigade attached to 1st Infantry Division.

After Dunkirk it was part of 27th Armoured Brigade until moving to join 8th Armoured in January 1944. The Hussars were equipped with Sherman D-D Tanks and played, as the narrative shows, a very active role in the battle for Normandy. After the war, the regiment served in Germany across the shrinking span of Empire (including the Malayan Emergency) before being amalgamated with 15th/19th King's Royal Hussars to form the Light Dragoons on 1st December 1992.

The Days Before

On the 21st April 1944, Hugh Franks and I were posted to the 13th/18th Royal Hussars, Petworth, Sussex. This was, for us, a secret triumph over the snooty little adjutant then at Borrington Camp. We had both squeezed out of Sandhurst together and had received our commissions just three weeks previous. The regiment we had chosen had not applied for us and so, after one week's leave, we found ourselves posted to the 52ND Training Regiment R.A.C. Borrington Camp, Dorset, where we duly presented ourselves in front of the adjutant in our consciously new cavalry outfits. The adjutant, although a young chap, was far too big for his boots; our appearance seemed to rattle him and he started ticking straight away. 'Why were we dressed up in cavalry clothes; why doesn't the War Office tell you chaps the position; surely we didn't expect to join a cavalry Regiment'. And he went on to say that we were unlikely to be attached to any regiment for a year, and even then certainly not the cavalry; and so he went on. We were much depressed and still more so when we met out fellow officers, many of whom we had already met at Sandhurst, and some had been in Borrington for over a year. We were very lucky, however, and able to smile at the adjutant: we were only to spend two weeks with him, which was more than adequate. We spent the two weeks letter-censoring and training troopers in tank tactics with infantry carriers to act as tanks!

Hugh Franks (Frankie) was seven years younger than I and full of youthful enthusiasm for life. He was a big chap, almost plump, with a babyish face, but this belied his true nature for he had plenty of courage and proved equal to his task in Normandy. I was very glad of his companionship and we had many a jolly evening together, discussing future plans and present situations. Monday 24th April found the two of us in very high spirits journeying to Petworth. We had lunched with Frankie's mother in town and, on reaching Petworth station, we were met by Lieutenant Pat Uttley, who took us to the camp in a jeep.

The 13th/18th Hussars were one of these regiments of the 27th Armoured Brigade, an independent brigade under the command of Brigadier Palmer. Lieutenant Colonel R.T.G. Harrap had recently taken over command of the regiment. He had a most attractive personality and was reckoned a very capable and efficient soldier. An armoured regiment consists of three fighting squadrons, A, B and C, with about nineteen tanks each and an H.Q. squadron. Two squadrons, A and B, were out on a week's exercise when we arrived. So we were temporarily attached to C Squadron under the command of Major Sir D.J.A. Cotter of Irish descent. The 27th Armoured Brigade had been chosen for the job of spearhead in the initial landings on the continent. For this, the Brigade had been specially trained in the employment of D-Day tanks, which were Sherman tanks adapted to float and move on the briny. Our brigade sign was of a very unique and picturesque pattern, being a golden seahorse on a blue background, and referred to by all and sundry as the 'Pregnant Prawn'. As was later disclosed a few weeks after D-Day, this brigade was looked upon as a suicide formation and was reckoned in the War Office books as a total loss after D-Day. The other two regiments of the brigade sharing this favoured hangout were the Staffordshire Yeomanry and the East Riding Yeomanry. Frankie and I were somewhat awed on learning these broad secrets and just a little uneasy, since we were not exactly familiar with amphibious tank tactics. It tickled us pink and we enjoyed many a laugh conjuring up the possibility that both of us might be leading a troop of D-Day tanks onto the French coast in anything from a week's time, when we had been told at Borrington that we were not likely to see a regiment for at least a year.

The regiment were camped under canvas in a fairly dense wood on the outskirts of Petworth. I shared a tent with Stewart Watson, who was the regiment's signals officer. He was a very efficient and conscientious type and later became adjutant of the regiment. I experienced a lot of trouble in canvassing for a batman.

Stewart's man, a chap by the name of Hayes, was a fellow sufferer with me during my early training days as a trooper in Catterick, and he managed to persuade a bespectacled and homely trooper by the name of Musson to take on the job. He has been with me ever since.

The Regiment were well up to officer strength and Frankie and I were more or less left to our own devices for the first week. We were not really wanted and felt horribly in the way: the elder officers were experienced cavalry officers of the regular army and not very communicative. There was a distinct division between these pukka cavaliers and the troop leaders who made up the younger section of officers. We quickly made friends with the latter but, although first impressions are seldom wrong, the pukka cavaliers were first class in the liberation. During this limitation period we did pretty much as we pleased, poking our noses into whatever smelt pleasant. We supervised a map-reading scheme, watched the waterproofing of tanks and went for walks to Midhurst and Petworth.

It soon became obvious that we were not to command a troop on D-Day and, on the 13th May, we were ordered to report to the then newly-formed 266 Forward Delivery Squadron, under the command of Captain Mitchell. The 266 F.D.S. was to justify its existence on D-Day by replacing battle casualties, both tanks and personnel, which occurred in the brigade. It consisted of 3 regiments' sections, the section belonging to the 13th/18th Hussars having some 100 troopers but no tanks. The personnel were either untrained or check-outs from the regiment, and were chiefly servants, clerks, storemen and anything but tank crew. Gale Windy was the section with two other officers, Lieutenants Edwards and Peerless, and there were a few NCOs. Windy spent the first two days interviewing the personnel. On the 15th May, thirty-two tanks arrived. They required a complete waterproofing job, which normally took ten days and with trained crews. We were given exactly six days to complete the job because on the seventh day the camp was to be sealed (an obvious clue that D-Day was near) and 266 F.D.S. were to move on to the coast before the sealing. We worked like slaves from dawn to dusk and Windy gave Frankie and I additional work by selecting our tanks for inspection of the kind the Brigade could expect before the camp was sealed. We just finished the job in time, as one always does in the army – but I did not see the King because I was sent on another job the day before her inspection. Frankie remained with the F.D.S. and I did not see him again until we both found ourselves attached to B Squadron a few days after D-Day.

I was sent on another rush job, this time even move disorganised than the F.D.S. It was suddenly realized by the powers that be (three weeks before D-Day) that a formation would be necessary to keep the Forward Delivery Squadrons supplied with tanks and personnel, as they in turn tended to the needs of the brigades. Accordingly, it was decided to form a Corp Delivery Squadron and each F.D.S. in the Corp was to supply some five to six dozen men as a basis of formation. After much discussion Windy selected thirty men from the already doubtful ranks of the 13/18th section, choosing those possessing the least amount of experience; a very difficult feat. I took them down to Hove where 255 C.D.S. was to make its headquarters. This was not such an easy journey as might at first be imagined. In the first place, there were two similar parties to accompany us from the Staffs and the E.R.Y. with two officers, Lieutenants Frank Biddle and Eric Pead, both of the E.R.Ys. It was decided by coin that I would be responsible for the luggage. I soon discovered that almost every trooper had at least double the regulated scale of kit packed very badly and insecure. There was also a considerable supply of raw and loose foodstuff, being the unexpired portion of our rations. The journey entailed three changes, which meant that all luggage had to be carted from platform to platform. an operation which invariably meant that at least one unfortunate's kit would find itself displayed to the smallest item on the permanent way, and that several pounds of sugar and flour would form a trail to guide the unknowing to their awaiting train. Major King was officer commanding 255 C.D.S. and he was already in Hove with a small staff, so we were fortunate in having a truck to carry our gear from the station. I managed to get my proteges billeted in a very pleasant road by the sea. They were a bit crowded... all thirty in one house. The officers had two houses, one for the mess and the other for sleeping. Before we had been there a week, we were joined by personnel from the 4th Armoured Brigade and a Canadian Brigade. In all, there must have been five to six hundred of us, and we had some two hundred tanks to maintain and waterproof. The 13/18th section were allocated eight tanks, so I split the boys into eight crews. Some of them had never worked on a tank before being transferred from other services and it was a difficult problem to find drivers for all the tanks. We were given a time limit to be ready by, which meant working from dawn to dusk and during the night with some tanks. They all worked with a true spirit and most of them proved useful members of the regiment on the continent.

We waterproofed our tanks in the streets of Hove and drove them up and down the roads to try them out. It was a novelty for the inhabitants of Hove, even if it were a bit noisy, and a friendship quickly developed between householders and the 'boys'. One old lady told Eric and I that she had never seen such hard workers as the boys. I don't expect to hear that again in the army. We were kept well supplied with tea and cakes all day long.

I chambered up with a John Pratt of the Staffs, and Frank Biddle. We used to spend our evenings enjoying the entertainments of Brighton, which were pretty adequate even in those times. Eric Pead had managed to smuggle his wife to Hove, so we saw very little of him. The arrival of the Canadians brightened up the mess considerably. It was not until we were within sight of Normandy that we finally finished the waterproofing.

The regiment, meanwhile, were sealed up in Petworth. They had the band with them during their enforced detention, while they awaited the commencement of their journey of liberation. Hugh Franks and the F.D.S. were somewhere outside Tilbury. We were waiting for the words 'Proceed with Operation Overlord.' [Overlord was the code word for the initial landings].

The Move Across

On the 1st June, Major King held an O Group and we were told to be ready in two days' time. (An 'O Group' is an Order Group held between the commanding officer of a unit and the officer class B sub-units.) The 3rd June brought us news of our move. Throughout the country units and formations had assembled, in a like fashion to us, in what were known as 'concentration areas'. In most cases, such as the regiment's, for example, these areas were sealed, but we were fortunate in being still at liberty. The procedure after 'concentration' was a move to a selected 'marshalling area', where units were sent on to a 'pre-embarkation' area as ships and transport became available.

We were ordered to move to a marshalling area just north of Gosport on 4th June. The day before, we tested out our waterproofing by running the tanks through a four-foot water dip. This was not highly successful in the case of three of my tanks, one of which filled up to a depth of two feet inside the tank: the fools had not sealed up the dump valve in the floor of the tank.

The selection of drivers for the move was a problem, only two of my group being trade-tested drive mechanics, and it was necessary to employ men who had not driven a Sherman before. Driving a Sherman tank is relatively easy but, although no great skill is required, great determination and power of endurance is necessary because of the physical strain imposed on a long run, especially at night. Actually, the run was done very well. Booton's tank caught fire but he quickly got it out again. Nearly every tank had to change at least one road wheel on the way, but all tanks arrived at the marshalling area before dusk. It was raining when we arrived. We parked our tanks in numbered spaces along the road and did a last maintenance parade. We then mounted a guard, collected our gear and tramped a good three miles to the camp. The camp was closely guarded and the tanks were actually outside the camp area. For obvious security reasons it was not a good thing for the troops to have contact with the local populace and, while we were there, we had much difficulty in obtaining permission to take the crews down to their tanks in order to finish off waterproofing. The weather was foul and it rained most of the time, in fact D-Day had to be postponed twenty-four hours owing to the rough seas. We slept in Bell tents and there was a large marquee for use as an officers' mess. A cinema gave entertainment throughout the day for those who were lucky in having no work to do. A loud-hailer erected in the centre of the camp announced any important news and the summons of officers to O. Groups. While I was in the mess that evening I was overjoyed to meet Belly Bennett, a lieutenant in the 8th Hussars. He was a friend of mine at Sandhurst. It livened the evening up considerably.

We managed to get most of the tanks in order during the two days we were there, although there was still much waterproofing to be completed. We were all issued with twenty-four-hour ration packs consisting of dehydrated meat, porridge, chocolate, sweets and ready mixed tea, sugar and milk cubes. These were for use on landing. In order to cook, we were each issued with a little Tommy cooker, which consisted of two plates of tin and a supply of fuel. For the actual sea voyage we were given a crude pair of water wings, most of which needed repairs, and I was glad that I could swim. We were also given a waterproof paper bag per man 'for use on the boat'.

The tanks were given a last look over on D-Day, craft serial numbers written on the tanks, and final orders issued in the command tent, together with maps. The 255 C.D.S. were to move in packets over a period of several days, commencing with my group of eight tanks and Eric Read's tank on D+1. On landing, we were to make for an assembly area nearest the landing point, where we were to de-waterproof our tanks and wait for the arrival of the rest of the formation. Good news was then coming through of the initial landings, in which the 27th announced Brigade were playing a leading part, and this buoyed up our spirits considerably.

It was not until the late afternoon of D+1 that we moved to the pre-embarkation area at Gosport, where we arrived at dusk. We received quite a welcome from the town and there were many free beers to be had. Our Landing Craft Tank (L.C.T.) was not then ready for us, so we parked ourselves in a side street and attempted to sleep. Even at this stage some of the crews had to carry on working, but there was no grousing possibly because they realized they were saving themselves a wet skin by ensuring that there were no leaks. Just before midnight, a despatch rider was sent to guide us to an awaiting L.C.T. Eric had somehow managed to meet his wife in Gosport in spite of the strict censorship and, of course, he was missing just as we were due to work. He was discovered after a frantic search and we moved onto the hard.

An L.C.T. is nothing more than a large wooden box with a pointed nose: the back lets down, forming a run-up for the tanks. When aboard, the tanks are shackled down to the deck. With a fairly calm sea, nine tanks can be taken but, if at all rough, only seven can be safely transported. Eric took his tank on first and I remained behind to stow my eight tanks. This was a difficult and wet task. I had to guide the drivers backward down the slope from the hard, across five or six yards of sea and then up the ramp into the narrow back entrance of the L.C.T. Since it was pitch black and the noise of engines made shouting impossible, I had to follow the wretched tanks into the water so that the drivers could see my directions. The captain of the L.C.T. sent word that he would only take seven tanks, so I had to leave two behind. These I put in the charge of Corporal Simpson, who I had promoted while we were in Hove. He followed on about twelve hours later and met us safely in Beny sur Mer.

Soon after we started, Eric and I went and chatted with the captain. This was his second trip to Normandy and during his first trip he had seen the 27th Armoured Brigade making their initial assault. The sea had been very rough and most of the casualties resulted from the unseaworthiness of the D-Day tanks in rough weather. The resistance on the beaches had been light and, had it not been for the bad weather, the operation would have been up to schedule.

The L.C.T. was now making full speed in an endeavour to catch up a convoy before dawn. We were issued with rations for the journey, consisting of five composition packs and two boxes of self-heating soup. A 'compo' box, as it was called, consists of tinned food sufficient for fourteen men for three days. The food is very good and varied; the boxes being labelled A to E. There is a 'K' box containing turkey and Xmas pud.

We quickly got to sleep for the remainder of the night and awoke to brilliant sunshine in the early morning. We lit a wood fire in the middle of the deck and had a brekker of sorts, then set-to doing the final stages of waterproofing. We had caught up with the convoy. It was quite an impressive sight to watch the armada advancing. The driver and co-driver have to be sealed in for the actual wading, since they are below water. It was a job to get the crews working, the sea was rough and most of them were feeling sea sick. In the afternoon we could glimpse the French coastline. Eric and I had tea with the captain, so we undid our maps and orders and the captain told us where he reckoned to land up. He promised he would go in as close to the shore as possible; for which I was very thankful, knowing the state of our waterproofing. The coast was now very clear and we were probably two miles away. There were ships of all shapes and sizes everywhere, and the navy was busy giving fire support to the troops on land. They also maintained a smoke screen continuously to blank off our operations from the high ground to the east. Apart from this gunfire and an occasional burst of Ack Ack at a jerry aircraft, the beach seemed comparatively peaceful and not nearby as aggravated as I had imagined. There was a fair amount of smoke about and the sky was clouding over. Our L.C.T. backed in, stopped and let down its ramp. We had about 600 yards of sea to cross. The first tank moved down the ramp. There was between five to six foot of water, not too bad, but a bit deeper than I liked, and I certainly expected one tank to come a cropper. Fortunately, we all made the shore and touched down just west of the mouth of the River Seulles, near the village of Graye-sur-Mer. There were a few bits of wreckage on the beach, some burnt-out vehicles and a beached L.S.T. but there was nowhere near the amount of damage one would expect from the German impregnable defences.

Eric took the lead and I the rear, and our seven tanks moved gracefully off the beach, along mine-cleared tracks and through the village of Graye-sur-Mer. It was not too battered and there were a few peasants in the houses; a young girl and her mother threw roses on our tanks as we passed. We went to an assembly area just south west of the village at a point 955835 and dismantled most of the waterproofing gear. When this was completed we left for Beny-sur-Mer, crossing the Suelles into Courseulles-sur-Mer. The roads were very congested and Eric, who was leading (I was bringing up the rear), was separated from the second tank by several vehicles. Consequently, when he turned right at Courseulles for Beny, he was not observed by the tanks that followed. All of them went straight on along the coast road and I had to follow them, since I could not stop them by radio, as it was not functioning. It was not until we were nearing Langrune-sur-Mer, 7km along the coast, that the column was held up and I was able to take over the lead. Rather than turn back I decided to turn south to Douvres, which I had heard was freed from enemy, and then to cut across west to Beny. At Douvres we met a platoon of the 6th Para Division and, since the tanks were in no condition to fight (being stacked up with extra ammunition and petrol so that the turret would not revolve), I enquired if the route to Beny was open. They said that it was, and so we set off. Half way across this route our way was barred by one of our gliders, which had burnt out across the road. I jumped down to inspect the verges for mines, with a view to going round the glider. I had only just commenced the inspection when five Spandaus opened up on us from the wood. I took rapid cover in a ditch and motioned to the tanks to turn round. Almost before the words were out of my mouth, they had turned round in a body and fled back along the track... I only just managed to scramble on the near tank. This fleeing may sound a little timid because, after all, Spandau fire in no way affects a tank, but I reckoned that there might be a few anti-tank guns in the vicinity and none of the tanks was fit for action, nor the crew trained to fight. In any case, we were bringing tanks over for reinforcements not to get them involved in private battles. We learnt afterwards that the fire had come from a German Radar station which held out as a strong point for nearly three weeks after D-Day, and delayed the laying of an airport near that position. We soon reached Douvres and by this time it was getting dark, so I took the tanks back along the coast and spent the night at an assembly area. We had no tents with us, so we took what cover we could under the tanks. For the first four hours of darkness we were entertained by a heavy raid and A.A. fire, after which I fell asleep and awoke to a grey dawn and rain. We found ourselves very wet. We had a quick brekker and set off early for Beny, this time without any mistakes, arriving there about 0900 hrs on 9th June. I found Eric harboured just off the road and not feeling too comfortable, although he was relieved to see us. There was quite a bit of suffering in the village still, and several French-women collaborators were captured that day. They had evidently married Germans during the occupation and knew that death awaited them anyway.

No other party of 255 C.D.S. had arrived, so we made a temporary harbour near the church. We made a pretty good dinner from our 'compo' rations and kept a guard posted for the arrival of our friends. The Canadian boys arrived in the afternoon and they harboured in an adjacent field to ours. We had made a few improvised tents with gas capes and ground-sheets when Corporal Simpson arrived with the two tanks about 1900 hrs. He proved a most efficient NCO and later became a sergeant in the Rekkie troop.

That night there was another air raid but otherwise a dry night. On 10th June, the rest of the 27th Armoured Group arrived with Frank, Pratt and Major King. Headquarters was established and contact made with 266 F.D.S. The 13/18th Hussars had received many casualties but more so in tanks than in personnel and they were harboured at Ranville 1073, with the 6th Para Division. The 266 F.D.S. were established at Hermanville-sur-Mer 0779 and were badly in need of tanks from us, since they had just replenished the regiment. There was another night of raids on our shipping and, the next morning, I took my eight tanks to 266 F.D.S. and was delighted to meet Wendy and Frankie. We chatted and compared notes: Frankie's lot had a 'flop' on the way over. Mitchell told that things had gone very badly and that they were to organize themselves into troops and fight their way to the regiment. This of course was a lot of hooey and they had no trouble in arriving at Hermanville. I asked to stay with 266 but the request was not granted. We arrived back at the C.D.S. in the afternoon and moved our gear over to the main body. Food was running short and we were forced to fall back on the twenty-four-hour packs. Corporal Simpson and Mockford managed to scrounge some eggs, meat and butter off the locals, which supplemented our fire. On 12th June, communal cooking was organized and a Naafi pack arrived. By 15th June, we were all getting fed up when, in the evening, I was sent with twelve of my section to join the 266 F.D.S., who had since moved to Periers-sur-le-Dan.

We arrived during an air raid and a bomb dropped within yards as we did so, but with no ill effect except discomfort. Frankie had just left to join the regiment a few hours earlier. I slept the night with Windy, who had a very decent dug-out, and in the morning we set to work repairing two damaged D-Day tanks. In the late afternoon we watched the dropping of airborne supplies to the 6th Para Division, who were occupying the lowlands east of the Caen canal.

I had been in Normandy over a week now and had seen nothing of the fighting.

The Attack on St Honore le Chardonneret

That same evening, on 16th June, a Don. R. arrived with orders to escort 10 O.R.s and me to Major Cordy-Simpson (Cordy) who was officer commanding A Echelon. A Echelon supply the squadrons with ammunition, fuel and other replenishments. When the squadrons are fighting it is harboured a few miles behind the lines, always ready to replenish the tanks. Cordy had already given his name in the regiment to Cordy's Rifles, organised from the Echelon personnel during an emergency in the first week after D-Day. He gave us a few words of welcome, saw that we were completely equipped and then sent us onto Regimental H.Q. situated at Ranville. I reported to the Adjutant Captain Julius Neave and was sent to B Squadron, who were harboured outside Ranville.

Just before my arrival, the colonel had been killed by a bomb when riding in a jeep. The second in command of the regiment, the Earl of Faversham (known as 'Sim'), took command and Major Price (Dag), the head of B Squadron, acted as second in command. Captain Peter Lyon of A Squadron was transferred to command B Squadron in Dag's place. Squadron organization in the earlier days consisted of five troops each with three tanks and an HQ troop with three tanks. There was an officer in charge of each troop with a sergeant and corporal on the Able and Baker tanks respectively. In Squadron HQ there was the Squadron

Leader, a second in command, and 2nd Captain. Bobby Neave was the second in command and Billy Wormald the 2nd captain in B Squadron. There were four troop leaders in B Squadron at the time of my arrival, a Lieutenant Knowles, a tall lanky individual known as 'Norse' who I had known in my trooper days in Catterick; Frankie; Lieutenant Jeff Oldham, a serious bespectacled chap, and Lieutenant Peerless.

When I reached B Squadron, Peter Lyon was in bed underneath his tank. I gave him a dig and told him I'd arrived. He told me to make myself at home with 5th Troop, which I was to take over, and he would see me in the morning. So I made my way over to 5th Troop area. There were two tanks which had just arrived from F.D.S. crewed by new personnel, most of which had come over with me. Besides these two tanks, there was a D-Day tank with its original D-Day crew in the charge of Sergeant. Macglouglin. They were the sole survivors of 5th Troop and I could see I was going to feel a little inferiority complex with Sergeant Mac. For a time since, he had already tasted blood, while I had scarcely seen a jerry except a few women! I spent a very peaceful night, having at last got a troop and a definite job to do.

The next morning, as soon as we had finished brekker, I got the sergeant and captain together, and we organised the crews. The old 75mm Sherman carried five. We discussed signals and troop formations, and then got to work on the tanks. Peter and Bobby came round in the morning to give me the form. The squadron were harboured just north east of Ranville in a field, C Squadron were giving the Highland Division moral support in Boue du Bevant, and A Dquadron were with Regiment H.Q. in Ranville. The regiment, together with the 6th Para Division, were responsible while in harbour for the final defence of the bridge over the Caen canal (which was the only link with the rest of 30 Corp). In the event of a counter-attack, 5th Troop were responsible for the northern approaches to this bridge and Mac and I made a rekkie to locate suitable positions for this purpose. All around us were elements of the Para boys and we were their only armoured support. We harboured in Ranville for several days so I was able to get the troop in some kind of order, both in maintenance and crew control. We also did a little troop training among the numerous gliders in the vicinity. Sergeant Spencer, who was in charge of the fitters, was very helpful in making modifications to our tanks and fitted a very fine luggage grid to the back of my tank. Jeff Oldham was a bit of an old woman in some ways and would sit for hours yarning with his troop on the philosophies of life. One evening a crazy airborne chap was playing with his Sten gun and accidently let a round off, which hit Jeff on his bottom while he was in his favourite position round the camp fire. He was absent for a few days.

We were constantly mortared during our stay in Ranville and the night of 23rd June was a particularly nasty one. Most of the troop slept in a trench dug underneath their tanks, with the exception of Tatlow and myself, who had dug private trenches outside. I had been asleep sometime in my little hole when, all of a sudden, I was lifted up bodily and my head bumped down with no little force, followed by several pounds of earth raining on top of me. When I recovered, I got up to examine the cause. There was a large mortar hole between Tatlow's and my trench, which were only a yard apart. Then, to my consternation, I saw that Tatlow's trench was entirely obliterated. I frantically shoveled up the earth with my hands until I came to his blankets, but there was no sign of Tatlow. Then I realized with relief that he must be on guard. During all this time a most terrific noise was going on and shells were whizzing in all directions. A large ammunition dump belonging to the airboys, and one of our own ammunition lorries, had been hit and were burning merrily. The position became very dangerous and it was necessary to move the tanks. Two officers of the Airborne Division lost their lives in trying to extinguish the fire.

The airborne chaps were very decent: they gave us one of their two bikes, which the troop leaders shared between them, and quite a bit of their gear when they returned home. The situation on the front had become fairly stable.

The 24th June brought news of an impending battle and the next two days were busy with preparations, rekkies and O. Groups. It was whilst on one of these rekkies that I first experienced the 'moaning minnie'. We were up a tree with the

Squadron Leader at the time, being shown our fire positions when a bunch of these were delivered to us. They are more or less terror weapons and no more dangerous than the 3" mortar. The moaning minnie consists of several tube-like mortar bombs, fired from a multiple gun on the rocket principle. During their progress through the air they emit the most terrifying moans. Fortunately, this moan gives one ample time to take cover, unless of course you are up a tree.

The regiment, with units of the 6th Para Division and the Highland Division, were to make a diversionary attack on St Honore le Chardonneret in order to encourage jerry into thinking that our attack on Caen would come from east of the canal. Meanwhile, the Canadians were to put in the main attack on the west flank. A squadron and infantry were to attack St Honore directly, whilst B and C Squadrons were to set on the flanks to give fire support and trap any reinforcements in the way of armour which we hoped the enemy would bring up.

About tea time on 25th June we moved to Herouvillette and harboured in an orchard. Early the next morning, at 0300 hrs, we moved slowly and as silently as possible into our positions, which were just west of Escouville, lining a hedge and facing southwest. We were more or less full down to anything coming up the broad valley from Demouville and could deal efficiently with a counter-attack from Colombelles. A Squadron went in from the north just before dawn and were quickly in occupation of St Honore. The expected counter-attack followed quickly afterwards, supported by armour, which we could only just discriminate through the thin dawn. They presented a lovely broadside to our guns and didn't advance very far, but were soon beating a hasty retreat. I had an extra tank in 5th Troop commanded by Corporal Pendulberry from HQ Troop. He brewed up one Mark IV tank and Corporal Eddison reckoned that he'd hit one also. Later we were able to distinguish four tanks knocked out by the Squadron. Three counter-attacks in all were made during the day but none was successful. Captain John Wardlaw, second in command of C Squadron, was acting as observation officer, and had a post on the high ground in Bois de Bevant. Many times he reported movement of tanks and vehicles in the areas of Demouville and Cuverville which were quickly engaged and dispersed by our artillery, and on three occasions by the Royal Navy. On one occasion during the day, some forty or more tanks, both Mk IVs and Panthers were observed approaching St Honore from the south. These were adequately dispersed by H.M.S. *Rodney* before we even saw them; so it was a pretty easy day for us.

The village was still in our hands by nightfall, with infantry and A Squadron in defence. We started back to harbour in Ranville for the night and C Squadron returned to Bois de Bevant. When we were half way to Ranville, a most heavy barrage, including mortars and moaning minnies, was laid down on our positions in Bois de Bevant and soon afterwards jerry launched an attack on the woods from the direction of Bevant. The affair lasted an hour, during which time we took up defensive positions in the form of a square. C Squadron had a most unholy time in the woods and, since they could be of little use in the trees at height, they retired to our positions. The Black Watch and 6th Para units successfully held off the attack and afterwards managed to gain a little extra ground.

We had no time left for sleep that night and we set off just before the dawn to take up defending positions to protect St Honore, Escouville against any more counter-attacks. We stayed in these positions until 1st July and had a very quiet time. This diversionary attack had the desired effect and the Canadians had made fair headway in the west. Caen had still to be taken however.

On 1st July we changed positions with C Squadron in Bois de Bevant, where the periodic quotas of moaning minnies were still arriving. My troop was attached to a company of the Black Watch, who gave us a cooked meal on arrival and were very hospitable during our stay. Our role in the wood was a combined one of simple patrol work and a morale booster for the infantry. We were situated hear to Peerless and his troop plumb in the middle of the wood. Horse held a position in the southeast corner of the wood, which was right opposite the jerries and did not permit of any laxity, although it contained a farmhouse with some excellent cider. Poor old Hugh was stuck right up in the northeast corner in a very uncomfortable position. Peerless and I went with Peter to crew positions we would take up in the event of an attack on Escouville. Escouville had been taken by the regiment in the first week: it was very much a shambles and there were plenty of dead cattle and huns still lying about. Peter always combined his rekkies with a tour of cellars and gardens. The gardens especially in Escouville were very plentiful with fruit and vegetables.

On July 8th we were relieved by the Staffs and proceeded to a rest area on the coast viz Luc-sur-Mer. I bagged a little chalet to myself with spring bed, sheets and mattress; it was heaven. A squadron mess was set up and Billy Wormald made M.C. There was plenty of red and white to be had, also cream, cream butter and other luxuries. The four days didn't last long but they were very enjoyable. We bathed twice a day and watched the continual stream of Ducks taking supplies from the boats to the dumps island. This whole operation was screened from the west by continual smoke twenty-four hours out of twenty-four.

Frankie, Horse and I visited a few local towns in the jeep. Most of them were battered, but the inhabitants were slowly coming to life and many shops were opened. After we had been there three days all officers of the brigade met in a school hall and the brigadier gave us a lecture on the use of 'Funnies', which were flails (mine-clearing tanks); crocodiles (flame-throwers) and AVREs (Assault Vehicle Royal Engineers). These were to be employed by us in the next push. After the lecture we had an O. Group and befriended our respective 'Funny' crews. Maps were issued in the evening and Jeff and I were ordered to move off and harbour that night (12th July) in the wood south of Gazelle.

The Battle for La Bijude and Caen

This was to be the big push for Caen and perhaps a breakthrough. Anyway, it would make Rommel keep his forces around in the east while the Americans made good headway in the west.

Jeff and I took our tanks down to Gazelle in the evening of 12th July and harboured with some infantry in the wood just south of the village. The reason for moving in parts was to avoid detection of a large concentration of armour. The next morning, we went with Peter on a rekkie and we were given some idea of our job. The squadron was to slant the push for Caen by capturing a small village just north of Epron called la Bijude, and we made observations of this village from the roof of a much-battered chateau.

Many jerries could be observed in La Bijude, but the presence of armour was not obvious. A final O. Group was held on 14th. The Staffs and E.R.Y. were supporting infantry on either side of us and the Canadians were performing on our west flank. The regiment were to work with the Suffolks and Norfolks. When B Squadron had secured La Bijude, C Squadron would pass through to capture Epron and Couvre-Chef. 2nd and 5th Troops were to be on the start line well before dawn on 15th July to join in the barrage. At zero hour, 5th Troop was to advance and take up positions on the track on the southern edge of the village, and 2nd Troop on the right flank. The infantry were going in from the right flank i.e. west of the main road, supported by 1st and 3rd Troops. Accordingly, on the evening of the 14th, Jeff and I moved our troops to a temporary position near the chateau, under the cover of dusk, to the noise of RAF bombers who were softening up the Caen area. We were to take up final positions on the S.L. under the cover of artillery fire at 0300 hrs. The artillery, however, didn't play and we were unable to move to the S.L. until the initial barrage for the attack commenced at 0400 hrs. On reaching the S.L. we pumped shells into La Bijude and at the ordered time, as the barrage lifted, we moved forward onto the village. It was still dark and the barrage had made it virtually impossible to see. It was all I could do to keep direction. Mac went over a mine halfway down the track, but it did no serious damage. After much searching, we located the track south of the village and took up positions. We could still only see a few yards in front of us. Corporal Eddison had not arrived and, just as I could see his tank vaguely in the distance, a bazooka hit him in the side and set an H.E. round off. This set up a sheet of flame and was probably very alarming for the crew, who tumbled out immediately and left the tank slowly rolling backwards. There was no sight of the infantry and I guessed the reason for this: as our barrage lifted the bosch had plonked down a mortar strike right on la Bijude, and it was still falling. After what seemed like an hour, it was beginning to clear slightly and we fired our Browning guns into the hedges, since we were more or less isolated and could see Germans every now and again in our flanks and front.

Later, the visibility became more normal and I suddenly observed a Mk. IV tank advancing from the southwest and more or less towards 2nd Troop's position. I wondered why they hadn't fired, but I learnt later that they had been unable to take up their proper position, and were just north of the village. I immediately got Mockford onto it and in three shots we had it nicely blazing. Now unfortunately there was a tank behind the one we had shot, hidden by the smoke of the burning tank. He engaged us and hit us in the gear box. I immediately jumped out to get Mac to give us a tow out. Before I had reached the ground two more shots landed. Luckily they were all low and I gave the order to scram. When Tatlow and Cawthray emerged, they were covered with oil and Cawthray reckoned he had actually seen one of the shots coming towards him through the periscope. We took cover in a shell hole and surveyed the position. There were still no infantry with us, although they could be heard firing in the village behind us, but what they were firing at I could not imagine, as la Bijude was just a mass of rubble and what jerries there were had been creeping about in front of us, not behind. Some of the crew had bailed out with their weapons and I had only my revolver. The jerries in the hedges started firing at us, so I got Mac to see them off. Our tank was burning merrily, and all our gear with it, but fortunately the tank which had hit us was now being engaged by 3rd Troop.

I sent Wilton back to contact our infantry. The rest stayed in the shell hole while I reported the position over Mac's wireless, and the presence of about five 'dug in' tanks which we could now see to our southwest. We were given no orders so I decided to make contact with our own infantry. Wilton had not yet shown up so I decided to go and look see, but did not go for, no sooner did I get to the end of the track, than I found myself looking at four jerries and a Spandau just ten yards off. So I returned, and we all retired back under the protection of Mac's tank, slowly reverting back to 2nd Troop's position. We ran into Wilton, who had been taken prisoner by our own infantry. He was in tank overalls with no badges but, since his hair was close-cropped, did not look unlike a hun. We soon persuaded them to release him. I went and saw Jeff who now had only two tanks, so we got in communication with Peter and transferred Mac to 2nd Troop.

I contacted the company commander of the infantry who had more or less left all their outposts and were huddled round Jeff's tanks. The situation by this time was pretty uncomfortable. The infantry had only landed a week ago and this was their first battle. Jeff and I tried to persuade the captain to get his men positioned since, by now, the snipers were creeping in on us. It was getting on for midday and it was with relief that the Norfolks were withdrawn and Jeff was left with a new lot of 'feet'. I looked round for my crew but they had gone on, so I left the village and caught them up. On the way back, we found Corporal Eddison and his crew (no casualties) and also Jeff's corporal and his crew. We had a bit to eat with them and then returned. We had a good deal of trouble with R.S.M. Hind, trying to get our kit replaced, at least sufficient for our immediate needs, but he coughed up in the end. The R.S.M. was office in command of Echelon which carried the stores, cooks and other non-essential gear. The battle for Caen went on into the next day but we remained with R.H.Q. I gave a hand to the technical adjacent Tony Hyon Clark and on the second day I went to view the damage to our tank with Sergeant Spencer. La Bijude was by then cleared.

My tank was an absolute write-off, with two shots through the turret and five through the hull front. It was completely brewed up and none of our kit was salvageable. I had a look at the jerry Mk. IV which we had accounted for and that also was a write-off, with three of the crew dead on the ground. A little way along the hedge was a row of four dug-in tanks, all accounted for by the regiment the day before. The corporal's tank took a bit of finding. It had reversed back some 200 yards into a sunken road and the batteries were right down. The fire caused by the bazooka had miraculously gone out and, by towing the tank with the A.R.V. (Armoured Rescue Vehicle), we were able to start it up and ride it back. The corporal secured a rocket over this because it looked as if he had evacuated his tank before it was immobilized, but I pointed out to Peter that the sheet of flame set up by the bazooka made the incident appear far worse than it actually was. While rescuing the corporal's tank I stepped accidently on a phosphorus mine, which exploded. Fortunately, I threw myself on my back and not by my face, and only received burns in my pants. On returning to R.H.Q. we were met with some sad news: Tony had been killed by a shell dropping on his dug out.

The Squadron returned that evening. Caen had been captured and the battle had gone very well, although a breakthrough had not been effected. Peter discussed troop organization. When it was decided to form four troops of four tanks my heart sank because I realized that I would be without a troop, but he then said that Peerless was to return to F.D.S. and I was to have 4th Troop. I only had 4th Troop for 2 hours. That night Lieutenant T.A.S. Anderson ('Andy') arrived back from England. He had been a casualty on D-Day and had to be evacuated. He now expected to return to B Squadron, but it was left undecided.

On 16th July we moved to a large chateau for a period of rest and maintenance.

An Attempt to Break Through Beyond Caen

We remained at the chateau for six days. Lieutenant Colonel Vincent Dunkerley arrived from England and took command of the regiment, Sim returned to second in command and Dag to B Squadron. Peter assumed his old position with A Squadron. The time was mainly spent on tank maintenance. Andy took over 4th Troop, as I feared, and I was given another tank with my old crew and tacked onto Andy's troop for the time being. The colonel started with a rush and told us that, as there might be a fair period of rest before the next conflict, we were to commence courses of instruction and generally be smarter over turnout. We had one or two parades for turnout and drill and a squadron parade every morning. We fixed up a very nice officers' mess in a small house on the estate which accommodated us for eating and sleeping. We also made a few trips into Luc-sur-Mer for luxuries. Horse took over the job of mess caterer.

I put in a claim for my burnt kit, £45 in all. When it finally came through I got £17, which was about right. There was a cheerful old gardener chap attached to the chateau, who told us many yarns about the occupation. Over 100 men from the town had been shot as hostages and burned in the chateau grounds. They didn't shoot him because he supplied the bosch with vegetables.

The airborne mo-bike which the Echelon brought along for us was very useful. During our stay we paid a visit to the Canadian sector and, in one area alone where the Canadians had been fighting, we counted over a dozen German tanks which had been knocked out. These included four Panther tanks which we inspected carefully. Their design was good, all the plate-armour being sloping and not like our vertical sides. The welding, however, was poor and, where our shots had scored a hit, whole plates had been torn off. Their armour proved too thick for a frontal attack by our tanks and they had been accounted for by sneaking round and then shooting up their rear. While in this area we met the commander of the Guards Armoured Division, which had just arrived in Normandy and expected to be in action in a week's time.

We commenced O. Groups again on 21st July. This time a breakthrough to Falaise and beyond was to be attempted from the east side of the Caen Canal, and so we were to cross over to Ranville once again. On the evening of 22nd we moved to some fields just outside the town and awaited the cover of darkness for the move over the canal. The weather had been so dry that movement during daylight couldn't be carried out without detection because of the dust. All that night we travelled eastwards and only just managed to reach the familiar village of Hérouvillette before the dawn broke. We quickly had ourselves in an orchard and camouflaged up. A troop of flails were already in the orchard. They were to accompany us in the present conflict. The day was spent by the officers on rekkies and our trouble was to find a route through the minefields beyond Escouville, where the push was to commence. The regiment were to commence the attack by taking Touffreville and Sannerville. Meanwhile the

Guards Armoured and the 11th Armoured Division were to push by and see how far they got.

The morning of 24th July was a glorious one and as the dawn broke, the RAF commenced their softening-up raids. At 0800 hrs we moved out of our hiding to take up positions just outside Escourible. The roads were blocked with all sorts of vehicles and units, and we had much difficulty in reaching the S.L. on time. C Squadron were attacking Sannerville and we were taking on Touffreville. 2nd and 4th Troops were to support the infantry approaching Touffreville through the woods to the east, and 1st and 3rd Troops had the job of clearing entrenchments just southeast of Cuverville.

All went well at the commencement, and Andy and I both scored a hit on a Mk. IV. Five hundred yards from Touffreville we hit a minefield and Frankie and his troop supported the flanks while they cleared a path to the village. When Hugh reached the village, he supported the infantry in clearing it, and was afterwards highly congratulated by the infantry commanding officer. It was about 1600 hrs when Touffreville was finally captured. C Squadron were not quite so fortunate and Eric Smith, Troop Commander of 4th Troop in C Squadron, had lost three tanks all by A/Tk fire.

The guards did not make their expected breakthrough and, after a short advance, they came up against an anti-tank screen. Between the two divisions about three hundred tanks were hit.

The enemy mortar fire was getting very heavy towards the evening, so the regiment was withdrawn back some few hundred yards to a hollow, and some attempt was made by my crew to prepare a meal. This was not very successful. An unfortunate splinter from a mortar went through the open porthole in the tank and hit an artery in Cawthorp's arm. We shoved a tourniquet on and got the Doc to him. He was evacuated on the half-track. A few more casualties occurred through the mortar fire, so by dusk we were dispersed as troops to strategic positions of defence. Near our position was a knocked-out Mk. IV, which on inspection provided many souvenirs for the crew. During the night, our Echelon received a visit from the Luftwaffe and had a few casualties. The next day we followed up the Guards to Frenouville, but we were only needed for defence positions there. We started the night there and experienced a severe air raid, suffering three casualties. On 26th July we were ordered back to harbour in Bois de Bevant. The breakthrough was abandoned. During the ride back, two tanks in the squadron were immobilized by riding over our own minefield. Corporal Eddison was one of the unfortunates.

The Squeezing of the Pocket

We spent the night in Bois de Bevant and heard the unwelcome news that the 27th Armoured Brigade was to be split up. In fact, since D-Day it hadn't existed according to the War Office's book. The Staffordshire Yeomanry and the East Riding Yeomanry were to be sent home (they had already spent several months in North Africa) and we were to join the 8th Armoured Brigade. The 24th Hussars of the 8th Armoured Brigade were also being sent home and we were taking their place. Brigadier Prior Palmer was to transfer his command to the 8th Armoured Brigade. The remaining two segments of the Brigade were the 4th/7th Dragoon Guards and the Sherwood Rangers (Notts Forresters).

The next day, 27th July, we moved from the Caen area via a special tank route to Carcagny southeast of Bayeux. Here we were to have a complete overhaul and exchange of tanks, replenishment of kit and personnel, and enjoy a short rest before joining the brigade. Everyone worked like merry hell from the start because they imagined that the sooner the regiment was in order again, the longer would be the rest period. There was plenty to do, eight new tanks were taken over by B Squadron, every tank was to have a kit and ammo check, and all personnel were to have their gear checked and completed. We were halfway through the work when we got the order to join the 8th Armoured Brigade immediately.

The colonel got the regiment together and gave a little speech; he told us how 'Monty' had praised the 27th Armoured Brigade and that he reckoned we would do well with the 8th Armoured Brigade. Early on the morning of 29th July we moved to the rear of La Belle Epine. I travelled with HQ Troop and, when we had harboured, I was transferred to C Squadron. Major Sir Delaval Cotter was commanding C Squadron; an Irishman with an unreasonable temper at times but a very fine leader in spite of this, and I grew to like him very much. Captain John Wardlaw was second in command and Captain Gale (Windy) was 2nd Captain. The troop leaders were Dan Riviere 1st, Eric S? 4th, Roddy Horrish 2nd, and the 3rd's troop leader I never met. S.S.M. Park was a broad Scotsman and the Quartemaster Sergeant was S.Q. Lyme. We had an O. Group that evening. The Falaise gap had been almost closed by this time and it was a case of squeezing the pocket. The bosch were proving very stubborn in our present area and we were to do a little pushing. The regiment were to support infantry of 43rd Division, the Hampshires, the Dorsets and Devons in a drive through the close Bocage country, starting from the area of St Germain through 790600 to pt 174 west of Villers-Bocage. Captain Wardlaw was put in command of Troops 2 and 4 and was responsible for the right flank with the Hampshires. Windy was in command of Troops 1 and 3, working on the left flank with the Dorsets. My job was to act as rear link (radio set up) in the scout car between John and Windy and the squadron leader, who was operating with Infantry Brigade HQ. We received a pile of maps of the area and then had a good night's sleep. Nothing happened the next day except that, just before we moved up to positions, I had to rush round in the scout car in an attempt to locate some flails which had been allocated to us. I never found them. We moved off at dusk, Major Cotter and I going to Brigade HQ, Windy and John to their respective S.L.s.

At dawn on 31st July the push started and the bosch proved very stubborn. Reinforcements were needed and, in the afternoon, I led our Rekkie Troop (Stewart tanks) and three Ack-Ack tanks to Captain Gale and John, where they were used as additional fire support. Windy looked all in; he had had a very tough time. He came back in a Stewart tank with me, we went right over a minefield by accident but nothing happened. Casualties were very heavy that day and scarcely any advance had been made. Three of the troop leaders were wounded and only Roddy remained. Windy was sail all in. The troops were withdrawn for the night and reorganised. Roddy took Windy's place as a/c of 1 and 3 Troops, the troop sergeants acting as troop leader, and I was put troop leader of 2nd and 4th Troops. We had a very hurried

O. Group with the Hampshires and Devons and then snatched a quick sleep. We were up two hours before the dawn and we moved up to the S.H. There was a very dense fog which made progress slow. 2nd and 4th Troops were to push through to pt. 174. On the S.H. I liaised with the infantry commanders and with the break of dawn we pressed forward. The country was very close, consisting of small fields with thick hedges and small woods. The method of advance we had decided on was for the tanks to 'brown off' the hedges to the sides and front, when the infantry then crept forward to the next hedge in front, followed by the tanks. The next field was then treated likewise, and so on. In practice, we had to advance with the infantry, since the fog was so thick that we could only see six yards, and in the first field we started going round in circles. We experienced very little opposition and, since the fog gradually changed to bright sunshine, we were not long in reaching our objective.

The bosch had evidently retired overnight. The objective gave good observation for some dozen or more miles but there was no sight of the bosch. I quickly arranged the tanks in defensive positions and reported back.

We received orders to support an infantry patrol which was to make a forward rekkie. No huns were seen during this patrol. With dusk, we harboured back in a small wood and the Hampshires did a right advance on their own. The next morning we moved to a farm near Le Belle Epin where we harboured for two nights and reorganised the troops: Lieutenant Edwards from R.H.Q. was put a/c of 1st, Roddy still kept 2nd, Sergeant Dwir 3rd and I was put a/c of 4th Troop. Windy had retired to the Eschelon for a rest and Pip Coates took his place as 2nd Captain. At the time we only had three tanks in 4th Troop.

Captain Peter Lyon MC was killed during the last incident and we buried him near La Belle Epin. He was sadly miss by all in the Regiment.

The Moonlight Advance: Mount Pinçon

I soon got to know the crew and troop during our short stay at La Belle Epin. None of them needed driving and they were all good workers, except perhaps Ames who we got rid of eventually.

Sergeant Haygarth (George) was a very energetic and efficient sergeant. He is married. We soon learnt that another incident had been planned. On 4th August we left harbour and, by a short morning march south, arrived at the hilly woods of Bois du Hourne, where we harboured temporarily to plan the next move. There were rumours of a night attack.

In the afternoon we received a bundle of maps and, as was the usual procedure, directly we had commenced a meal I was summoned to an O. Group. The worst had been confirmed; we were on a moonlight advance with infantry of the 43rd Division. We were to strike southeast and keep going until we reached the River Orne. The start was rather a fiasco. We collected our infantry and carried them on the outside of the tanks; 15 men on each tank. The moon was high and we met with practically to opposition. Each squadron had been allotted slightly different out parallel routes. We proceeded as a regiment down the main road and then were to take parallel routes east at pt 295 (745478). It was at this point that opinions differed and owing to bad map-reading on somebody's part, and also bad rekkie on the part of corporal HQ (which resulted in a few tanks becoming logged) there was one colossal block in the area, where we were forced to spend half the night. There was a quite a community of peasants in this village and they were overjoyed to see us. The hun had left only a few hours before. When the situation became clear, the troop was called off and we settled down in a field to await the dawn in one hour. We then moved to defensive positions to await orders for the advance.

Rekkie parties reported that the bosch was making a stand on Mount Pincon, a Radar station 835458, but that the route was clear as far as Duval. We had a quick O. Group. A Squadron were to do the assault on Mount Pincon while C Squadron defended the crossroads at Le Quesne and prevented reinforcements from reaching the hill.

At the S.H. we distributed the infantry and fired them across the stream into Le Quesne. This was particularly tough going for the infantry, owing to enemy mortar fire right on the bridge, and there were glowing accounts in the newspaper some days later praising the lieutenant colonel for his bravery in getting his men across. Delaval ordered me to take my troop further south to another fire position on the S.H., which meant turning into an orchard. We had so sooner entered the orchard than a dozen or more jerries emerged from a hut and gave themselves up. Sergeant Haygarth checked them over while we covered them with our guns. We didn't get much booty off them, so we sent them back along the line. When the infantry were all safely across we followed in troops and took up positions just off the road at Le Quesne, facing south. Edwards and Roddy, with their troops, were to take up positions facing Le Plessis Grimoult but they were unable to do this effectively. Edwards and his troop were badly bogged and only managed to get two tanks out. They had an awkward time with German infantry and two of their troop were killed. Roddy could not find a suitable position owing to the low lying ground, and devoted his time in evacuating Edward's troop. The village of Le Quesne was still occupied by jerries and, from our position near the cross-roads, we could see their movements and often had a few pop shots. Later in the afternoon an enemy self-propelled gun suddenly appeared and made a dash across our front, about 50 yards away. It was forced to stop because of a sunken road and Sergeant Haygarth got it first shot.

The battle for Mount Pinçon was going well. The infantry had been heavily mortared and were unable to make the top, but A Squadron had got a troop sitting on the top. They had lost several tanks, including the squadron leader's tank (Major Wormald). So that evening my troop was sent to A Squadron. We did practically nothing. When we were half way up Mount Pincon, Major Wormald told us to return to the crossroads and wait for him. He also asked we locate his knocked-out tank and salvage two bottles of whisky in it. There were still a few 88mm rounds whizzing by the crossroads.

We spent the night by the crossroads with a strong guard because of the jerries in Le Quesne. The next morning my troop was given the job of shooting up Le Quesne. We went down the road to Crepigny and shot the village up from there. We then advanced through it and back to the squadron. We burnt a few houses but had met very few bosch. We stayed in defence for the remainder of the day and in the evening we were relieved by Rekkie Regiment.

We harboured that night in troop blocks in the area 790455 and, after staying there the whole of next day, we moved in the evening and darkness to Villers-Bocage by the route through Aunay sur Odon. Both of these two had received a severe pounding by the RAF and Aunay was just one heap of rubble with no visible signs of any roads. We expected to stay in Villers-Bocage for a few days' maintenance but the next day the Brigadier gathered us together, gave us a pep talk and told us we were to do little attack the next day.

The Push from Le Plessis Grimoult

That afternoon, Delaval took troop leaders to meet the C.O. and company commanders of the 6th D. L. I. who we were to support in the next advance. We had continued O. Group and then rekkied the ground of advance and discussed methods. Since the attack on Mount Pincon, Le Plessis Grimoult had been captured but the bosch was still hanging around the southern edge of the village. Our job was to make a push south of Le Plessis Grimoult for about 1½ miles down the road to Conde-sur-Noireau, where we were to make a stand while the rest of the Brigade pushed through. B Squadron were to be on our left with another regiment of the D.L.I. and they were on the extreme left of 43 Division. To B Squadron's left were to be the units of the 7th Armoured Division. I contacted the major of the company I was supporting and we decided on the usual hedge to hedge advance.

The morning of 9th August was bright and warm. The attack was scheduled for 12 o'clock. 4th and 2nd Troops were to lead the attack, so Roddy, Del and I went early to le Plessis to meet our friends the D.L.I. and finally tie up. While we were waiting in Plessis for the arrival of our troops, jerry commenced a very heavy bombardment which actually went on all day.

We took what cover we could but it was very unpleasant. Our tanks arrived together with the infantry at 11 o'clock. The D.L.I. sustained many casualities walking to the S. L. Their colonel was a fine chap and openly encouraged them all the way in the heavy five. The attack went forward without a hitch. About half way to the objective the bosch had taken up positions along a sunken road. This we thoroughly brewed up and then we charged it with the infantry. They gave themselves up, and there were well over a hundred in our sector alone. There was no stopping the D.L.I. and they were one of the best bunch of infantry we worked with in France. We consolidated on the objective and awaited the arrival of A/Tk guns. When they arrived we could retire.

My troop was situated by a farm which we afterwards exploited for cider and eggs. The shelling was heavy most of the time and it was 105mm stuff. One of these caused a sad incident back at HQ. Both Captain John Wardlaw and the F.O.O. (Forward Observation Officer) were killed by one hitting a tree when they were underneath. B. Squadron were in a bad plight. Jeff Oldham's troop were next to move, so I paid him a visit in the afternoon to see it he could locate the guns which were firing at us. B Squadron were advancing on one side of the slope of a valley. Now the 7th Armoured Division should have advanced with them on their left flank, but unfortunately the 7th Armoured Division had failed to push forward, so B. Squadron were exposed on their left to all the 88mm jerry had. By the end of the day they were left with only five tanks. Gerald Wilton, my old operator, was killed that day.

The A/Tk guns did not arrive until late evening and so we were forced to remain on the objective until dusk, when we withdrew about one thousand yards and harboured for the night. We remained back in our harbour the next day because the rest of Brigade had gone through. There was much shelling around us but most of the stuff went over our heads into Plessis. Toward evening Mac and I decided that it was fairly safe to venture out, since most of the shells were passing well over us. We had decided to cook a really decent meal so Mac and I went into on adjacent field to dig up some spuds. While we were digging, a salvo of 105mm stuff landed right in the field. We flattened immediately and were OK. We should have taken this as a warning but we reckoned that Jerry had mislaid his aim and so we continued digging. Almost at once another load arrived and this time we were both hit in the leg and the back. It made us limp quite a bit and was very uncomfortable, but we managed to make our way back to the Regimental Aid Post (R.A.P.). Fortunately, the splinter in my back had hit the shoulder blade and had therefore not penetrated very far, but

Mac's was lower down. Del was very decent: I had quite expected a dressing down from him for not staying under cover. We were both transported back through the various clearing stations and I finally finished up at 97th British General Hospital at Bayeux. Mac was evacuated to England and I did not see him again for several months. The shrapnel was removed from my back but the piece in my thigh was so small and had penetrated so deep that it was best left in. It was very pleasant while I was at Bayeux. The hospital was staffed with Queen Alexandra nurses and it was nice to see English women again. I was only there for ten days.

On 17th August I was fit again and commenced my journey back to the regiment. I called at the Regimental Training unit for a few hours, which was staffed by several old 255 C.D.S. officers, including Frank Biddle. We exchanged news and I had tea there. I then went on to Corp Delivery Squadron, who were just outside Villers-Bocage. This is the usual route back to the regiment, via R.T.U.; C.D.S.; F.D.S. Echelon; Regiment. I had supper at C.D.S. and was just about to find a bed there when Captain May arrived from F.D.S. Since he was returning that night I went back with him. I slept the night at F.D.S. who were encamped near Aunay-sur-Oden. If ever a place has been bombed it is Aunay. There was not a brick left in place, the roads were completely obliterated and our engineers had made new ones over the rubble. I chatted with some French peasants there and they had no idea where their own house had stood! I met a few familiar faces at the F.D.S. the next morning, including Captain Glass. At midnight on 18th August I was roused from a pleasant slumber and ordered to proceed at once to A Echelon. I thought the regiment must be hard up for personnel to call for me at this hour. We were going to A Echelon, who were at St Honore. During my absence the regiment had had one engagement near Conde-sur-Noireau and had since then been in harbour. They were ready to commence the race to the Seine. The German 15th Army had been routed and it was essential to entrap them.

BIBLIOGRAPHY

Published sources

Alexander, Field Marshal the Earl, *The Alexander Memoirs 1940–1945* (London, 1962)

Ambrose, S.E., *Pegasus Bridge* (London, 1985)

Arthur, M., *Men of the Red Beret: Airborne Forces 1940–1990* (London, 1990)

Arthur, M., *Forgotten Voices of the Second World War* (London, 2005)

Badsey, S., *Normandy 1944* (Oxford, 1990)

Bailey, J.B.A., *Field Artillery and Firepower* (London, 1989)

Baldwin, H., *Battles Lost and Won, Great Campaigns of World War Two* (London, 1967)

Baverstock, K., *Breaking the Panzers, the Bloody Battle for Rauray* (Stroud, 2002)

Beale, P., *Death by Design, British Tank Development in the Second World War* (Stroud, 1998)

Bidwell, S., and Graham, D., *Firepower, British Army Weapons and Theories of War 1904–1945* (London, 1982)

Bishop, C. and Drury, I., *Combat Guns* (London, 1987)

Bond, B., *France and Belgium, 1939–1940* (London, 1975)

Braddock, D.W., *The Campaigns in Egypt and Libya* (Aldershot, 1964)

Bruce, C. J., *War on the Ground 1939–1945* (London, 1995)

Bryant, Sir Arthur, *The Turn of the Tide* (Vols I and II; London, 1957–1959)

Bullock, A., *Hitler, A Study in Tyranny* (London, 1952)

Calder, A., *The People's War, Britain 1939–1945* (London, 1969)

Carruthers, Bob and Trew, Simon, *The Normandy Battles* (London, 2000)

Carver, M., *The Apostles of Mobility: The Theory and Practice of Armoured Warfare* (London, 1979)

Chandler, D.G., and J. L. Collins, (editors) *The D-Day Encyclopaedia* (Oxford, 1994)

Churchill, W., *The Second World War* (6 Vols; London, 1948–1954)

Cooper, M., *The German Army 1933–1945* (London, 1978)

Cruickshank, C., *Deception in World War Two* (Oxford, 1979)

Deary, T., *Dirty Little Imps – Stories from the DLI* (Durham, 2004)

Defence Operational Analysis Centre, *The Combat Degradation and Effectiveness of Anti-Tanks Weapons – Interim Analysis* (Vols I and II Study 670)

—— *The Effectiveness of Small Arms Fire* (Defence Study No. M 83108)

—— *Historical Analysis of Anti-Tank Battles – The Battle of Snipe* (Study N 670/201)

D'Este, C., *Decision in Normandy* (Connecticut, 1983)

—— *Bitter Victory* (London, 2008)

De Guingand, Major-General Sir Francis, *Operation Victory* (London, 1949)

Dodds-Parker, D., *Setting Europe Ablaze, Some Accounts of Ungentlemanly Warfare* (London, 1984)

Doherty, R., *Normandy 1944 – the Road to Victory* (Staplehurst, 2004)

Ehrman, J., *Grand Strategy, Volume V, August 1943–September 1944* (London, 1956)

—— *Grand Strategy, Volume VI, October 1944–August 1945* (London, 1956)

Ellis, J., *Brute Force: Allied Strategy and Tactics in the Second World War* (London, 1980)

—— *The Sharp End of War: The Fighting Man in World War Two* (London, 1980)

Ellis, L. F., *The War in France and Flanders 1939–1940* (London, 1953)

English, Major I. R. and Moses, H., *For You Tommy the War is Over* (Durham, 2006)

Fletcher, D., *The Great Tank Scandal: British Armour in the Second World War Part 1* (HMSO, 1989)

Foot, M. R. D., *SOE in France; An Account of the British Special Operations Executive in France 1940–1944* (London, 1966)

Ford, K., *D-Day 1944: Gold and Juno Beaches* (Oxford, 2002)

D-Day 1944: Sword Beach and the British Airborne Landings (Oxford, 2002)

Forty, G., *The Royal Tank Regiment – A Pictorial History* (Tunbridge Wells, 1989)

—— *World War Two Tanks* (London, 1995)

—— *British Army Handbook 1939–1945* (Stroud, 1998)

Fraser, D., *Alanbrooke* (London, 1982)

—— *And We Shall Shock Them: The British Army in the Second World War* (London, 1983)

—— *Knights Cross: A Life of Field Marshal Erwin Rommel* (London, 1993)

French, D., *Raising Churchill's Army; The British Army and the War Against Germany 1919–1945* (Oxford, 2000)

Guderian, H. and Others, (editor D. C. Isby), *Fighting in Normandy: The German Army from D-Day to Villers-Bocage* (London, 2001)

Harris J. P. and Toase, F. H. (editors), *Armoured Warfare* (London, 1990)

Harrison-Place, T., *Military Training in the British Army, 1940–1944: From Dunkirk to D-Day* (London, 2000)

Hastings, M., *Nemesis* (London, 2008)

Hilary, R., *The Last Enemy* (Pimlico Edition, London 1997) p. 82

Hills, S., *By Tank into Normandy* (London, 2002)

Hinsley, F. H., *British Intelligence in the Second World War* (abridged ed. London, 1993)

Hogg, I. V. and Weeks. J., *The Illustrated Encyclopaedia of Military Vehicles* (London, 1980)

Holt, Major and Mrs., *Battlefield Guide to Normandy* (Barnsley, 2004)

Horrocks, Lieutenant-General, Sir B., *A Full Life* (London, 1960)

Howard, M., *Grand Strategy, Volume IV, August 1942–September 1943* (London, 1972)

Howarth, D., *Dawn of D-Day* (London, 1959)

Instructions for British Servicemen in France 1944 (the Foreign Office London, 1944, reprinted 2005)

Irving, D., *The Trail of the Fox* (London, 1977)

—— *Hitler's War* (London, 1977)

Jackson, W. G. F., *'Overlord' Normandy 1944* (London, 1978)

Joslen, Lieutenant-Colonel H. F., *Orders of Battle: Second World War* (HMSO, 1960)

Keegan, Sir J., *Six Armies in Normandy* (London, 1978)

Kershaw, R. J., *Piercing the Atlantic Wall* (Surrey, 2009)

Lewis, P. J., and English, I. R., *Into Battle with the Durhams: 8 DLI in World War II* (London, 1990)

Lewis-Stemple, J., *The Autobiography of the British Soldier* (London, 2007)

Levine, J., *Operation Fortitude* (London, 2011)

Liddell Hart, Sir B. H., *The Tanks: The History of the Royal Tank Regiment and its Predecessors, Heavy Branch Machine Gun Corps, Tank Corps and Royal Tank Corps, 1914–1945* (2 Vols; London, 1959)

Lovat, S., *March Past* (Weidenfeld & Nicolson, London 1978)

McKee, A., *Caen: Anvil of Victory* (London, 1984)

MacDonald, J., *Great Battles of World War Two* (London, 1986)

Macksey, K., *Rommel: Battles and Campaigns* (London, 1979)

Miller, R.A., *August 1944, the Campaign for France* (Novato, CA 1988)

Montgomery, Field Marshall the Viscount B.L., *Memoirs* (London, 1958)

Morgan, Lieutenant-General, Sir Frederick, E., *Overture to Overlord* (London, 1950)

Moses, H., *Faithful Sixth: A History of the 6th Battalion DLI* (Durham, 1998)

—— *Gateshead Ghurkhas: A History of the 9th Battalion Durham Light Infantry 1859–1967* (Durham, 2002)

Myatt, F., *The British Infantry 1660–1945: the Evolution of a Fighting Force* (Poole, 1983)

Neillands, R., *The Battle of Normandy* (London, 1993)

North, J., *NW Europe 1944–1945: The Achievement of 21st Army Group* (London, 1953)

Parkinson, R., *Blood, Toil, Sweat and Tears* (London, 1973)

—— *A Day's March Nearer Home* (London, 1974)

Osprey Elite Series 105: *World War II Infantry Tactics: Squad and Platoon*

—— Elite Series 122: *World War Two Infantry Tactics: Company and Battalion*

—— Elite Series 124: *World War Two Infantry Anti-Tank Tactics*

—— New Vanguard 28: *Panzerkampfwagen IV Medium Tank 1936–1945*

—— New Vanguard 46: *88 mm Flak 18/36/37/41 and Pak 43 1936–1945*

—— New Vanguard 98: *British Anti-Tank Artillery 1939–1945*

Rissik, D., *The DLI at War – History of the DLI 1939–1945* (Durham, 1952)

Rommel, E., *Infantry Attack* (London, 1990)

Russell of Liverpool, Lord, *The Scourge of the Swastika, A Short History of Nazi War Crimes* (London, 1954)

Salmond, J.B., *The History of the 51st Highland Division* (Bishop Auckland, 1994)

Saunders, T., *Hill 112: Battles of the Odon (Gold Beach – Jig; Jig Sector and West – June 1944* (Barnsley, 2002)

Smith, M., *Station X – The Codebreakers of Bletchley Park* (London, 1998)

Terraine, J., *The Right of the Line* (London, 1983)

Toase, F. H., and Harris, J. P., *Armoured Warfare* (London, 1990)

Tout, K., *The Bloody Battle for Tilly* (Stroud, 2000)

Turner, J. F., *Invasion '44; the Full Story of D-Day* (London, 1959; Shrewsbury, 1994)

Van Creveld, M., *Supplying in War: Logistics from Wallenstein to Patton* (Cambridge, 1977)

Wilmot, C., *The Struggle for Europe* (London, 1952)

Young, D., *Rommel* (London, 1950)

Useful websites

https://witness.theguardian.com/assignment/53884eeae4b0bd8f35189225?page=2

http://www.ddaymuseum.co.uk/

http://sgmcaen.free.fr/resistance/douin-robert.htm.

http://www.culture24.org.uk/places-to-go/yorkshire/art21992

Archive Sources:

The National Archives

The D-Day Museum, Portsmouth

'Listen to the Soldiers' DLI Oral History, Durham County Record Office

Royal Northumberland Fusiliers Archive Alnwick Castle

The King's Own Scottish Borderers Museum, Berwick Barracks

The Green Howards Museum and Archive, Richmond

The Museum of the Light Dragoons Newcastle upon Tyne

NOTES

Chapter 1 Introduction

1. Hilary R., *The Last Enemy* (Pimlico edition, London 1997), p.2.
2. Foreign Office, London 1944 (reprinted 2005), p. 4.
3. Sadler, D. J., *Dunkirk to Belsen* (JR Books, London 2010), p. 1.
4. Ibid., p. 2.
5. Ibid.
6. Bond, B., 'The Army Between the Two World Wars 1918–1939' in *The Oxford History of the British Army* (Oxford, 1994), p.257.
7. http://heritage.stockton.gov.uk/stories/battle-stockton-1933/ retrieved 28 March 2018
8. Ward, S.G.P., *Faithful – A History of the Durham Light Infantry* (Durham, 1962), p.449.
9. Arthur, M., *Forgotten Voices of the Second World War* (London, 2005), p. 7.
10. General Sir John Moore, killed at Corunna in 1809.
11. 'A History of the Light Infantry' *Illustrated London News* 20 November 1948.
12. Ward, p.461.
13. Lewis, P.J. and English, I.R., *Into Battle with the Durhams: 8 DLI in World War Two* (London, 1990), p.2.
14. Ward, p.p.460–466.
15. Lewis and English, p.2.
16. Ward, p.462.

17. Forty, G., *British Army Handbook 1939–1945* (Stroud, 1998), chapter three.
18. BBC, WW2 People's War A8557103.
19. Ibid.
20. Arthur, p.19.
21. The *Maschinen-pistole* MP38 and MP40 were superior to anything the UK possessed at the start of the war. The development of the ubiquitous Sten gun was a response.
22. Arthur, p.19.
23. *Laws of the Rear* – anonymous
24. BBC, WW2 People's War A3696087.
25. Forty, pp.28–29.
26. BBC, WW2 People's War A3696087.
27. Forty, p.13.
28. Ibid.
29. BBC, WW2 People's War A8557103.
30. Ibid., A3696087.
31. Oskar Hutier was a successful Great War German general who'd pioneered the use of infiltration tactics.

Chapter 2 Overture

1. Montgomery writing to Bradley and Dempsey, 14 April, 1944.
2. *Instructions etc.,* p. 5.
3. http://sgmcaen.free.fr/resistance/douin-robert.htm retrieved 29 March, 2018.
4. The Todt Organisation was named after its creator Fritz Todt, an engineer, and the group carried out many of the major Third Reich military undertakings, often using slave labour; death rates amongst these workers were very high indeed.
5. These were literally harbours, temporary and dismountable, an IKEA version, a brilliant and extraordinary innovation. Churchill had thought of the idea as far back as 1917.
6. Website of the D-Day Museum, Portsmouth, www.ddaymuseum. co.uk, retrieved 29 March, 2018.
7. http://www.historylearningsite.co.uk/world-war-two/world-war-two-in-western-europe/d-day-index/cossac-plan/ retrieved 29 March 2018.

8. Supreme Headquarters Allied Expeditionary Force.

9. http://www.culture24.org.uk/places-to-go/yorkshire/art21992, retrieved 24.01.2018

10. Major-General Percy Hobart (1885–1957), a military engineer by training, acerbic and apt to be contentious, he was retrieved from obscurity to head 79th Armoured – nonetheless, his designs saved thousands of Allied soldiers.

11. Alan Brooke, 1st Viscount Alanbrooke (1883–1963), Chief of the Imperial General Staff, brilliant soldier and foil for Churchill's overbearing and often mercurial temperament.

12. Interview with the late Thomas Walling, August 2004.

13. Eben-Emael, this fortress complex was Belgium's answer to the Maginot Line and just about as effective.

14. A Monitor is effectively a floating inshore battery delivering concentrated firepower for naval bombardment.

15. DLI Sound Recording Project, Durham County Record Office

16. Ibid.

17. Website of the D-Day Museum, Portsmouth, www.ddaymuseum. co.uk, retrieved 29 March, 2018.

18. DLI.

19. Large-scale D-Day rehearsals.

20. PLUTO = Pipe Line under the Ocean.

21. DLI.

22. Website of the D-Day Museum, Portsmouth, www.ddaymuseum. co.uk, retrieved 29 March, 2018.

23. Ibid.

24. Ibid.

25. Ibid.

26. Website of the D-Day Museum, Portsmouth, www.ddaymuseum. co.uk, retrieved 29 March, 2018.

27. Howarth, D., *Dawn of D-Day* (Wren's Park Publishing, London 1959), p. 13.

28. DLI.

29. Ibid.

30. Website of the D-Day Museum, Portsmouth, www.ddaymuseum. co.uk, retrieved 29 March, 2018.

31. Ibid.

32. Ibid.

33. Ibid.
34. Ibid.
35. Ibid.
36. Ibid.
37. Ibid.

Chapter 3 H-Hour, The Airborne Drop

1. *Instructions etc.,* p. 5.
2. Horsa Glider: The Airspeed AS.51 Horsa was a British troop-carrying glider developed and manufactured by Airspeed Limited; named after Horsa, one of the 5th Century Saxon chieftains who invaded southern England (Hengist being the other).
3. Halifax Bomber: The Handley Page Halifax was an RAF four-engined heavy bomber, developed by Handley Page to the same specification as the contemporary Avro Lancaster and the Short Stirling.
4. Stirling Bomber: The Short Stirling was a British four-engined heavy bomber. It had the distinction of being the first four-engined bomber to be introduced into service with the RAF.
5. Website of the D-Day Museum, Portsmouth, www.ddaymuseum. co.uk, retrieved 29 March 2018.
6. From John Howard's *Pegasus Diaries* originally published by Pen and Sword and featured in *D-Day and Normandy, Sixty-Five Years On,* Wharncliffe History Magazines, Barnsley 2009), p. 61.
7. Website of the D-Day Museum, Portsmouth, www.ddaymuseum. co.uk, retrieved 29 March 2018.
8. *Sixty-five Years On,* p. 62.
9. Ibid., p.p. 44–50.
10. Ibid., p. 64.
11. D-Day 50th Anniversary *Soldier Magazine* Supplement.
12. Website of the D-Day Museum, Portsmouth, www.ddaymuseum. co.uk, retrieved 29 March 2018.
13. Ibid., Ashby went on to take part in the Battle of Arnhem in September 1944 and the crossing of the Rhine in March 1945. Married in 1944, he retired as Surrey's county librarian in 1978.
14. The cemetery contains 2,236 Commonwealth burials of the Second World War, 90 of them unidentified. There are also 323 German graves and a few of other nationalities. The churchyard contains 47

Commonwealth burials, one of which is unidentified, and a single German grave.

15. Website of the D-Day Museum, Portsmouth, www.ddaymuseum. co.uk, retrieved 29 March, 2018.
16. Ibid.
17. Howarth, p. 63.
18. Website of the D-Day Museum, Portsmouth, www.ddaymuseum. co.uk, retrieved 29 March, 2018.
19. Howarth, p. 65.
20. Ibid., p.p. 62–67.
21. Ibid., p.p. 52–53.
22. Ibid., p. 54.
23. Ibid., p. 58.

Chapter 4 Sword Beach, Morning
1. *Instructions etc.*, p. 6.
2. He was commissioned in 1946, transferred to the RAF in 1949 and subsequently rose to the rank of group captain.
3. By Kind permission of The Light Dragoons, Charge! – The Story of England's Northern Cavalry, Discovery Museum, Newcastle upon Tyne.
4. Website of the D-Day Museum, Portsmouth, www.ddaymuseum. co.uk, retrieved 29 March 2018.
5. Howarth, p. 234.
6. Ibid., p.p. 235–236.
7. Ibid., p. 237.
8. Craggs, Tracy (2008) *An 'Unspectacular' War; Reconstructing the History of the 2nd Battalion East Yorkshire Regiment During the Second World War,* PhD thesis, University of Sheffield.
9. A US-manufactured self-propelled gun, mounting a 105mm gun, the bulbous nose is said to have resembled a pulpit.
10. *Sixty-five Years On,* p.p. 47–48.
11. Ibid., p. 49.
12. Ibid.
13. Ibid., p.p. 53–54.
14. Ibid., p. 52.

15. KOSB, *A Short History of the* 1st *Battalion 6th June 1944–8th May 1945* by kind permission of the Trustees of The King's Own Scottish Borderers Museum and Archive.
16. *Sixty-five Years On,* p. 53.
17. Ibid.
18. Ibid., p.p. 54–55.
19. The Bren or Universal carrier, a lightly armoured tracked reconnaissance vehicle, built by Vickers-Armstrong.
20. *Sixty-five Years On,* p. 55.
21. KOSB
22. Ibid.
23. Ibid.
24. Ibid.
25. Website of the D-Day Museum, Portsmouth, www.ddaymuseum. co.uk, retrieved 29 March 2018.
26. Howarth, p.p. 204–206.
27. As in *The Longest Day,* a 1962 movie, based on the 1959 book of the same name by Cornelius Ryan.
28. Lovat, S., *March Past* (Weidenfeld & Nicolson, London 1978), p.p. 309–310.
29. Lovat, p. 211.
30. Ibid.
31. Ibid., p. 313.
32. Website of the D-Day Museum, Portsmouth, www.ddaymuseum. co.uk, retrieved 29 March 2018.
33. Lovat, p.p. 313–314.
34. Ibid., p. 314.
35. Ibid., p. 316.
36. Ibid., p. 316.
37. Website of the D-Day Museum, Portsmouth, www.ddaymuseum. co.uk, retrieved 29 March 2018.

Chapter 5 Juno Beach, Morning
1. *Instructions etc.,* p. 9.
2. Website of the D-Day Museum, Portsmouth, www.ddaymuseum. co.uk, retrieved 26 April 2018.

3. Ibid.
4. Ibid.
5. Ibid.
6. Ibid.
7. https://www.junobeach.org, retrieved 26th April 2018.
8. Medics perform a triage system, patch the walking wounded, evacuate the treatable cases and set aside those who won't survive and make them as comfortable as possible.
9. https://www.junobeach.org, retrieved 26 April 2018.
10. Website of the D-Day Museum, Portsmouth, www.ddaymuseum. co.uk, retrieved 26 April 2018.
11. The Churchill (Infantry Mk. IV) tank; built by Vauxhall, heavily armoured, long chassis, all round tracks with multiple bogies and still armed with the obsolete 2- pounder gun.
12. A fascine tank carried a cargo of timber beams, an extension of the ancient idea of bridging enemy ditches and wet gap crossing with bundles of brushwood.
13. Howarth, p.p. 218–219.
14. Ibid., p. 220.
15. Ibid., p. 222.
16. Royal Marine Commandos; formed from Royal Marines Infantry battalions in 1942, a total of nine commando units (designated 40–48) were formed.
17. Howarth, p.p. 224–225.
18. Ibid.
19. Ibid., p. 228.
20. Ibid., p.p. 228–229.
21. Ibid.
22. Ibid.
23. Ibid., p. 231.
24. Ibid., p. 232.

Chapter 6 Gold Beach, Morning

1. *Instructions etc.*, p. 44.
2. http://users.clas.ufl.edu/snod/DouglasIntroductionNB.071815.pdf, retrieved 19 April 2018.
3. Bowen, R. *Many Histories Deep,* (London Associated University Press 1995), p. 90.

4. DLI Sound Recording Project.

5. Ibid.

6. Website of the D-Day Museum, Portsmouth, www.ddaymuseum. co.uk, retrieved 20 April 2018.

7. DLI Sound Recording Project

8. Website of the D-Day Museum, Portsmouth, www.ddaymuseum. co.uk, retrieved 26 April 2018.

9. Rissik, D., *The DLI at War 1939–1945*, (Durham, 1952), p. 241.

10. Website of the D-Day Museum, Portsmouth, www.ddaymuseum. co.uk, retrieved 26 April 2018.

11. Howarth, p.p. 167–168.

12. Ibid., p. 176.

13. Ibid., p. 177.

14. Bobbin was another of the 'Funnies', a track-laying variant.

15. Petard was a bunker-busting tank with a stubby howitzer-type gun very effective at close range, although alarmingly, it had to be loaded externally!

16. Howarth, p.p. 180–181.

17. Ibid., p. 181.

18. Ibid., p. 185.

19. Ibid., p. 186.

20. Ibid., p. 188.

21. Morgan, M., *D-Day Hero,* (Stroud, Spellmount 2004), p. 59.

22. Ibid., p. 60.

23. Ibid.

24. Ibid., p. 61.

25. Ibid., p. 62.

26. Ibid., p. 63.

27. Projector Infantry Anti-tank – 'PIAT', a weapon manufactured by ICI, of all people, a development of the Spigot Mortar, and which entered service in 1943; it was an absolute swine to operate.

28. Morgan, p. 67.

29. Ibid.

30. Citation, quoted in Morgan, p. 68.

31. DLI Sound Recording Project.

32. Ibid.

33. Ibid.

34. Ibid.

Chapter 7 Getting a Grip, the Afternoon and After
1. *Instructions etc.,* p. 37.
2. Website of the D-Day Museum, Portsmouth, www.ddaymuseum. co.uk, retrieved 26 April 2018.
3. Fortunately, such important buildings such as the great castles and the two abbeys holding the remains of Duke William and his wife survived, otherwise the devastation was terrible.
4. Light Dragoons.
5. KOSB.
6. *By Air to Battle,* Official History of the British Paratroops in World War II (2012 Edition, Pen and Sword, Barnsley), p. 141.
7. Ibid.
8. Ibid.
9. Ibid., p.p. 142–143.
10. https://www.gliderpilotregiment.org.uk/ retrieved 10 April 2018.
11. *By Air to Battle,* p. 144.
12. Ibid., p.p. 144–145.
13. The General Aircraft Limited, GAL. 49 Hamilcar or Hamilcar Mark I was a heavy glider capable of lifting light vehicles and guns.
14. The Tetrarch was a light tank produced by Vickers Armstrong, equipped with a 2-pounder gun. It was of limited use to 6th Airborne, outdated and no match for a *Panzer Mark IV.*
15. *By Air to Battle,* p. 146.
16. 51st Highland Division had suffered badly at St Valery in 1940.
17. *By Air to Battle,* p. 149.
18. KOSB.
19. Ibid.
20. Ibid.
21. Allied tank crews could expect that to knock out one Tiger would cost five or six Shermans/Cromwells.
22. The Museum of the Light Dragoons.
23. Ibid.
24. Lovat, p. 317
25. The dreaded German *Nebelwerfer.*
26. Lovat, p.p. 318–319.
27. Ibid. p. 319.
28. Ibid., p. 320.
29. Ibid., p. 322.

30. Ibid.
31. Website of the D-Day Museum, Portsmouth, www.ddaymuseum. co.uk, retrieved 26 April 2018.
32. Trustees of the Museum of the Northumberland Fusiliers.
33. Ibid.
34. Ibid.
35. Ibid.
36. The condenser was used to conserve water for the water-cooled barrel.
37. Royal Northumberland Fusiliers.
38. Ibid.
39. Ibid.
40. Ibid.
41. Ibid.
42. Ibid.
43. Ibid.
44. The Green Howards Museum.
45. Ibid.
46. Ibid.
47. Website of the D-Day Museum, Portsmouth, www.ddaymuseum. co.uk, retrieved 26 April 2018.
48. Ibid.
49. Ibid.
50. https://www.theguardian.com/world/2014/jun/05/-sp-d-day-memories-from-the-front-line retrieved 10 April 2018.
51. Website of the D-Day Museum, Portsmouth, www.ddaymuseum. co.uk, retrieved 26 April 2018.
52. Ibid.

Chapter 8 The Battle for Normandy

 1. *Instructions etc.*, p.10.
 2. Tout, K., *The Bloody Battle for Tilly* (Stroud, Sutton 2000), p.205.
 3. These still remain.
 4. The DLI Sound Recording Project.
 5. Ibid.
 6. Ibid.
 7. Ibid.
 8. Ibid.

9. Villars-en-Bocage, scene of a traumatic British defeat; see note on Michael Wittman below.

10. The DLI Sound Recording Project.

11. Rissik, D., *The DLI at War – History of the DLI 1939–1945* (Durham, 1952), p.246.

12. Ibid.

13. Ibid. pp.246–247.

14. Michael Wittman (1914–1944) SS *Hauptsturmführer* (Captain), leading *panzer* ace with 168 kills; some mystery surrounds his death in action in Normandy on 8 August.

15. The DLI Sound Recording Project.

16. Ibid.

17. Ibid.

18. *Panzerfaust* ('armour fist' or 'tank fist'): a cheap, effective, hand-held, recoilless German anti-tank weapon.

19. The DLI Sound Recording Project.

20. Ibid.

21. Operation *Cobra* on 25–26 July heralded the successful US breakout from the west.

22. Operation *Bagration* launched on 22 June, three years to the day since the Germans invaded Russia.

23. The DLI Sound Recording Project.

24. Quoted in Rissik, p.253.

25. Lewis, P.J., and English, I.R., *Into Battle with the Durhams: 8 DLI in World War II* (London, 1990), pp.272–273.

26. VI Rocket: the flying bomb, commonly known as a 'doodlebug'; these were spreading terror in south-east England.

27. V2 Rocket: one of Hitler's 'super' weapons, its arrival caused consternation in England, though it was less effective than feared – the need to eliminate launch sites in France spurred the Allied advance. The perceived need to do likewise in the Low Countries was a spur to 'Market Garden'.

28. The DLI Sound Recording Project.

29. Ibid.

30. Ibid.

31. Von Rundstedt managed to stabilise the German position in the west – 'the Miracle in the West'.

32. DLI Sound Recording Project.

33. Ibid.
34. Ibid.
35. The Light Dragoons.
36. DLI Sound Recording Project.
37. Ibid.

Chapter 9 And Now
  1. *Instructions, etc.*, p. 42.
  2. http://www.arromanches360.com/, retrieved 3 April 2018.
  3. https://www.combinedops.com/pluto.htm, retrieved 3 April 2018.
  4. Extracts reproduced by kind permission of Mrs Mary Pinkney.

INDEX